Suzy Gershman's

BORN TO SHOP

ITALY

9th Edition

Hungry Minds™

Best-Selling Books • Digital Downloads • e-Books
Answer Networks • e-Newsletters • Branded Websites • e-Learning
New York, NY • Cleveland, OH • Indianapolis, IN

For Richard, who helped make this one possible—with many thanks and a million jars of tuna fish.

Produced by:

HUNGRY MINDS, INC.
909 Third Ave.
New York, NY 10022

Copyright © 2001 by Suzy Gershman
Maps copyright © 2001 by Hungry Minds, Inc.

Find us online at **www.frommers.com**.

ISBN 0-7645-6447-1
ISSN 1066-2804

Editor: Alice Fellows
Production Editor: Tammy Ahrens
Photo Editor: Richard Fox
Design by Michele Laseau
Cartographer: Roberta Stockwell
Production by Hungry Minds Indianapolis Production Services

SPECIAL SALES
For general information on Hungry Minds, Inc.'s books in the U. S., please call our Consumer Customer Service Department at 1-800/762-2974. For reseller information, including discounts, bulk sales, customized editions, and premium sales, please call our Reseller Consumer Service Department at 1-800/434-3422.

Manufactured in the United States of America

5   4   3   2   1

CONTENTS

MAP LIST

ABOUT THE AUTHOR

Suzy Gershman is an author and a journalist who has worked in the fiber and fashion industry since 1969 in both New York and Los Angeles, and has held editorial positions at *California Apparel News, Mademoiselle, Gentleman's Quarterly,* and *People* magazine, where she was West Coast Style editor. She writes regularly for various magazines; her essays on retailing are text for Harvard Business School. She frequently appears on network and local television; she is a contributor to National Geographic *Traveler* and *Where Paris*.

Suzy now lives in Paris.

TO START WITH

Now that I live in Paris, I am a simple hop, skip, jump and train ride from Italy—so *mamma mia*, here's a brand new revision of *Born to Shop Italy*, and look at what the neighbors are doing. During this revision period, the dollar has been laughably strong, so I've been having a good giggle while I buy shoes, shoes, shoes. Oooops, I mean while I do research for this update.

I'm still very committed to Milano, despite the fact that many other guides have begun to cut back on their Milan coverage because they feel that tourists just don't care. What they're forgetting, however, is that Milan is still Italy's number one city for shopping and style. (Milan is also the gateway to factory outlet shopping in northern Italy, so there's more outlet coverage in the Milan chapter, too.) So basta and pasta, andiamo!

While this book has always been different from other titles in the series, because Italy has so many primary shopping cities, this edition is packed with even more destinations . . . with luck, next time around we'll go to two books and even more details. I feel like more and more people are interested in driving around, in summer rentals, and maybe even second homes or retirement purchases. More to come!

This edition does have a cruise chapter at the end—not a list of major port cities, such as Venice (which has always been part of this book), but Capri, Positano, and the little-known ports, such as Taormina and Sorrento. Naples gets more and more attention, partly because Faith promises me that the days when someone tried to grab my handbag are long over, and that Naples is her favorite city. And I listen to Faith Heller Willinger, I do.

I hope some of my extra side trips have inspired you to reach out past the big cities and to slow down, smell the slow food, and buy a little olive oil. There're more and more factory outlets in this edition, and also more information about arranging for someone to drive you into in the countryside if you do not want to drive yourself.

Many thanks to the guys who help me do my job: Karen Preston at Leading Hotels of the World and Vincenzo Finizzola at the Four Seasons in Milano, my long-lost general manager friend from the Gritti who turned up in Milan in one of the best luxury shopping hotels. Thanks to my oldest buddy as in hotelier buddy in Italy—Paolo Guardeni whom I have followed from Milan to Florence and back to Milan and who still takes good care of me in Milan at the Principe de Savoia. In Florence, the trip was made better by the help of my old buddy Maria Teresa who now runs Tuscany by Tuscans and can arrange anything and make it seem simple . . . and Rolando Fallani, general manager of the Grand Hotel Villa Medici, and Vincenzo Pagano from Naples. To one and all, my heartfelt thanks.

Thanks also to my personal team, generous with information and secrets: Alan Heller (Milan), Patricia Schultz (Venice), Faith Heller Willinger (Florence), and Logan Bentley Lessona (Rome).

Big *baci* to all; the next pizza is on me.

Chapter One

....

THE BEST OF ITALY IN AN INSTANT

Italy has more style per square mile than you can shake a *formaggio* at, especially in the northern regions. The south has more *limoncello*, that delectable lemon vodka brew that makes me tipsy after one thimbleful . . . so wherever your travels take you, I know you'll find a lot to buy and a lot more to enjoy.

I'm sure I don't need to tell you that the dollar is under the influence of something far stronger than lemons or vodka, so you will also be dizzy with just how many lire you get and get to spend.

Even if you're on a cruise and don't get to do much shopping, you'll still find specialty items to put a smile on your face—and your wallet. Welcome ashore, mates.

If you're in a hurry, you may want to breeze through what I consider some of the highlights of the whole country, so when you stop by these places, you can worship and shop and feel like you've indulged. By no means is my list comprehensive; it will take years for me to perfect it, so bear with me while I shop, shop, shop.

The Best Store in Italy

10 CORSO COMO
10 Corso Como, Milan

No, that's not a typo; the store's name is its address.

There's much more written about this store in the Milan chapter (see chapter 8), but suffice it to say that this is a

1

bazaar, a magic act created by one of Italy's most famous fashion editors and stylists who turned to retail and hasn't looked back.

The store is well bought, but for people who shop a lot, there are no surprises in terms of merchandise. What's yummy is the way it's laid out and presented and served on your platter. You can gawk and enjoy and not buy a thing, but don't miss it. Note the new cafe, speaking of served on a platter.

The Second Best Store in Italy

STVDIVM VENETIA, VENICE

Fortuny-inspired pleated silks made into wraps, bags, tassels, and treasures . . . a wonderland of fairytales and dreams in colors that will make you swoon. Two shops in Venice and one in London (go figure).

The Best Grand-Scale Shopping City

MILAN

Milan may not be adorable or overwhelmingly charming or flashy, but the shopping is divine. One reason is that Milan offers high-quality goods in many different price ranges. Milan has excellent alternative retail—street markets, jobbers who sell discounted designer clothing, and more—all of which help you to make do with less. Less is always more, as Mother used to say.

The Best Small Shopping City

DERUTA

Italy is filled with tiny cities, devoted to craftspeople and artists, where shopping has been elevated to an art form. But the best of them all is the city of Deruta, in Umbria, where every store sells hand-painted faience. Deruta is about an hour from Rome.

The Best Port City for a Quick Spree

VENICE

Venice is not included on every Mediterranean cruise, but if you can get here, even if only for 1 day, do—it is magic. The shopping isn't bad either.

The Best Factory Town

COMO

Perhaps because Como is ever so much more than a factory town, it wins my vote for the best factory town in Italy. It's gorgeous, it's upscale, it's got a lake, it's got Switzerland nearby, and it's got silk factories galore. Prices are laughably low on the biggest names in designer fashion fabrics, including French names. Go home with fabric by the yard or ties, scarves, and shawls for at least half their regular retail price. The best factory in town? Ratti.

Como is about 30 minutes from Milan by train; do remember that **FoxTown,** one of the many outlet malls selling designer things at a discount, is located across the Swiss border between Como and Lugano (see chapter 8).

The Best Airport Shopping

LEONARDO DA VINCI INTERNATIONAL AIRPORT, ROME

It's virtually a shopping mall, with all major designers represented. Furthermore, a guide to its shops, which lists prices, is made available once a year. Use it to comparison shop. Not everything is a bargain, but you'll have a great time finding out which items are well priced.

The Best Sales

FENDI
Via Borgognona 39, Rome

You haven't lived until you've wandered into the Fendi store in Rome at sale time (twice a year; January and July). There are mounds of goodies (some of them a few seasons old) selling at a fraction of their regular price. Affordable luxury goods!

While Fendi sales are good at all Fendi shops, the best sale is in the Rome store. From a design perspective, it is the most fun-to-look-at shop in the Spanish Steps luxury shopping district; to get a sale and an eyeful of glamour at one time is indeed to see the face of bliss.

The Best Department Store

LA RINASCENTE
Piazza del Duomo, Milan

In response to competition, La Rinascente has redone its image in recent years. The store is a lot like an American department store and may not impress you at first. Wait till you experience its details—that's where its greatness lies. The store offers non-Italian passport holders a flat 10% discount on health, beauty, and makeup treatments on the first floor. And there's a tax-free office upstairs, as well as a travel agency, hair salon, and full-service bank. Its cafe overlooks the Duomo and will drench you with magic and memories.

The Best Historical Shopping Experience

ANTICO SETTERIA, FLORENCE

You will step back in time when you enter this 18th-century silk factory that was renovated by the Pucci family. It still produces damasks, silks, and cottons on looms that have hummed for hundreds of years.

The Best Street Market

VIALE PAPINIANO, MILAN

Fun? It just doesn't get much better than this! On Tuesday and Saturday, you can enjoy this fabulous street market, which sells fruits and vegetables in one part and designer goods in the other. Arrange your visit to Milan so that you're in town for one of the market days!

The Best Museum Shop

THE VATICAN
Vatican City, Rome

No cheap pope scopes, but beautiful reproductions of precious treasures.

The Best Free Postcards

HOTEL EDEN
Via Ludovisi 49, Rome

Postcards from Il Papiro created in medieval style with a bright blue background, lots of gold stars, flowing borders, detailed insets and design school whoop-de-do.

The Best Gifts for $10 or Less

- Designer pasta in fashion colors. Find it in all sorts of brand names, in all Italian cities in grocery stores, *entocas* (wine/food shops), and TTs (tourist traps); $6 to $10 a package.
- Caldo Caldo brand of coffee—even coffee with grappa— or hot chocolate in a "magic" cup that heats itself when you employ (or deploy) the push-in bottom, about $1 per cup.
- Soap. Try "Weekend Soap" from Santa Maria Novella or any of Rancé's soaps sold from their freestanding store in Rome at Piazza Navona. The Weekend Soap is available at Farmacia Santa Maria Novella stores in Florence and Rome and costs $10. The package consists of three bars of soap, one each for Friday, Saturday, and Sunday. Rancé sounds French because the firm was started in France a hundred years ago but is now Italian, although they specialize in Marseille process soaps.
- Limoncello liquor. Sold most readily in southern Italy but also all over Italy and in most supermarkets and airports,

this is a wonderful souvenir to bring home, about $9 a bottle. It's like lemon vodka with a pucker; serve chilled.

- Cardinal's socks. Sold only in Rome, at $6 a pair. Fine cotton knits; they come in red.
- Marble paper pinwheel. A Florentine souvenir for $10. Yet another (new) use for this marbleized paper.

The Best Extravagant Gifts

- Mantero scarf, in the shawl size; printed with so many screens of gorgeous color that you will weep for its beauty and finesse. Come to think of it, anything from Mantero will tickle my extravagance bone. Buy yours at the outlet store in Como for savings.
- Important blown glass. Venice or Murano.
- Gucci dog collar.
- Etro paisleys. Silk or cashmere is what you want. Available in all Etro stores, in most major cities . . . don't miss the Etro outlet in Milano.

Chapter Two

....

DETAILS

WELCOME TO ITALY
....

I was discussing new products with my friend Tom, the editor of a magazine, and he thanked me for sending him the Italian-made Caldo Caldo instant espresso magi-cup, which he says he keeps on his desk. As he marveled over what a wonderful invention it is—some sort of witchcraft enables a plain old plastic cup of coffee to become boiling hot by merely pressing and shaking—he finished his exclamations with the words: "What a country!"

Indeed: Hot chocolate and coffee with grappa or espresso come in magic presto-cups. Restaurants on the autoroute feed truck drivers from buffet tables that celebrate the mushroom every fall. Women wear tiny skirts and tops and giant fur coats. Everyone shops with great passion.

What a country.

In fact, it's possible the Italians invented shopping—maybe not trade, but certainly browsing and the refined art of shopping. Marco Polo brought magic to the Old World; Alitalia can now bring magic to your life . . . or Air France or Swiss-Air or American Airlines.

The French may have invented haute couture, but only the Italians can create both wit and whimsy—you get both in the contradictory notion that those fake Prada handbags sold from street vendors may just turn out to be real.

7

The Italian ability to set aside the traditional and adapt to the new is mind-boggling. The results are spectacular and stimulating. As you shop, you can appreciate views of hills as old as the ages, peeling palazzi with tile roofs and handmade wrought-iron gates and window grills, masterful antiques, and then whammo—smack in the middle of it all, tables perched precariously on bent triangles, clothes in medieval colors, shoes and bags in styles you've never thought of, and a pride of craftsmanship in absolutely everything.

Stand back in awe of the extension of lines only Italians could create: Jeweler to the jet set, Bulgari added handbags, then sunglasses, and now dishes to the line; Prada makes everything from their traditional shoes and leather goods to fur-lined sleeping bags and travel-sized cosmetics and beauty products; Giorgio Armani now has makeup (as does Versace) as well as a virtual department store of line extensions and icons to merchandising and marketing. Hey, even Bottega Veneta has expanded and now has clothes.

Roberta di Camerino is not only alive and well and back in business, she has the hottest cult item to come out of Italy since MiuMiu came on the scene. Benetton is in business with Mercedes Benz to produce the Smart—it's a car. They also own the Autoroute chain of fast-food restaurants on highways. Pucci has been bought by LVMH (*c'est vrai*) and is now able to expand with smart new shops in most Italian cities. Global domination can't be far off.

At the same time, in today's Italy you'll find that flea markets and antiques fairs are bigger than ever, and that Italians have taken seriously to outlet shopping—several new outlets and even outlet malls have opened recently.

GETTING THERE

From the U.S.

You'll get the best fares from the U.S. to Italy if you latch on to a new gate or a promotional rate, so watch local papers closely. It may even pay to make a domestic hop to a nearby city if direct flights to Italy have just begun to be offered from there. Ask your travel agent. You can always go via New York; explore other options if you are looking for a price break. Note that deregulation of intra-European flights has brought on all sorts of new choices.

You might also want to remember that Italians still have a tendency to declare a strike—or even threaten a strike—every time someone gets PMS. Back-up plans (and planes) are a good idea; also stay away from those carriers that are more prone to strikes than others.

Alitalia, the Italian national carrier, has various flights and connections from the U.S. to Italy, but doesn't play by the same promotional rules as U.S. carriers. They are also being denationalized in the new century, so they may get competitive in new ways.

Alitalia and **Continental** have come up with the gimmick of the century for their new code-sharing scheme. Book a seat through either airline, and you're likely to get a jet that is painted with the Alitalia logo on one side and the Continental logo on the other.

I usually fly Delta Air Lines, partly because I can go into one Italian city and come out of another without much ado. My style is to fly into Milan and out of Rome, but with Delta's many gateways you have many choices—including Nice; see "Nice Girl Trick," below.

American flies through Chicago to Milan, which is not too convenient for those on the East Coast of the U.S.

Off-season travel always offers better value; sometimes packages do too. Alitalia has an "Escape Package" for the off-season that includes airfare from the East Coast of the U.S. and 5 nights in a hotel in Rome or Florence for $599; you can add on Venice for $100 more. Check it out at www.italia-tour.com. This package is also in cooperation with Continental Airlines.

Nice Girl Trick

The city of Nice (France) is only 229 miles from Milan. If you are a Delta customer, as I am, note that you can fly into Italy through Nice, Milan, or Rome—the Nice International Airport is only about an hour's drive from the Italian border.

If you are driving around northern Italy, or combining the two Rivieras, this is even better—as you're in Turino in no time at all.

You can take the train from Milan to Nice, or even from Venice to Nice (this is an overnight journey and saves on a hotel room!), or you can fly. It's a 1-hour flight.

If you're headed elsewhere in Italy, look at local flights and fares. I buy tickets on Air Littoral, which flies from Nice to all cities in Italy and has bargain airfares, especially on advance purchase. Round-trip tickets from Nice in and out of Italy, with a Saturday night stay, are in the $200 price range. Note: Air Littoral has no U.S. office, so book reservations through your travel agent or online, or through Lufthansa at ☎ 800/645-3880.

From London & Continental Europe

From the United Kingdom, you can fly via **British Airways** or **Alitalia,** or any of the new low-cost carriers such as Richard Branson's **Virgin Express** or **BA's Go Air.**

You can also cross the channel and connect to sleeper trains, which are usually routed through Paris. At certain times of the year, British Airways does a promotion that offers a free layover in London to passengers with ongoing outbound flights. These fares are dramatically priced and should be considered, even if you hadn't at first thought about adding on a British stopover.

Now that I am spending so much time in Paris, I tend to book through **Air France** or on a Delta code share—I was recently able to book an Air France flight from Paris to Venice for just under $200 round-trip!

As the European skies loosen up, many airlines are trying to create new European hub cities. They offer some amazing deals to get you to connect through them. Often these deals include a free layover (as in a free hotel room for a night or two). **Sabena** doesn't say, "From Brussels sprouts the rest of Europe . . ." for nothing: They have an extensive network of travel through their hub. Call ☎ 800/955-2000.

I recently did an extensive trip with **Swissair,** using Zurich as the hub city. If you look at a map, you'll note that Zurich is just a straight hop from Milan—I was into Milan in less than an hour. (I also got to use Linate Airport, which may not work for you.) Prices on Swissair are a flat rate per segment from the hub city, so they can be quite reasonable; call ☎ 800/221-4750.

Check other carriers as well.

If you are coming from another European country via train, try combining your U.S.-bought train passes. A complete Eurailpass may be a wasted value, especially if you are just visiting two countries (say, France and Italy). Nowadays there are so many different types of rail passes that it pays to figure out which kind is best for you.

If you are flying between connecting European cities, price your tickets carefully. I needed to go to Rome and priced the airfare from Zurich and from Nice and found Nice offered me a $500 savings. If I had the Swissair pass program, it would have been less money, but since I didn't, I could just call my travel agent and pray. French prayers were answered.

For Americans, the various air-pass systems offered by different carriers can be a lifesaver, surely a fare saver. But they do have restrictions and must be bought in the U.S. before you depart.

GETTING AROUND ITALY

....

By Plane

Most intra-European flights are outrageously expensive. However, as European skies deregulate, new local services are popping up. There are now air wars over business travelers flying between Rome and Milan, a 20-minute flight. **Alitalia** flies this corridor, of course, but so do some upstarts, and now **Lufthansa** has gotten into the action by going into partnership with **Air One.** Check with your travel agent. Note that prices may vary based on the time of day. Usually, flights between 11am and 3pm are 40% cheaper than early-morning and late-afternoon flights.

Alitalia also has a deal where if you buy your tickets 7 days in advance you get a 40% discount; 14 days, 50%; and 21 days, 55% off. Not bad.

By Train

I've been using Italian trains for years and swear by them. I just can't imagine driving around Italy when you can take a train to the big cities and then rent a car to explore the countryside for a day or two. While train fares from city to city are not expensive (especially in second class, which is how I travel), your best buy is an Italian Rail Pass, which can be bought from a travel agent in the U.S.

The price of this pass, which is good for a certain number of days, depends on the class you choose. On my first trips to Italy, I purchased first-class passes; thereafter, I switched to second class. I usually pay about $150 for a 5-day second-class pass, and it's good for unlimited travel on all trains, including the faster IC (InterCity) trains and the *rapido*.

If you have a first-class ticket and a reservation, which are two completely different things (and are even purchased separately), you will not have to worry about finding a seat on a train—which can be hairy, especially if you are schlepping some luggage with you. If you are footloose and fancy free, or just going on a day trip, a second-class seat is fine. If you need more space, pay extra and go first class. And yes, spring for a reservation: It costs another $10, but it's worth it in stress-free train time.

To revise this edition a few years ago, I bought a three-country Eurailpass and splurged on first-class seats. Most people going to Italy just think about Italy, but after you look at a map, you realize that France and Switzerland are a sneeze away. I now like to fly into Milan and out of Nice, and use the Eurailpass to connect me to Venice, Geneva, and Monte Carlo before returning to Nice. I got five train rides for about $300, which I thought was a fabulous bargain. Call ☎ 800/4-EURAIL for tickets and more information.

For this edition, I was more casual and usually bought my train tickets on the day of travel. Doing this cut down on the confusion about the different types of trains offered in Italy, as I simply chose the best train for my schedule and paid what I was told to pay.

Do note that some trains are called **Eurostar Italia.** These trains do not go through the Chunnel, but they are new, fast, and deluxe. And expensive. They even come with a cute little boxed snack. Such trains are marked "ES" on the schedule or the big board.

By Car

If you want to drive around, reserve your car in the U.S. before departure, using a prepaid plan. It'll be half the price you'll be charged in Italy—even if you reserve through an American rental agency, such as **Avis** (☎ 800/331-1084) or **Hertz** (☎ 800/654-3001). **Thrifty By Car,** the Italian division of Thrifty, has beefed up promotions with fair daily rates and special 2-day weekend rates. Call them in Palermo at ☎ 091/605-7160.

Fly-drive packages may offer the best prices; check to see if your airline has a fly-drive affiliation with a car-rental agency.

The best deal I've ever found is available from **Kemwel** (☎ 800/678-0678); our car rental in Italy went smoothly . . . and inexpensively. Before I wax on about the glories and low prices of Kemwel, let me first remind you that because of the crime rate in Italy, car rentals there are far more expensive than in other European countries, and various insurance plans are mandatory. You have no choice. Furthermore, American Express and credit- and bank-card firms that offer car insurance automatically with your membership have now waived coverage in Italy. *Do not assume you are covered by your credit card!*

Now then, to let Kemwel's value really sink in, I think you should know that my travel agent tried to talk me out of renting a car in Italy, even though she would have been paid commission. She priced Hertz for me, went into a 10-minute rap about driving in Italy and the problems of renting a car there, and then left me dangling with a quote of $150 per day.

To make a long story short, I got the same car from Kemwel for $107 for 3 days! Furthermore, the Kemwel rental desk was right next to Hertz's in the Rome train station, and the drop-off point was in the same building as Hertz at the airport. We drove 500 kilometers (310 miles) and spent a total of $23.75 for gas!

To be fair, all the big rental firms have weekly rates and European plans that are far less expensive than a daily rental. None of them compares with Kemwel, but you may want to call around before you book, or leave it to your travel agent. *Remember:* Even if you want a car for 1 day, the Kemwel 3-day price is less than anyone else's 1-day rate. Pay for 3 days but use the car 1 day, and you'll still save money, since the major rental companies charge about $150 per day.

Rates vary with the size and type of car you rent, the number of days you rent, and the time of year. Also, all car rentals are taxed 19% in Italy! This tax should be included in the rate quoted you, but ask to be sure. You may luck into a promotion: Kemwel offers a "presummer sale" if you book a summer rental before the end of April. The last time I took advantage of this offer, the 3-day economy-sized rental was $59, including unlimited mileage. Kemwel has partnerships with various airlines (Air France, Delta, and United are just a few) and may offer totally free rentals when you purchase a plane ticket on one of their partner airlines. Ask!

Car & Driver

If you can afford it or you want to splurge, a car and driver are a wonderful way to do a day trip or to connect to other parts of Italy. I certainly wouldn't want to be driving the Amalfi Pass on my own. And sometimes I have so much luggage that a trek through a train station could be a nightmare.

However, make sure your driving company knows where they are going. I recently used a service to drive me to Como and to outlets along the way . . . not only did the driver not know where anything was, but he didn't speak English, refused to call the factories for directions, and wouldn't cross the border into Switzerland to get to FoxTown. *Urrrrrgggh.* Although I felt I could communicate adequately in French, Spanish, English, and a few words of Italian, and I had an agenda with phone numbers of all destinations, this guy refused to call the places and spent about 2 hours lost in space . . . and I was expected to pay for this! When we got back to Milano, he was equally lost and again refused to call, saying that he knew he was near. And I knew we were in Italy.

For involved shopping trips, consider taking a train to the destination city and then hiring a local taxi driver for a flat rate.

SLEEPING IN ITALY

While there is specific hotel information in each of the following city chapters, for those who like to make all or most of their reservations with one hotel chain or one phone call, there are a few firms that can help you out. Ask each if it has promotional deals.

Concorde: French hotel chain that owns the Crillon also has a few hotels in Italy in main destinations such as Rome, Milan, Florence, and Como (☎ 800/888-4747; www. concorde-hotels.com).

Jolly Hotels: Leading 4-star hotel chain in Italy, also with hotels in other European cities (☎ 800/247-1277; www.jollyhotels.it).

Leading Hotels of the World: Also represents Leading Small Hotels of the World, with a wide selection of the fanciest hotels in the world, sometimes multiple choices in the same city (three hotels in Florence, three in Milan, and five in Rome; ☎ 800/223-6800). Note that most of the hotels have their own websites, posted in the annual Leading Hotels catalog.

Meridien & Trust House Forte: These chains have merged; they have many luxury hotels around Italy (☎ 800/543-4300; www.leMeridien-hotels.com).

Orient Express: Although they only have three hotels in Italy, they are winners . . . and the train ain't bad either. Note that most of the hotels are also members of Leading Hotels of the World (☎ 800/237-1236; www.orient-expresshotels.com).

Relais & Châteaux: With some 30 properties all over Italy, you'll rest in a luxury property and eat awfully well (☎ 800/735-2478; www.relaischateaux.fr).

Sofitel: Hotels in Venice, Bologna, Florence, and Sardinia; part of France's Accor Group (☎ 800/763-4835; www.sofitel.com).

Westin: Westin ended up with the old CIGA hotels from Starwood or is part of Starwood (or something)—who can keep all this straight? Anyway, they do have several luxury hotels in key cities and are more than able to take care of your needs with one swift phone call (☎ 888/625-5144; www.westin.com).

MORE INFO

The *International Herald Tribune* now publishes an English-language Italy supplement called *Italy Daily*. This supplement is automatically inserted into *International Herald Tribune*

Electronically Yours

The Internet is a great source for tourism information. Here are a few addresses you might want to check out before you begin your Italian adventures:

The Vatican — www.vatican.va Dial a prayer.

Made in Italy — www.made-in-italy.com Made in Italy online is Logan Bentley Lessona's fashion and design-related site, with information on wine and food, travel, and shopping.

Condé Nast Traveler — www.epicurious.com This website, one of the most stylish and best on the Web, publishes original reports by Faith Heller Willinger and other food writers on where and what to eat in Italy.

Italian National — www.masternetit/itwg This is the Italian National Tourist office's official online source for information—find a hotel or look up a train schedule.

Italian Wine — www.ulysses.it Information about Italian wine.

CNN — www.CNNitalia.it News in Italian from CNN.

Italian furniture — www.italydesign.com California firm that can help you learn and price Italian furniture and design, which may be cheaper in the U.S.

papers in Italy. It does not come with your subscription if you receive your paper in the U.S. Not only does this section report news, it also offers cultural listings, including events and even movies in English. The Travel Update section lists transportation strikes and slowdowns.

If you are worried about strikes or bad weather—both of which can affect your travel plans—consider going to your airline's website: You will probably get more information than you will get on the phone, if you are even able to connect.

PROFESSIONAL HELP

If you are looking for guidance in making travel plans, there are a few organizations that specialize in showing you the insider's Italy. The good ones are usually regional.

Try contacting these people, whom I know, trust, and have personally worked with:

In Venice: Samantha Durrell
fax: 39-041/523-23-79
(See chapter 7)

In Tuscany: Maria Teresa Berdondini
Tuscany by Tuscans
Villa L. Galvani 13B
51016 Montecatini Terme Italy
☎/fax 39-0572/70467; e-mail: tuscany@italway.it

Other Resources

The Best in Italy is a service that primarily rents villas but can help with all your travel plans. Contact American-born Contessa Simonette Brandolini d'Adda (☎ **39-055/223-064**; fax 39-055/229-8912; www.thebestinitaly.com). Note that this is the best, and the best costs plenty: Prices begin at $7,000 per week; there is a 2-week minimum in summer.

Rentvillas.com rents villas all over Europe, including Italy. Chefs can be added into the equation, as can baby-sitters;

special events can be arranged upon request (☎ 800/726-6702; fax 805/482-7976; www.rentvillas.com).

Okay, this one I haven't worked with, but since they have tours of Italy that cost $60,000 per person, I thought you'd want to know about them (☎ 212/860-3400; www.italicus.org).

GETTING CONNECTED

Note that the phone system in Italy was changed in the middle of 1998. This affects calls to Italy from outside the country and from within the country as well. A zero has been added before the city code for *all* calls.

Also remember:

- International phone calls made from the U.S. to Europe are far less expensive than those made from Europe to the U.S. Your best bet is to call home and ask family or friends to call you back.
- Hotels usually charge a flat rate for a fax—it often comes to $10 or $15 per page. This rate is often less expensive than a phone call, but it is still outrageous!

Phone cards can be the cheapest way to call home, if you don't mind making phone calls from a phone booth. I buy a SIPS card at any *tabacchi* (tobacco shop) in Italy and use it in Italian pay phones. USA Direct is a marvelous gimmick and is often a lifesaver, but it doesn't necessarily give the best rate possible.

If you prefer to use your American long-distance carrier, the access codes for the major carriers in Italy are: **USA Direct** (AT&T), ☎ **172-1011; MCI Direct** (MCI), ☎ **172-1022; Sprint,** ☎ **800/825-8745.** Please remember that each carrier charges a flat fee for providing this service; it appears on your monthly phone bill.

As for the nitty-gritty of using a pay phone in Italy, a 200-lire coin now replaces the traditional *gettone.* If you were worried that you might have to go to a bar to get the proper coins for phone calls, relax—Italian phones have been revamped and now take various forms of payment, including phone cards.

For calling Italy from abroad, the **country code** is **39**. The access codes (area codes) for the major cities are: **Florence,** 055; **Milan,** 02; **Venice,** 041; **Rome,** 06; and **Naples,** 081. For example, to call Rome from the U.S., you would dial 011 + 39 + 06 (the access code for Rome) + the number. For long-distance calls, you add a "0" before the access code. All Italian phone numbers listed in this book include the 0.

If you are using your laptop computer to connect to e-mail, work with your hotel front desk or business center directly. I have had great difficulty with the difference between digital (European) lines and analog lines (which AOL uses). More modern hotels often have better facilities for getting connected; Four Seasons Hotels & Resorts even have 110-volt electricity and direct dataports in all rooms. Older hotels undoubtedly will have a business center where you can connect to their T-line.

I now use a tri-band mobile phone, which allows me to receive calls on my portable anyplace in the world. When I make local calls in Italy, I am connected to a local carrier and just pay that fee. Since my phone is based in France, if you call me in Italy your call goes to me in France, and then I pay the satellite relay from France to Italy. But if I am making local calls, I am charged according to local rates.

You may want to try a service called VoiceStream (☎ 888/787-3267), which means you can be reached on your phone all over Europe and Asia.

If you have a U.S. tri-band portable phone, also called a "3-way," you can use your phone in Italy after changing the band on arrival in Europe. Look under "change network" in your phone memo system. If you have a regular U.S. phone, it will not work anywhere outside the U.S.

After changing the band on your 3-way phone, you will pick up an Italian roving system and can make local calls within Italy; to dial outside of Italy, press 00, then the country code, and then the rest of the phone number.

Chapter Three

....

MONEY MATTERS

THE EURO, THE LIRA & YOU

Although prices are now offered in both lire and euros, this really will not affect your shopping style in any manner until after January 2002, which happens to be around the corner. If you have been sitting on lire, you will want to trade in your lire for euro paper money, but such paper will not be available before then. Right now, the euro is purely an electronic currency. After 2002, you will get euros whenever you use a bank machine or change money in Italy, and the lire will supposedly disappear from circulation within a year.

Just so you know, the euro/lira exchange rate has already been set; it's quite good for Americans—1 euro is pegged at 1,936.0 lire to the U.S. dollar. So it's pretty safe to figure parity with the euro when you are figuring out prices; I have also pegged prices in this book at 2,000 lire to the dollar.

During part of the research for this edition, I actually got 2,300 to 2,400 lire to the dollar, but I won't be greedy. By the time you read this book, the dollar could be in the toilet. There was still plenty to buy in Italy when the exchange rate was 1,500 to $1, so don't fret.

PAYING UP

For the most part, I recommend using a credit card, especially in fancy stores. Plastic is the safest to use, it provides you with a record of your purchases (for U.S. Customs as well as for your books), and it makes returns a lot easier.

Best yet, credit-card companies also give the best exchange rates. The price you pay is converted to U.S. dollars on the day your credit slip clears at the credit-card company (or bank) office, not on the day of your purchase.

Another advantage to paying by credit cards is that your purchase may be protected. The American Express card offers Purchase Protection. This plan, which automatically accompanies every card, assures you of extra insurance coverage for the first 90 days from the purchase date if the item you bought is stolen or damaged. Remember to save all your receipts. You must prove the purchase date and the fact that you used your American Express card, although you can always call AmEx for your "record of charge." To file a claim, call ☎ 800/322-1277.

Traveler's checks are a must—for safety's sake. Shop around a bit, compare the various companies that issue checks, and make sure your checks are insured against theft or loss. While I like and use American Express traveler's checks, they are not the only safe game in town. Barclay's is another reliable provider of traveler's checks.

Because I am a member of AAA, I get my AmEx checks without a fee; this makes a big difference to me. I also like the fact that American Express is extremely well organized and highly visible in Italy. Their offices are centrally located (usually in main shopping districts of all large Italian cities) and keep regular hours.

Bancomat

Bring along your bank card: All Italian cities have banks with ATMs. It's very easy to use an ATM in Italy; this remains your single best way to get lire (or euros) at a good rate. The only caveat is that there are a few different types of bank machines that look similar but offer different functions—only a **bank machine/ATM** (usually marked *bancomat*) will give you a good rate. Those machines that exchange your dollars for foreign currency will cheat you, so don't be fooled.

There is a fee for using these machines (usually $1.50), just as there is at home, but you do get a good rate of exchange. Most of the ATMs operate on a 24-hour basis. Call your bank and find out if the PIN you have now will work in foreign locations, or if you need a new number. I have never had any trouble using my same old PIN with my Cirrus card.

Most bank machines/ATMs are located alongside a bank so that you need not enter the building. If you need cash for a big purchase in a specific store, ask the sales clerk where the nearest ATM is located. Very often a small store will give you a sizable discount if you pay cash and are willing to forego your VAT refund. Of course, they do this because they have another set of books that Brussels knows nothing about, but what else is new?

Cash & Carry

If you must carry cash with you, use a money belt. I use a Sport Sac, large enough to hold a passport, traveler's checks, and cash. I won't tell you where I wear it, but most of my valuables are not in my handbag, which can be rather easily stolen. I've heard of extra-large brassieres, under-the-arm contraptions, and all sorts of more personal and private inventions. You're on your own here.

Currency Exchange

As already mentioned, currency exchange rates vary tremendously. The rate announced in the newspaper is the official bank exchange rate and does not apply to tourists. Even by trading your money at a bank you may not get the official rate. Here are a few points to bear in mind:

- While hotels give a less favorable rate of exchange than banks, they don't charge a fee to guests, are convenient, and rarely make you wait. Your time may be worth the difference. The rate of exchange you get is usually not negotiable at a given establishment. Hotels do not give a more favorable exchange rate to regular patrons, etc.

- If you want to change money back into dollars when you leave a country, remember that you will pay a higher rate for them. You are now "buying" dollars rather than "selling" them. Therefore, never change more money than you think you will need, unless you plan to stockpile for another trip. At the airport in Rome, you must have the original receipts in order to get dollars for lire.

- Keep track of what you pay for your currency. If you are going to several countries, or must make several money-changing trips to the cashier, write down the sums. When you get home and wonder what you did with all the money you used to have, it'll be easier to trace your cash. When you are budgeting, adjust to the rate you paid for the money, not to the rate you read in the newspaper.

- Do not be embarrassed if you are confused by rates and various denominations. Learn as much as you can, and ask for help. Take time to count your change and understand what has been placed in your hand. The people you are dealing with already know you are an American, so just take it slowly. Use a calculator to avoid being cheated. I was once cheated out of $60 in Milan. The cashier was giving me my change, counting it out in Italian, very rapidly, with a great deal of hand motion, and fooled me totally. My husband caught the error immediately.

- Memorize comparative rates for quick price reactions. Know the conversion rates for $10, $50, and $100 so that you can make a judgment about whether to buy something instantly. I know many people who type up their own cheat sheets on a computer. If it helps you, do it.

Countdown to the Euro

At midnight on December 31, 2001, those EU countries that are participating in distribution of the euro will ship the new currency to banks and post offices.

For a month and a half in the beginning of 2002, both local currency and euros will be accepted.

On February 18, 2002, local currency will cease to circulate.

If you are hoarding lire, you have until June 30, 2002, to get to a bank or post office to change your money. You will have 3 years during which you can change Italian coins for euros and 10 years for exchanging bills.

Bad Money

When I see money being handed to me from under the inside tray of a cash register, I know one thing immediately: This is outdated currency that is either useless or cannot be redeemed anywhere, except perhaps at a bank. In short, I am being cheated. During the euro–lire transition period, you may also be assured that lire are just fine. (They will be for 6 months, but you will have to go to the bank to change them yourself.)

Tipping Tips

Service may or may not be included in your restaurant bill. Even if service is included, I leave a few thousand lire extra for the waiter. Note that whether you tip in lire or USD may influence how big a tip you are giving.

The porter who takes your luggage at the train station has a set fee (usually posted prominently) per bag—do not bargain with him. The bellman who takes your luggage at the hotel gets 2,000L per bag. The man in the fancy uniform who gets you a taxi in front of your hotel gets 1,000L per taxi.

In taxis, round off the fare to tip the driver. If your driver charges you a negotiated flat fee, his tip has already been included in the price. Tip extra only for extra services he provides, such as helping you with your bags.

To thank your hotel concierge for providing very simple services, leave him an envelope with 10,000L in it. If he makes many dinner reservations and takes care of you, leave him 20,000 to 40,000L. If he has provided tickets to a sold-out performance at La Scala or rescued you from a closed airport, he deserves a lot more.

Personal Checks

It's unlikely that your hotel will take your personal check, unless the staff knows you very, very, very well and you are (a) famous, (b) rich, or (c) both. Be prepared to cry, whine, or go to extraordinary lengths to get your hotel to provide this service. But carry your checkbook anyway, because all sorts of other places will take your old-fashioned American checks (couture houses, for example).

The best bets are mom-and-pop stores where the owners are anxious to have funds in a U.S. bank account. Since the amount of money they can take out of Italy is limited, they never deposit the money in Italy.

You will also most likely want to write a check to U.S. Customs to welcome yourself home.

Never travel without your checkbook!

Send Money

You can have money sent to you from home, in about 2 days. Money can be wired through Western Union (bring cash or a certified check and Western Union does the rest, but it may take up to a week) or through an international money order, which is cleared by telex through the bank where you cash it. Money can be wired from bank to bank, but this is a simple process only with major big-city banks that have European branches or sister banks. Banks usually charge a nice fat fee for doing you this favor. If you have a letter of credit, however, and a corresponding bank that is expecting you, you will have little difficulty getting your hands on some extra money.

In an emergency, the American consulate may lend you money. You must repay this money. (There's no such thing as a free lunch.)

Italian Tax Refunds

Italy really does have an export tax credit, and you really can get it. If you've shopped in Italy before, you may know that up until a few years ago it was virtually impossible to get a refund on the tax. Now, thanks in part to unification and a business called **Europe Tax-Free Shopping,** which is running the refund operation for various European countries, claiming the credit—and actually getting your refund—has become a lot easier. Note that Europe Tax-Free Shopping has changed its name to **Global Refund,** but all printed materials may not have been changed over. The logo remains the same.

But first, let's start at the beginning so you understand the system. European Union (EU) countries have a system that allows foreign shoppers who buy goods and take them out of the country to receive a tax refund. In France, the tax is called TVA. In England, it's called VAT (value-added tax). In Italy, it's called IVA.

The amount of the tax credit varies from country to country, although major efforts have been made in recent years to bring it to a flat 15% in all EU countries after unification. England offers a flat rate (17.5%), but Italy has a sliding rate, which continues to change, by the way. The IVA was recently lowered on luxury hotels, yet raised from 18% to 19% on other items. As Italy gets stronger and the euro becomes stronger, it is expected that the IVA rate will fall to 15%.

Many designer shops now automatically say to you, after you inquire as to the price of a leather handbag, "but you get a 19% discount from the tax." Furthermore, the minimum expenditure for a refund has been lowered. Whereas it used to be that you had to spend 930,000L, plus 18% IVA, to get back a refund of 18%, now you only have to spend 300,000L to get back a refund of 19%. That's a big difference!

You can pick up a free brochure from the Global Refund people; they are often given away in stores or hotels. The brochure not only tells you the rules of the game, it also lists the addresses for refunds and provides maps of airports. If you are driving, road border stations are also listed.

However, you only claim the refund when you depart the EU for the duration of the trip. So if you are driving from Italy into France, you are still in the EU and can't claim the refund until you leave the EU for the U.S. If you go into Croatia, a non-EU country, you get the paperwork stamped at the border.

For local information services, try any of these numbers in Italy (use the 39 country code if dialing from outside Italy):

Head Office:

Calls from Italy: ☎ **167/01-84-15**

Calls from abroad: ☎ **39/0331/28-35-55**

Florence: ☎ **055/21-15-67**

Milan: ☎ **02/86-02-10**

Rome: ☎ **06/67-93-899**

Global Refund prides itself on providing a cash refund as you depart the EU. While this sounds attractive, it is foolhardy, as you will lose money on the conversion unless you take local currency. Whenever possible, have the refund applied to your credit card.

- When you are at the airport but before you check your luggage, go see the Customs officer. This is a breeze in Rome; the last time I used Malpensa International Airport in Milan, it was a nightmare. The new and improved Malpensa is getting better.
- Mail the papers from the airport if you want a credit-card refund.

- If you want an immediate refund in cash, find the cash refund desk. Look for the desk bearing a red, white, and green logo and the sign "Tax Free for Tourists."

Please note that there are two ways for you to receive a refund: a tax-free check, which you can cash or deposit at any bank; or a voucher, which can only be redeemed in currency. The voucher can be tricky because you will lose money on the conversion and have no chance to get a credit-card refund.

If you are leaving Italy via train or car, there are refund desks at the borders. Remember that you only do tax-free declarations at your final point of exit from the EU. If you plan to hit another EU country before departing for home, you don't need to worry about Italian tax-free plans. *Ciao*, baby.

U.S. Customs & Duties Tips

- You are currently allowed to bring in $400 worth of duty-free merchandise per person. Before you leave home, verify this amount with one of the U.S. Customs offices, as there is currently a bill to change the amount to $1,000. Each member of the family is entitled to the deduction; this includes infants.
- You pay a flat 10% duty on the next $1,000 worth of merchandise. It's worth doing—we're talking about the very small sum of $100.
- Duties thereafter are based on the type of product. They vary tremendously per item, so ask storekeepers about U.S. duties. They will know, especially in specialty stores. Note that the duty on leather goods is only 8%.
- The head of the family can make a joint declaration for all family members and should take responsibility for answering any questions that the Customs officers may ask. Have receipts ready, and make sure they match the information on the landing card. If you tell a little lie, you'll be labeled as a fibber, and they'll tear your luggage apart.

- You count into your $400 per person everything you obtain while abroad—this includes toothpaste (if you bring the unfinished tube back with you), items bought in duty-free shops, gifts for others, the items that other people asked you to bring home for them, and—get this—even alterations to clothing.
- Have the Customs registration slips for things you already own in your wallet or someplace easily accessible. If you wear a Cartier watch, you should be able to produce the registration slip. If you cannot prove that you took a foreign-made item out of the country with you, you may be forced to pay duty on it!
- The unsolicited gifts you mailed from abroad do not count in the $400-per-person rate. If the value of the gift is more than $50, you pay duty when the package comes into the U.S. Remember, only one unsolicited gift per person.
- Do not attempt to bring in any illegal foodstuffs—dairy products, meats, fruits, or vegetables (coffee is okay). Generally speaking, if it's alive, it's verboten. Dried mushrooms happen to be okay.
- Antiques must be at least 100 years old to be duty-free. Provenance papers will help (so will permission actually to export the antiquity, since it could be an item of national cultural significance). Any bona-fide work of art is duty-free whether it was painted 50 years ago or just yesterday.
- Thinking of "running" one of those new Italian handbags? Forget it. New handbags shout to Customs officers.

Chapter Four
....

SHOPPING & STYLE

SHOPPING HOURS
....

Shopping hours in Italy are similar to those in other major European countries: Shops open at 9 or 9:30am and close at 1:30pm for lunch. They reopen at 3 or 3:30pm (or even 4pm) and stay open until 7:30pm. Some stores close on Saturday from 1 to 4pm. Stores are open on Saturday afternoon in winter and are closed Saturday in summer. Some stores do whatever they please.

The notion of staying open all day is catching on in big cities, but not the countryside. You never find shops open all day in the south, where it is too hot to think in the afternoon, let alone shop.

Stores that do not close for lunch write their hours as "non-stop" or "continual hours," which is usually spelled out in Italian. In all cities, major department stores stay open at lunchtime.

Sunday Shopping

Just when you thought nothing ever changes in a country slow to change, well, whammy, Sunday shopping comes to Italy! Not everywhere, mind you, but more and more stores in big cities are opening on Sunday, especially the big department stores such as **La Rinascente.**

Sunday shopping hours vary dramatically from city to city. Venice is the most wide open, but most of the major Italian towns now have some shopping on Sunday. In towns where stores open on Sunday, expect those same stores to be closed all day Monday . . . or, at least, until 4pm on Monday. You can't have it all ways.

Surviving Monday

Monday mornings are a total write-off for most retail shopping in Italy. With the rare exception, most stores open at 3:30pm on Monday.

But wait, that's why God invented factories. Because factories are open on Monday mornings, most factory stores are also open. Not all, just most. Call and ask, or have your hotel's concierge call. If you are in Milan on a Monday, fret no more, my lady—you are off to Como (see chapter 8).

Surviving Summer

Summers in Italy have two problems: It can be too hot to shop, and stores can be closed!

Also, August is the official summer vacation season, especially in northern Italy. Most shops in Milan and many in Rome close between August 1 and September 1. Shockingly, some stores close for a longer time.

In southern climates, especially in summer, expect stores to close from 1 until 5pm, during the heat of the day, but to be open until late in the evening.

Holidays

Keep track of local holidays (when you check into a hotel, always ask the concierge immediately if there are any holidays approaching and how they will affect the banks and stores!), since shops will close then. Cities celebrate religious holidays with differing amounts of piety. Shops that are closed in Rome may be open in Milan. (December 8 is a big holiday in some towns, a medium holiday in others.) August 15 is a big religious holiday (one of the feasts of the Virgin), and all stores are closed.

If Christmas falls at the beginning of the week, stores in big cities will most likely be open on the Sunday before the holiday and quite possibly all the Sundays in the month of December.

Watch Out!

As a vacationing visitor to Italy who wants to believe in magic but doesn't speak the language well, you are vulnerable to scams. Most of them are small-time shopping scams, but they are annoying nonetheless, and can be expensive if you get taken.

Reputable shops (and hotels) are usually safe. But even in classy establishments, be careful when you talk to strangers. I've met some wonderful people in hotels and on airplanes around the world, but there is a rather well-known scam in which the con artist pretends to be just the kind of person you'd like to know and then—whammo—takes you for a ride.

Remember:

- Merchandise, especially name merchandise, selling at a price that is too good to be true is usually too fake to be true.
- If a person volunteers to go shopping with you, to steer you to some real "finds," to help you find some long-lost family members of yours, or whatever—don't trust him or her! There are more tourist scams of this nature in Italy than any-place else, except maybe Hong Kong. Be safe—not sorry.
- No matter how well dressed the person is, no matter how friendly the person is, no matter how helpful and endearing—the answer is still "No." If such a person is following you or becomes a real nuisance, call the police, duck into a prestigious hotel and ask the concierge for help, or walk right into the American embassy.
- Likewise, if a person volunteers to take your money and buy an item for you cheaper than you could get it because you are an "Ugly American," forget it. If you want the concierge of a reputable hotel to handle some shopping for you and you know the hotel well enough to trust the concierge, by

all means, do so. (Don't forget to tip for such a favor.) Otherwise, you are taking a risk.

- Always check your purchases while they are being packed by the store, and when you return to your hotel, unwrap them to make sure you got what you thought you were getting. Mistakes occur, but occasionally someone will switch merchandise on you. Return to the shop the next day if an error has been made. Bring your sales slip. If you anticipate a language problem, have the concierge call the shop for you and explain the situation, then have him tell the shop when you will be in for the proper merchandise.

- Don't forget the old newspaper scam. A poor person (or two or three) spots you with an attractive shopping bag. He is reading or holding a newspaper as he passes you on a crowded street—or worse, on a bridge. The newspaper passes over your shopping bag while the thief's hand goes into your bag for the goodies. The person reading the newspaper may or may not be the thief—this scam is worked by mothers with three or four children in tow. We've also heard it worked so that the person reading the newspaper passes you, grabs your glasses, and then runs off while several children pounce on you, take your shopping bags and handbag, and dash away while you are left wondering what hit you.

- Watch out for the old subway trick. You know the one, where some "boys" pick a fight among themselves between subway stops, and your pocket is picked, and they are out the door before you know what has happened.

- There is a variation of this one that I call the "Ice-Cream Trick." Someone bumps into you and knocks his ice cream cone all over you. He's very apologetic and helps clean you up. He also cleans you out.

- And then there's the old Mama Mia! scam. You are involved in a transaction being conducted in Italian, which you barely speak. If you question the mathematics, the vendor rolls his eyes, waves his arms, and screams at you. You feel like an idiot and leave, not wanting to cause a scene. You have just been cheated out of $50 in correct change.

It's a Crime

I don't want to put a damper on your shopping spree before you even start out, but I do feel compelled to point out that the hard times in Italy have brought more and more criminal elements to the front. They are in front of, and behind, your handbag. And your rental car.

I was accosted not once but several times by thieving bands in Milan. Two incidents occurred on different days, but in full daylight, in the area immediately surrounding the Duomo. In one case, it was a Saturday, and I was surrounded by a throng of shoppers. When I screamed out, none of the other shoppers even gazed in my direction.

Keep handbags close to your body and under your coat or sweater. Don't put valuables in a backpack or fanny pack that is beyond your watchful eye. Don't sling shopping bags across a shoulder and away from your body so that their contents can be lifted from the rear. Leave nothing in your rented car, and be careful where you park it. Last time I rented a car in Italy, I was told which cities, such as Naples, were considered unsafe for parking a car on the street or in an unattended lot. If you're given a similar warning, heed it.

Buying Boutique Lines

Big-name designers have boutique lines that may not have their names on them. There's Mani, a boutique line by Giorgio Armani; and GFF by Gianfranco Ferré. The players remain the same, but the names change. You'll find these lesser lines in department stores like Rinascente or even in the duty-free shops at the airport.

If you see a name you don't know, ask about it. The Flexa line happens to be the young style division of Fratelli Rossetti. The Marina Rinaldi line is the large-size version of Max Mara. A. Testoni is a rather traditional line, but the Duckling line is anything but. Malizia is a lesser-priced lingerie line from La Perla, which has its own advertising so that people don't know the brands are actually competitive.

Buying from Duty-Frees

While intra-European duty-free has been outlawed, this does not affect travelers leaving the EU through Italy and may not affect those traveling within the EU, depending on airport policy. On my recent departure from Paris to Milan, one of the French duty-free shops was allowing the discount for EU travel, and the other one was not. Go figure.

It's easier upon departure from Italy, especially if you are indeed flying back to the U.S. or out of the EU. The Rome airport is virtually one giant shopping mall once you pass through immigration. While there are tons of stores and the selection can be huge, the savings are not a sure bet. Perfume and cosmetics may be cheaper at the duty-free you left behind in the U.S. or London, or in the in-flight magazine. Not every shop in an airport selling area is duty-free (or, more accurately, tax-free; you may pay duty on what you buy in a "duty-free" shop when you take it home). Many of the designer shops are not duty-free shops. Ask! Not every shop offers a bargain—many are outrageously expensive; some just charge the going rate.

You may get a flat 19% discount off regular Italian retail on Trussardi, Enrico Coveri, and Ferragamo shoes as well as many other things. The catch here is that the Italian retail price might be so inflated that a discount of 19% is meaningless. If you buy at the Ferragamo sale, you'll do better than at the airport.

Don't forget that whatever you buy at the duty-free shop must be declared when you return to the United States. Unless you eat it on the plane. And never forget that duty-free shopping no longer ends when you leave the airport. All airlines now have duty-free shopping on the plane. The price list should be inside the in-flight magazine. *Buon viaggio.*

Mailing & Shipping from Italy

Shipping anything from Italy begins before you get there. If you are smart, or serious, you will do some homework before you leave and have your shipping arrangements partly made before you even arrive. You'll complete the transaction once you arrive in Italy with a preselected and guaranteed broker.

Contact a shipper in your hometown, or in New York, London, or your chosen port of entry for your goods, and work with them to make sure all your shipping days are pleasant ones. The shipper should be able to act as your agent—the buying game will be much less tense once you have someone to take care of you.

Find out if you need a customhouse broker to meet your goods and clear them, or if the shipping agent does this, and if so, is it included in the shipping cost, or is there an additional fee? Likewise, make sure you pay for adequate insurance and do not assume that it is included in the freight price.

Small items should be shipped via Federal Express, DHL, or another courier service you know and trust. Italy does have a service called "express mail," but don't trust it.

Before I totally pooh-pooh the Italian mail system, I want you to know that all the postcards I've ever sent from Italy have been delivered home and abroad, sometimes in less than a week. I've also noticed that concierges have charged differing rates for a simple postcard stamp. Actual postal rates are posted at the post office.

The Moscow Rule of Shopping

The Moscow Rule of Shopping is one of my most basic shopping rules and has nothing to do with shopping in Moscow, so please pay attention. Now: Average shoppers, in pursuit of the ideal bargain, do not buy an item they want when they first see it, because they're not convinced that they won't find it elsewhere for less money. They want to see everything available, then return for the purchase of choice. This is a rather normal thought process. However, if you live in Russia, for instance, you know that you must buy something the minute you see it, because if you hesitate, it will be gone. Hence this international law: the Moscow Rule of Shopping.

When you are on a trip, you probably will not have the time to compare prices and then return to a certain shop. You will never be able to backtrack to cities, and even if you can, the item might be gone by the time you get back, anyway. What to do? The same thing they do in Moscow: Buy it when you see it, understanding that you may never see it again. But since you are not shopping in Moscow and you *may* see it again, weigh these questions carefully before you go ahead:

- Is this a touristy type of item that I am bound to find all over town?
- Is this an item I can't live without, even if I am overpaying?
- Is this a reputable shop, and can I trust what they tell me about the availability of such items?
- Is the quality of this particular item so spectacular that it is unlikely it could be matched at this price?

If you have good reason to buy it when you see it, do so.

Caveat: The Moscow Rule of Shopping breaks down if you are an antiques or bric-a-brac shopper or if you are shopping in a factory outlet. You never know if you can find another such item, or if it will be in the same condition, or if the price will be higher or lower. It's very hard to price collectibles and bargains, so consider doing a lot of shopping for an item before you buy anything.

Italian City Planning

If you are going to a variety of Italian cities, you probably are wondering which one offers the best price, the best selection, and the best value. There are no firm rules—the Moscow Rule of Shopping really applies—but I do have a couple of loose rules to guide you.

The City of Origin Axiom   An item usually is cheapest in the city where it's made or where the firm's headquarters are. That's because the trucking and distribution costs are less. Following this rule, **Pratesi** linens should be bought at the factory store in Pistoia; **Fendi** goodies should come from the mother store in Rome; and **Etro** should come from the factory near Como, or, at least, Milan.

The Milan Rule of Supply and Demand   If you don't know the city of origin for an item, or want to be safe, use the Milan Rule of Supply and Demand. Because Milan is the center of the fashion and furnishings business, it should have the best selection of big-name merchandise. If you are only shopping in one city or creating a schedule that allows only a 1-day spree, Milan is the city for you.

Milan is far more industrial than the other big cities. Its entire psychology is one of moving and selling goods and services. Furthermore, while in Milan you have the opportunity to shop at factories that are just outside of town, or at flea markets that sell leftovers from factories (you mean those ties didn't just fall off a truck?), or you can luck into very good sales that are created to move merchandise.

The Roman Holiday Rule of Shopping   If you just want designer merchandise and a good time, forget about the rest of Italy and just do Rome. You won't get the faience, the souvenirs, or the gilt wood trays, but you will find all the big names in one easy-to-shop neighborhood.

Venice and Florence are crammed with tourists, especially in the spring and summer months, and the shopkeepers know you are a tourist. Prices in Venice soar in season. Florence has changed dramatically in the last couple of years: The merchandise in the streets and stalls has gotten junkier and junkier.

If you're going on a cruise of Italy, please note that chapter 10 in this book has information on shopping in various Italian port cities. Unless you have a pre- or postcruise layover in Rome or Venice, you will not have an opportunity to do much traditional Italian-designer shopping.

Shopping for Fakes

In years gone by, some of the best buys in Italy were on fake designer leather goods and scarves. These items are harder to find and once found are often so inferior to the real thing that the game is no fun to play at all.

But wait—someone just told me that he read an article in the *Herald Tribune* (I did not see the article) that said that Prada (etc.) actually makes the fakes that are sold in the streets, and that they get enormous revenue from doing so. I personally do not condone fakes because I'd like to think you get what you pay for.

The bigger question is, why buy a fake when you can have the real thing through an outlet store or a sale? Fendi key chains were going for $16 at the sale in Rome. I mean, *really.*

In a less glamorous area, watch for imitation Kodak camera film. You'll see the familiar Kodak box and logo, only to discover on careful examination that you have bought a cheap rip-off labeled "Kolak"—but the "l" and the "d" look quite similar.

In the Bag

Shopping bags are freely given out at boutiques and department stores when you make a purchase. Not so in grocery stores. Either bring your own or expect to pay about 50¢ per plastic sack. The large can of olive oil that you came to buy comes with a handle, so you might not even need a bag.

If you score at a sale in a designer shop, you can ask for gift wrap and a designer bag, but you may not get them. Pucci gave me tons of attention and free wrap; Fendi settled on tissue and Fendi bags—no wrap or ribbon.

Bar None

This is not strictly a shopping secret, but is nonetheless a strategy: Next time you belly up to the bar, consider how much money you've just saved. That's right—eating at the bar (while standing) is a money-saving tactic.

If you see a bar you'd like to wander into for a coffee or a snack, remember that all bars in Italy have two systems: Either you order at the bar and stand and drink at the bar, or you order at the bar or a table and then sit down. To eat at a table will cost just about double the price of a meal at the bar. It is rude to order at the bar, pay at the bar, and then wander to a chair with your snack and sit down.

To Market, To Market

One of the difficulties of shopping in Italy is deciding which markets to visit and which to pass up. Italy is crawling with good markets. There are dozens of them, and it's impossible to get to them all unless you spend a month doing little else. Remember:

- Dress simply; the richer you look, the higher the price. If you have an engagement ring or one of those wedding bands that spells out "Rich American" in pavé diamonds, leave it in the hotel safe.
- Check with your hotel's concierge about the neighborhood where the market is located. It may not be considered safe to go there alone, or after dark. Beware Rome.
- Have a lot of change with you. It's difficult to bargain and then offer a large bill and ask for change. As a bargaining point, be able to say you have only so much cash on hand.
- You do not need to speak any specific language to make a good deal. Bargaining is an international language of emotion, hand signs, facial expressions, etc. If you feel like you are being taken, walk away.
- Branded merchandise sold on the street may be hot or counterfeit. If the deal seems an exceptionally fine one, suspect fraud.
- Go early if you expect the best selection. Go late if you want to make the best deals pricewise.
- Never trust anyone (except a qualified shipping agent) to mail anything for you.
- In Florence and Rome, most market areas are so famous that they have no specific street address. Usually it's enough

to give the cabbie the name of the market: Ask your concierge if you need more in the way of directions. Usually buses service market areas. Expect markets to be closed on Monday morning.

Outlet Shopping

All Italian factories have had outlet shops for their employees or the local community for years; these addresses used to be closely guarded secrets. Not anymore. They say the second most visited sight in Florence, after the Uffizzi, is the Prada outlet store.

There are now locally published guides to outlets. I use a book called *Lo Scopriaoccasioni* (*Bargain Hunting in Italy*), written in Italian, which is a listing of over 1,400 outlets, according to the cover. This book costs about $18; I got mine at the Rizzoli in the Galleria in Milan. Note that it's now on the fifth edition as we go to press in 2001, so don't be fooled into buying an older edition (as I was).

I have checked out many of the listings in this book and offer some fair warnings: I don't think that listing the January and July sales at Ferragamo in Florence counts as a true factory outlet, but there are names, addresses, and phone numbers of plenty of worthwhile places. You will need a car to get to most of them, of course.

Also note that one of the older of these new outlet malls, **FoxTown,** is technically in Switzerland—it's 5 kilometers (3.1 miles) from the Italian border and right near Como.

Also note that our Italian correspondent, Logan Bentley, has her own website, already mentioned in chapter 2, and she has a section on outlets; try www.made-in-italy.com and then click "factory outlets."

An American firm has gone into business with European partners and opened U.S.-style factory outlet malls in continental Europe; their Italian outlets began to open last year, the most exciting being **Serravale Scrivia,** a fake outlet village done in the style most Americans adore, not too far from Milan.

In reality, the outlet site was chosen to be 1 hour from Milan, Genoa, and Turin, since Italian law will not allow outlets too close to major retailers. Three or four more outlets are expected to open around Italy within the decade.

Mills & Thrills

Outlets can offer truly great bargains—if they are the real thing. There is a small business in hustling big-city locals through warehouses in industrial suburbs that sell fakes or are just normal businesses that market themselves as outlets. Know your stuff, know your regular retail prices, and know a few other rules of the road:

- Most true outlets close for lunch.
- Sales help in out-of-the-way, small communities may not speak English. It's not a bad idea to bring an Italian-English dictionary with you.
- Be sure you have a size conversion chart, or know the sizes you want in the continental sizing system. There is a size conversion chart at the back of this book.
- Many mills are open Monday morning but close in the afternoon; others are closed the entire day. Remember the Monday rule of shopping—anything goes. Call first, especially on a Monday.
- Mills are never open on Sunday; not all are open on Saturday. Some factory outlets are open on Sunday, however. In fact, in outlet malls, stores may be open 7 days a week. Welcome to the new Italy.
- Few mills will take credit cards. Many will take payment in currency other than lire, usually French francs or British sterling, rather than U.S. dollars. Outlets will take credit cards.
- If you have chosen a day trip with specific outlets in mind, do yourself (and me) a favor—call first. Actually, have your hotel concierge call in case your Italian isn't as good as his. Get hours, credit-card information, and confirmation of directions. Frequently you can find these places once you get in the town—locals always know where they are.

DICTIONARY OF ITALIAN DESIGN
....

Anna Molinari   The name you'll remember is not Anna's, but that of her label—Blumarine—which has been making waves for about a decade. There are now a few Blumarine boutiques. Check out the one in Milan for a peek at her hotsy-totsy, cutting-edge fashions with a hint of whimsy.

Benetton   Benetton can only be described as a phenomenon. They hang in there and continues to reinvent, if not the wheel, then the sweater and perhaps the future. The family-run Benetton enterprise churns out some 2,000 designs a year. Check out some of the Benetton superstores in Italian capital cities; they even have play areas for kids.

Cavalli   A longtime legendary talent in Italy, Roberto Cavalli just made it into the global scene about a year ago when his wild jeans were being worn by movie stars and rock artists. This guy was king of the world in the 1970s, so his flower-power position now comes from longstanding tradition and historical reference. Only this time around, the clothes are heavily featured on *Sex in the City,* and people in the street say he is the "new" Versace.

Dolce & Gabbana   Bad boys with reputations on the cutting edge of fashion, and highly influenced by their southern Italian roots. These are the guys who were responsible for launching the particular underwear-as-outerwear look Madonna made popular in the 1990s. Fashion editors count on them to be a little outrageous, yet their collections reflect the combination of street fashion and high-end esoterica that makes a look into a hit.

Emilio Pucci   Being dead doesn't mean much when you have a name brand in Italy, or children who can carry on the business. In the case of the late Count Pucci, his children did admirably with the struggle to stay alive, and have recently done the smartest thing they could for all of us—sold to LVMH so that the Pucci brand can be revived and expanded. Already new shops and styles are popping up, and the public is Pucci-crazed all over again.

Etro   Gimmy Etro's family has been in the paisley business with some of Italy's most famous mills in the Lake Como area for centuries. The "new" Etro line is composed of fashions so chic you could swoon. Their traditional paisley leather goods is now a small part of the line. Also on sale in these stores are paisley linens and shawls, and a complete fragrance line for men and women. Everything is deluxe beyond words and makes you feel like you're the kind of person who travels only on the Orient Express. The outlet shop in Milan will bring tears of joy to your eyes.

Fendi   Fendi is a sisterhood of five women who run various aspects of the family business, which includes leather goods, ready-to-wear, and furs; now their children are in the business. The furs, designed by Karl Lagerfeld, are fun and crazy. The newly redone flagship shop in Rome is fabulous and worth seeing (it's like a museum or temple); the other Italian cities have nice shops that are small and usually teeming with tourists. You can buy something in a Fendi shop for as little as $25. Less if you hit the sale! You may have more fun with the Fendissime line, which has its own freestanding stores in some Italian cities. This is a lower-priced bridge line.

Fiorucci   If you did not come of age in the Swinging '60s, you may not even know about the Fiorucci look or the furor it caused way back when. Now that the retro '60s and '70s look is back in vogue, Fiorucci is back in business, and the kids are loving it. The two-level store, right down the street from the Duomo in Milan, is filled with kitsch and wonder and real clothes too; the main store in Milan is actually on via Torino in the heart of teen shopping heaven. Hello Kitty everyone.

Gianfranco Ferré   A former architect, Ferré's work is identifiable by its construction and architectural lines. The store in Milan, which is the flagship, is gorgeous, and, of course, stunning from an architectural point of view. The clothes are divine but are crafted more for the tall woman.

Gianni Versace The line survives and thrives under Donatella's watchful eye and tender loving care. Despite Gianni's death, Versace defines shape and color, flair, drape, and humor. In most Italian cities, the men's, women's, and home design stores are separate boutiques. Yes, Virginia, there is a Versace Jeans line, now with some of its own stores. Check out the perfume and makeup business.

Giorgio Armani Giorgio Armani has been called one of the top five designers in the world. Armani got his start designing menswear with the Nino Cerruti line. He went off on his own with a partner (1974), then branched into women's wear, where he is credited with bringing a feminine version of the menswear look to women. His look has always been unstructured, soft, and easy to wear.

Armani lives in a palazzo in Milan and rules over Armani (black label), Armani Collezioni, Mani, Emporio Armani, and the A/X line (Armani Exchange) sold in America, and the AJ (Armani Jeans) line sold in Europe, as well as the new makeup range and mini-department store in Milano. There are men's, women's, and children's lines, home items as well as several fragrances, and international licenses.

Gucci Thanks to designer Tom Ford, Gucci is such a triumph that there's now a home collection as well as must-have items of whimsy and cool, such as dog dishes. Savings are minimal (about $60 on a $600 handbag), but the cachet is high. The new Gucci means status and a whole new look—if you haven't been keeping up, you should check it out. Besides shoes and leather goods, there's clothing, scarves, jewelry, etc.

Krizia No, Krizia isn't the designer's name—it's the name of a character from Plato. The designer behind it all is Mariuccia Mandelli, who has several licensees and creates many Krizia lines, including several fragrance lines. Imaginative, with a good sense of humor, Mandelli still manages to produce those drop-dead elegant clothes that rich women wear. Many of the boutiques around the world have been shuttered, but you'll still find a flagship store in Milan.

Laura Biagiotti   Although she shows couture and ready-to-wear, Biagiotti is best known for her cashmere knits. And her new passion: golf. In her cut-and-sew work, Biagiotti has been known to show a sense of humor. Many of her styles are loose (they make stunning maternity dresses!) and fit nicely on women with imperfect figures. Her cashmeres are expensive but sought-after. She has just announced plans to open shops in China!

Les Copains   Despite the Frenchified name, this firm is an Italian sportswear company, something on the order of an American bridge designer. They are pretty well known and pretty pricey, but not quite in the same league as Armani. The line is now designed by two young men from southern Italy—one from Sardinia and the other from Naples. It's this southern slant that makes the line hot, they claim.

Mariella Burani   She has a few Italian shops, but seems to be concentrating on opening in the big-time international cities (Paris, Tokyo, Singapore), instead of opening more local shops. Little wonder: She is a big-time talent, along the lines of Mr. cut-it-clean-and-simple Armani. The clothes are spare; the Milan shop is an architectural wonder; and the prices are equal to Armani's. Total chic. Note that the family owns a vertical operation; the mills that make her clothes also produce the Calvin Klein clothes for Italy.

Marni   Based in Forte di Marmi, the Palm Beach of Florence, the Marni family (actually named Castiglioni) has become well known in the U.S. only recently, partly because of the backing of a handful of New York specialty stores and now a shop in London. Marni does a cross between whimsy and silly, and provides clothes that people talk about, not the average bland garments—that's for sure. Lotsa flowers and bold prints.

Missoni   A family venture, the Missoni firm is famous for its use of knits and colors. They have become affiliated with architect-designer Saporitti, who has designed many of their boutiques, including the one in New York and the one in

Milan. The architecture of the Milan shop is worth seeing and is an incredible example of new Italian style. Prices are high. Missoni bed linens are sold in T&J Vestor boutiques around Europe (and Italy).

Moschino   The most successful ghost in Italy, Franco Moschino is actually dead, but his spirit lives on and thrives. If you have a good sense of humor and believe that fashion should be fun, you'll love the work inspired by bad boy Franco Moschino, who was what the French call a *créateur* (a big-name designer who doesn't create couture). There are freestanding Moschino shops; accessories and fragrances are sold just about everywhere. Prices are moderate to high; the really wild stuff frequently goes on sale.

Oliver   Oliver is the name of Valentino's pet bulldog, and the line is Valentino's interpretation of sporty and casual—a great look for those who can afford such stuff.

Valentino   The famous designer Valentino, known for his work in beige, is legally named Valentino Garavani. In some countries (for example, Japan), licensed goods are registered in his legal name. These are not necessarily the man's own designs. If you want true Valentino merchandise, you must buy it in Italy—either through Valentino couture, ready-to-wear, or a shop that sells ready-to-wear.

Chapter Five

....

ROME

WELCOME TO ROME

....

It's no coincidence that Rome and Romance are made of the same letters of the alphabet; nothing sounds quite as exotic—or did I mean erotic—as a few days in Rome. It must be the palm trees. No, maybe it's the handbags. My palms begin to itch.

Whether you come for a fling, a specific thing, a Fendi baquette or a loaf of bread, to bring the kids for a real life history lesson, whether you want pizza or pasta or shoes and more shoes, just remember: There's no place like Rome.

Rome, of course, has always had a great designer upscale shopping neighborhood, and with the dollar stronger than ever, well, who needs to eat anyway? Who even has time to eat? Maybe that's why some of the stores still close from 1:30 to 3:30pm—to give the sales help a bit of a rest from ringing up all those American purchases.

Part of the glory that is Rome is that while there are heaps of designer shops, there are heaps of everything else too. Even the magazine stands are fabulous to drool over. For me, well, too much designer shopping just puts me to sleep. But in Rome, you can be someone different every day, just by the places you choose to shop.

Actually, truth be told, aside from the Fendi store, I'm not that knocked out with the so-called luxury Spanish Steps district. My best shopping days in Rome are spent in older districts, in tiny alleys, on back streets. I prefer to buy alternative retail, funky designs, vintage clothes, and soap. I prefer to prowl the Campo dei Fiori.

A few years back, I found a vintage Pucci velvet skirt (it almost even fits me!) for $50. Vintage Pucci is selling in London and New York for $200 to $400 and upward. I recently bought a chic, resort-y, coral silk pants-pajama creation at Max Mara for $217—a buy not only in terms of price and quality, but because this type of clothing isn't as easy to find in New York as it is in southern Italy.

On a winter day, I bought a medieval-style velvet chapeau that would please both Romeo and Juliet, those great arbiters of Italian style. Last trip, I bought something called "Duck Shoes," pink and green suede clogs topped off with green fur. Each purchase reflects a different aspect of Italian style and what you can find when you prowl the streets of Rome . . . all at the best prices you've seen in years.

Rome's best shops are quite affordable these days and Rome's back streets are as much fun, if not more so, than Milan's for seeking out ancient architecture and charming shopping sojourns. It's not really fair to compare Rome and Milan, so I won't do it anymore. Just note: In olden days, it was my modus operandi to schedule Rome as the last city I visited in Italy, so by then I had already done much of my serious shopping. No more. I have seen the glories of the south and I love it. Is that a palm tree? Oh my!

Now I go in and out of Rome, or do a Rome/Florence/Tuscany/Umbria driving tour kind of trip. I can fly Paris–Rome and then take an Italian train to another city if I want to, or just fly back to Paris. Or I can book a cruise out of Rome. In short, I no longer need to rely on northern Italy for traditional shopping and fashion stimulation. I can now get everything I need out of a shopping spree in Italy by booking southern Italy alone.

ARRIVING IN ROME

....

By Plane

You can fly into Rome's airport from anyplace in the world. While the airport is quite a bit out of town, the strength of the dollar makes the taxi fare bearable, if you pick a legal taxi (see below). There's also a train, but I digress.

Before arrival, please note: A private car and driver cost relatively the same thing as a taxi, by the way (a little more but usually not much). As a result, many people book a car and driver to meet them or ask their hotel to provide this service. I've been given a source by my friend, Logan; you can call Gianni Ceglia on his mobile phone at ☎ 0338/80-89-397. My friend, Claire, books Europe Car Service for her boss and his business team—this is a more formal car service (see p. 196).

If you can manage your luggage on your own, you may want to take the train from the airport right to the central train station in beautiful downtown Roma. It costs about 15,000L and is a total breeze if you're not laden with heavy bags.

If you arrive in Rome from another EU country, there are no formalities. The color of your luggage tag is coded so that you don't even go through Immigration or Customs. You suddenly end up in the luggage retrieval area, watching fashion shows and car videos on large-screen TV monitors while waiting for your bags.

Trolleys are free. There's both a *cambio* for changing money and a bank machine (better rates than the cambio), although the lines can be long. Still, since you have to wait for your bags to arrive, you might as well stock up on cash and be done with it.

You can connect to the train from within the arrivals terminal (it is well marked), but you must forfeit your trolley to use the escalator, so again—make sure you can handle your luggage on your own or with your travel companion. You can also get to the train station from outside, which is easier if you are a bit bulky with bags, since there are ramps for trolleys and carts.

Before you even exit the terminal, be aware that you might be assaulted by taxi drivers: These are gypsy drivers who may even have official taxis with medallions and may convince you that they are legit. Furthermore, they will quote the price in an odd manner, further confusing you. For example, one such guy kept tailing me, beseeching, "Two fifty." This registers in strange fashions to a foreign brain and possibly even sounds like a bargain. What he means is 250,000 lire (about $115), when indeed the going fare is about 60,000 lire (about $40) and can be less—depending on the location of your hotel. So watch out!

There is an official taxi rank, but you must find it, which I happened to have had trouble doing over a period of many years (slow learner). In fact, I was almost in tears last trip and wished very much that I had booked a car and driver. If you end up on the curb wondering what to do—look right and then walk right, you will find the taxi stand. I promise.

By Train

All rail tracks do indeed lead to Rome, be it intra-Italian trains or any of the fancy intra-European trains, including Eurostar (see chapter 2 for more on this, as it's tricky). The Centrale train station has been spiffed up for the Jubilee Year and is looking far better than you may remember it.

As you emerge from the main train station, you'll see taxis everywhere; you may even be approached by some drivers who offer their services. Again, there is an official taxi stand with a very long line right in front of the train station. You wonder why you don't just hop into one of the waiting cabs, defying the queue. Why are all those people standing in line for up to 20 minutes?

Because they don't want to overpay, be cheated, or come to blows with aggressive taxi drivers.

Rome wasn't built in a day, nor were the taxi scams being run out of the main train station. All those people can't be wrong. Stand in line, and you'll get a legitimate cab.

By Ship

If by chance you are coming to Rome via ship, the port is Civitavecchia, along the coast north and west of Rome (say: *Cheat-a-veck-e-ahhhh*). It can take up to 2 hours to get into downtown Rome from here, although 1 hour is the no-traffic estimate. If you are going directly from your ship to the Rome airport, it will take 1 hour on a superhighway, and you will not actually go into Rome at all. (*Arrivederci, Roma.*)

And one final ship-to-shore report: During the summer, most stores close for the day on Saturday at 1:30pm. This isn't really a problem for you, however, because you arrive in port at 7am and make it to Rome by 9:30am, when the stores open. You have the whole morning to shop. You go to lunch at 1:30pm, when the stores close, and slowly eat a glorious Roman midday feast. Head back to the ship around 4pm and arrive in time for cocktails. Or stop off in Tarquena, a sneeze away from the port, where they have some cutie-pie retail, and yes, I thought you'd never ask, a few pottery shops.

There is a train station at the port, but you have to get from the boat to the train in order to connect (you can walk, but it's not a stroll—it can be a hike, depending on your ship's berth). Also note that part of the 2000 Jubilee created a major renovation and improvement of the port area. They even added on some shopping venues.

The Lay of the Land

The city of Rome is divided into 33 zones, working in circular rounds much like the *arrondisements* of Paris. The oldest part of the city is 1, Centro Storico. Rarely do tourists use these zones.

I have instead divided Rome into my own areas or neighborhoods; see below).

Technically speaking, Vatican City is a different city than Rome; that's why it has its own guards (who are Swiss) and its own postal service. (Whenever possible, use the Vatican's post office, which is superior to Italian mail.)

Rome

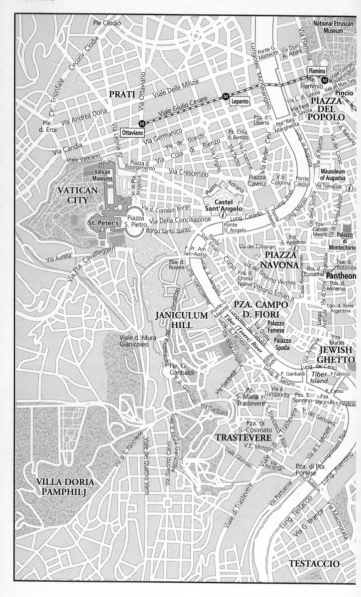

Addresses seem to bounce around from street to street; some alternate in a sensible way and some make no sense at all. Frequently, all the stores in a block have the same street number and are designated by letters. It's not unusual for a store to be listed according to its piazza or its street corner.

GETTING AROUND

Walk.

Okay, so it's too hot to walk that much, and the city's too spread out. So, the best time investment you can make is to organize your days so that you can do lots of walking; this keeps you out of crazy Roman traffic and on the streets so that you can count the fountains.

Taxi   Taxi drivers in Rome are known to be difficult, especially to tourists, especially to Americans who can't speak Italian, and most especially to women traveling without men. Be prepared to occasionally have to argue with the driver if you take cabs; be aware of when you should pay a supplement (for extra baggage and for rides after 9pm and on Sunday and holidays). I continue to have unpleasant situations with taxi drivers, enough so that I think the difference between Italy and France can be summed up in the way you are treated by taxis. But enough about me.

Legitimate taxis carry a shield with a number. Cars for hire are black with a shield. Taking any other car can be dangerous.

Metro   There is a metro, the Metropolitana. It's nice and gets you to all the touristy attractions, but it does not blanket the city. You may find the walk from your hotel to the nearest stop (look for the big red "M" sign) worthy of a taxi in itself.

To ride the metro, have change to put into the ticket machine, or look around for a machine that produces change. You must get your ticket from one of the machines; there is

---

Electronically Yours

Born to Shop Italian correspondent Logan Bentley has her own website with information on shopping and everything Italian: Bentley's Shopping Guide to Italy at **www.made-in-italy.com**.

Also note that the *International Herald Tribune* publishes an insert in its Italy-distributed papers called "Italy Daily"—it's also in English.

---

no booth selling tickets. (The newsstand will not give you change without a purchase.) Because the metro is not too involved, it is easy to ride and safe. A Metrobus card, which costs about $3 per day, allows you unlimited use of the metro and buses. It's sold in train stations.

Bus I love to take the bus in Rome, although many people will tell you that buses are slow and not dependable, especially in the rain. But the bus gives you a nice view of this gorgeous city and gets you easily to the main attractions. To find out which bus to take, you can buy a bus map at a newsstand, you can ask your concierge, or you can read the sign at the bus stop that lists all the stops. Also check inside the telephone book in your hotel room, which may have a bus and metro map.

I once took the right bus in the wrong direction—a typical mistake for those who don't speak the language or know their way around the city very well—but I had a great time and saw a lot of sights.

Rome has many bus islands that act as little stations where buses congregate. There's one such island in front of the Vittorio Emanuele monument in the old city, and another called San Silvestro, which is in the heart of the shopping district at the base of the Via Veneto and halfway to the Spanish Steps.

The bus system in Rome is similar to those in other Italian cities: You must purchase your ticket at a tobacco stand or newsstand ahead of time (they do not sell tickets on the bus or take money); you enter from the rear and cancel your own ticket in the box; and you exit from the center of the bus. Instructions in English and Italian are inside the bus.

SLEEPING IN ROME

....

American Chains

The American hotel chains have made a comfortable dent in the Roman scene; they often offer deals (in dollars, no less) that are too good to be true. While there are several chains (see below), note that with the addition of a spa, the Hilton has reached icon status. While it has a slightly screwy location, it has become a major, major player. See below for more on the Hilton.

Hilton   Originally, I thought this hotel would be inconvenient for a shopper, but years ago I decided to give it a whirl. After all, the hotel has a shuttle bus to the shopping districts as well as special promotional rates. Furthermore, it has its own swimming pool and a resort ambience—perfect for summer in Rome, which is always a scorching situation. The hotel has a fabulous rooftop restaurant, La Pergola. Last time I called Hilton to book, they had a deal that had to be booked in the U.S., for $129 per room per night. I don't need to tell you that $129 per night is about the least expensive 5-star room you can get in Rome.

But it gets better: Always famous for its swimming pool and parklike grounds, this Hilton now has a spa. Not just any old spa, as is the rage among all hotels, but a spa of such grand proportions that it was possibly created to make Cleopatra roll over in her grave. This spa has become so important in the local landscape that now zillions of celebs stay here. The buzz on the hotel has changed from that of insider's secret to bastion of hip.

Holiday Inn/Crowne Plaza   The Holiday Inn in Rome is the Minerva. It, too, is a 5-star hotel, so in some ways it competes with the bigger names listed here. Children up to age 19 stay free in their parents' room in all Holiday Inn properties, so this is something to consider. When I called Holiday Inn, they explained that prices change on a daily basis, depending on availability, but rates booked in U.S. dollars are guaranteed at that rate. Furthermore, I was offered an additional discount for being an AAA member, which brought my room rate for a fall booking to $309.25. Not bad, considering that the regular rate on these rooms is often over $380.

InterContinental   The Hotel de la Ville InterContinental Roma has the best location of any of the U.S. chains for shopping, as well as some rather good deals. Last time I looked, the Hotel de la Ville was booking at $250 per night, guaranteed in U.S. dollars. Note that you get breakfast with this rate, as well as 500 frequent-flyer miles. Also note that the Hotel de la Ville is next door to the Hassler, one of the most famous hotels in Rome, known for its excellent location at the top of the Spanish Steps.

Sheraton   Sheraton has long had an interesting position in Rome. They have a modern hotel in the middle of nowhere, halfway between Rome and the airport; it's frequently booked by cruise companies for turning around passengers. **Westin** has taken most of the Ciga properties that Sheraton was holding onto, including the Hotel Excelsior, well located on the Via Veneto and also often booked for cruise passengers. It is a gloriously old-fashioned grande-dame hotel worthy of royalty.

Please note that special rates almost always have to be booked before you arrive.

Cavalieri Hilton
Via Cadiolo 101
U.S.: ☎ 800/HILTONS

Crowne Plaza Minerva
Piazza della Minerva 49
U.S.: ☎ 800/465-4329

Excelsior Hotel (Westin)
Via Veneto 125
U.S. and Canada: ☎ 800/325-3535

Hotel de la Ville InterContinental Roma
Via Sistina 69
U.S.: ☎ 800/327-0200

Sheraton Roma
Vialle del Pattinaggio
☎ 06/545-31, or 800/325-3535 in the U.S.

Dream Hotels

HOTEL DE RUSSIE
Via del Babuino 9

While I am not a big fan of modern hotels, I admit to falling head over heels in love with this one, a recent entry from Sir Rocco Forte and as delicious and decadent as the Delano in Miami Beach. On top of all that: a fabulous shopping location at the Piazza Popolo. Sir Rocco Forte also re-created the Savoy in Florence (see chapter 6). U.S. reservations: ☎ **800/323-7500**; local phone ☎ 06/32-88-81.

HOTEL EDEN
Via Ludovisi 49

"Eden" just about sums up this hotel—paradise. If you want to combine luxury and personal service with location, this is the place for you. For some reason, the hotel often markets itself as being only steps from the Via Veneto—while this is true, I think it's a mistake to categorize the hotel in that manner. Walk one way (left if your back is to the front door) and you reach the Via Veneto, but walk straight and you connect more quickly into the heart of Rome's shopping district. Any luxury hotel that's also within walking distance of the dime store Upim is my kind of place.

The chef is famous; the food is fabulous. The concierge went to great lengths to find addresses for me, and someone from the front desk reprogrammed my computer so that I could connect online. When all airports in France were closed and I was stuck at the Rome airport, the concierge got me train tickets. Why would you stay anyplace else?

Note that the rooms are very uneven—you may want to see a few. Bathroom amenities are from Etro; there is an executive floor. Member of Leading Hotels of the World. For reservations in the U.S.: ☎ **800/223-6800.** Local phone ☎ 06/47-81-21; fax 06/482-15-84; online: www.hotel-eden.it.

HOTEL MAJESTIC
Via Veneto 50

This old-time grande-dame hotel has been recently renovated and stands ready to continue its new status in the celebrity market, a position launched when Madonna stayed here. Charmingly old-fashioned, with cage elevators, mixed matched prints in the rooms, big double windows, and huge tubs—this place is a dream come true with modern facilities.

On a more personal level, I must confess that I once left my makeup case in my bathroom here; it was recovered, and the concierge went to great lengths to send it on to me in France. That's the extra service and effort that make you a repeat customer. Doubles begin at $300. For reservations in the U.S., call Leading Hotels of the World at ☎ **800/223-06800.** Local phone ☎ 06/48-68-41; fax 06/488-09-84. E-mail: hotel.majestic@flashnet.it.

4-Star Finds

HOTEL CARRIAGE
Via delle Carrozze 36

This is just one of those "finds" that I discovered while shopping around in the Spanish Steps district. I stumbled on it, so I did not stay here but did do an inspection. This is indeed a find—a great shopping location and a nice little 4-star for those who would rather put their extra lire into their shopping sprees.

The hotel has the tiny, clubby, modest feel of home. Singles start at $150; a suite is about $250. Local phone ☎ 06/69-91-24; fax 06/678-82-79; online: hotel.carriage@fanet.it.

JOLLY VIA VENETO
Corso Italia 1

One of those newfangled, post–World War II, high-style modern Italian buildings, the Jolly gives you the best of both worlds. Your room overlooks the park, and you are situated at the top of the Via Veneto, so you just roll out of bed and into the stores. It's rare to find the American crowd here; the hotel is often frequented by businesspeople. Rates include a big breakfast buffet and start at around $200—a great price for Rome. There are also various promotional deals, including a package called Mitica Roma (available for all four Jolly hotels in Rome), which puts a room at less than $200 per night, and weekend nights, when added on, are about $120 per night for two. For reservations in the U.S.: ☎ **800/221-2626.** There is also a toll-free system within Italy, ☎ 167/01-77-03; local phone ☎ 06/84-95; fax 06/884-11-04; online: www.jollyhotels.it.

Snack & Shop

LA CARBONARA
Piazza Campo dei Fiori 23

This is one of the few places in Rome where it is as pleasant to eat inside as outside, where your experience is as special in winter as in spring. Located right on the Campo dei Fiori, this seems to be the nicest of the surrounding cafes. The interior is done in a rustic country style, with some tables overlooking the piazza. The daily fruit and flower market adds to the charm of the location and makes this restaurant a must. This is one of the few restaurants in the area that is open on Sunday, but the flower market is closed on Sunday.

For reservations, call ☎ **06/686-47-83.** Closed Tuesday.

McDonald's
Piazza di Spagna (near the Spanish Steps)

Stop laughing. I love this McDonald's, and not just because my son does. The architecture (it's in a fake villa) is astounding, the location is sublime, and the food is inexpensive for Rome, if not by U.S. standards. You can get the usual burgers and McNuggets, or load up at the salad bar, where you can get tomatoes and mozzarella. You have to see this place. The crowd it gets is amazing. It's a good place to rest between stores. Logan says to sit downstairs where it's less noisy, where Baci (the chocolates) are sold, and there's an ice-cream counter.

Nino
Via Borgognona 11

My favorite restaurant in Rome, Nino is a small bistro with dark wood walls, and it's located right in the heart of the Spanish Steps shopping area. It attracts a nice, fashionable crowd without being chi-chi.

Prices are moderate by Rome standards, which to me is incredibly inexpensive, especially for this location and style. I just got my Visa bill: My last lunch at Nino, an admittedly simple affair consisting of bottled water, one Coca-Cola, spaghetti, and a coffee, was all of $14. Tip included. The waiters are friendly; I often eat here solo and feel comfortable doing so. If you get here early (by local standards) for lunch, you don't need a reservation. Or you can plan ahead and call ☎ 06/ 679-56-76. Closed Sunday.

Ristorante Girarrosto Toscano
Via Campania 29

This country-style place is at the top of the Via Veneto (across the street from the Jolly, around the corner from the Excelsior). Sit down and feast on the antipasti, for which there is a flat charge per person, no matter how much you eat. After you've eaten more than you knew possible, they bring dinner. The cooking style is Florentine; the wine is Chianti (although there are plenty of others); the atmosphere is adorable (covered in tiles and charm); the crowd is well-heeled, although there are some tourists. And prices are moderate. Book a reservation, especially after 8pm, as the place does fill up (☎ 06/482-18-99). Closed Wednesday.

THE SHOPPING SCENE

Shopping is something you do in Rome while you are doing Rome. Aside from making a frontal attack on Via Condotti and the fancy stores in that area, you will find shopping ops as you explore Rome, and not vice versa.

Roman style is still a little bit old couture, but mostly Roman fashion reflects Rome's geographic location. Rome is philosophically the beginning of the south of Italy. As such, Rome is rather like the Beverly Hills of Italy, and the clothes for sale here have a glitz and gleam to them that you won't find up north. Colors are hot in Rome. Women are not flat chested in Rome. Skirts are shorter in Rome. Nailheads, studs, bugle beads, and sequins with, yes, truly, little bits of fur—faux and/or real—can be found sewn to clothing and, hmm, even shoes.

The globalization of money and designer franchises means that Italian designers sell their lines all over their own country, most certainly in Rome, and in just about every other country as well. The line may be most fully shown in stores in Milan, but you can find an excellent selection of these designer clothes in Rome. In a few cases, the Rome store is better than the Milan store. In other cases, something experimental is attempted in Rome to see how it will play—like Armani's Jeans store (Via del Babuino, 70A), which is a variation of Armani A/X being trotted out for the local/tourist mix on a look-see basis.

Best Buys & Power Ties

Rome doesn't have any cheap best buys, unless you are ready to spring for Italian designer fashions, in which case everything is a best buy. Oops, I lied.

Designer Fashions   You won't find too many designer bargains unless you hit a sale, but then things can really go your way. If you are bargain conscious, the best deals in Rome are at a few outlet shops (see below) or in the airport, which has a gigantic duty-free shopping area. If you are status conscious, the best buys are on every big name you've ever heard of.

Please note that items imported to Italy for sale at the duty-free shops at the airport (English sweaters, for example) are 19% cheaper than they are in a regular Italian store, but they are still outrageously expensive. Buy Italian when in Italy; forget everything else. Also note that not every store in the Rome Airport is a duty-free shop even though it may look like one.

Ties   I got caught up in how many status ties are for sale in various shops in Rome. Prices are less expensive than in the U.S. and the U.K. In fact, prices can be so low you may giggle. The average price of a power tie in New York, without New York State sales tax, is $95 to $135. The same ties in Rome cost $65 to $110. You can even buy a power tie in Rome for $35. I kid you knot.

Shopping Hours

Hours in Rome are the same as in all of Italy, but Sundays are really loosening up. In fact, La Rinascente is open on Sunday from noon to 5pm!

For normal retail days (Tuesday to Friday), shops open at 9:30am and close at 1 or 1:30pm for lunch. They reopen at 3:30pm in winter and at 4pm in summer. In the summer, stores stay open until 8pm. Because Romans (as do all Europeans) dine late, many people are out shopping until midnight. Do not let any hotel concierge or signpost lead you to believe that stores in Rome open at 9am—even if it says so on the door. This is Rome, remember?

If you don't like to give up shopping for lunch, the department stores and mass merchandisers stay open during these hours, and a growing number of high-end merchants are following suit. Fendi is open through lunch, as are many other stores on Via Borgognona and in the Spanish Steps area.

Now then, the odd days are Monday, Saturday, and Sunday. Some stores are closed Monday morning; in summer, they are often also closed Saturday afternoon. But that's not a rule. On my last Monday in Rome, I found that mass-market stores and chains are open by 10am on Monday. Designer shops open at 3:30pm on Monday. For Sunday shopping, except during big retail push months or special Sunday shopping days when everyone joins the act, again the big names are not open on Sunday—but many chains are. Considering that your choices used to be flea markets or museums, shopping on Sunday has vastly expanded.

Closed Out

Watch out for those August closures—some stores call it curtains totally. Only madmen go to Rome in August. The sales are in July.

Personal Needs

You will find neither grocery stores nor real-people department stores in the middle of the usual tourist shopping haunts, although there's a branch of **La Rinascente** and of **Upim** just near San Silvestro, close to the main tourist areas such as the Trevi Fountain and the Spanish Steps. But you have to know how to find them . . . or to even look for them.

Ask your concierge for the nearest pharmacy or grocery.

Note: The Centrale train station does have facilities to meet most needs, and Rome has several dozen all-night pharmacies, including one at the airport. The pharmacy at the main train station is open until 11:30pm daily.

Boxers or Jockeys?

So it happens that I was asked to run out and buy a few pairs of cotton boxer shorts for my gentleman traveling companion. First I went to Upim, where the small selection of boxer shorts was in knit cotton (not woven) and cut to fit a Calvin Klein model, not a middle-aged American man who gave up smoking 20 years ago and now has a Santa Claus belly. Next try: La Rinascente. No boxers. Next try: a men's haberdasher, where they finally clued me in—to buy men's underwear in Italy, you go to a shirtmaker. Voilà: They were well made, came in several styles, and cost about $15 per pair— less than at Neiman Marcus.

There are three branches of **Standa**—the Kmart-like department store locals rely on—in Rome; the one in Trastevere (Viale Trastevere 60) also has a supermarket.

Rome is more spread out than some of the other cities you'll visit; you may need to take a walk around your hotel to learn the whereabouts of your own minimart for buying water, snack foods, and all those things that cost too much from your minibar.

Since you will probably be visiting the Via Veneto, here's the name and address of the little grocery store that I use when I stay at the Hotel Eden or the Excelsior Hotel. It's called Santa Domingo (Via Lombardia 11). They sell everything from chips and bottled water to health and beauty needs to candy bars in wrappers that look like 50,000L notes (these are a great gift and cost a mere $3) as well as chocolate euros.

On this same little street—one of my faves in Rome because you feel so European, so real, so chic, so in the know just by being on it—you'll find a deli, **R. Gargani** (no. 15), as well as a fruit store and other real-people goods and services. There's even an office of **Europcar,** so you can get in your rental and head for the hills. The hills of Rome.

Special-Event Retailing

The most special of 'em all was the Jubilee year, Rome 2000, which had its own souvenir merchandise. This merchandise will be sold for many years and may become collectible. But don't count on it.

On a smaller scale, if you happen to be in Rome any year between December 15 and January 6, get yourself (and your kids) over to the Piazza Navona, where there is an annual Christmas fair. Stalls surround the large square and offer food, candies, and crafts. You can buy tree ornaments and crèches. *Warning:* Much of the Hong Kong–made merchandise is less expensive in the U.S. Stick to locally crafted items at the fair, and you won't get ripped off.

Because Easter in Rome is also a big deal, there are more vendors in Vatican City at this time.

Shopping Neighborhoods

Spanish Steps/Condotti No matter what season of the year, the Spanish Steps are so gorgeous that you can't help but be drawn to them. They are particularly magical because they lead to all the best big-name stores. Don't forget that there's an **American Express** office at the Steps, so when you run out of money on a shopping spree, you can get more without missing a beat, and then get right back to spending it.

The **Via Condotti** is the leading shopping street of the high-rent Spanish Steps neighborhood—but it is not the only game in town, or even in the block. The area between the Spanish Steps and the Via del Corso is a grid system of streets, all packed with designer shops.

Via Condotti has the most famous big names and is the equivalent of Rodeo Drive, but you'd be missing a lot of great stuff (and the American designer stores) if you didn't get to the side streets, all of which combine to make up the area I hereby name Spanish Steps/Condotti.

Note: There is one street that leads away from the Spanish Steps, the Via del Babuino (yes, it's the baboon street), which appears to be an equal spoke from the Steps but actually has a very different neighborhood feel to it, so I have separated it from the rest (see below).

If you have only a few hours to shop in Rome and you are seriously interested in designer fashion, your assignment, should you accept it or not, is to shop the Spanish Steps/Condotti area and to get to some of—or all of—the Via del Babuino and a block or two of the Via del Corso down at the Condotti end. By all means, make it into the newly refurbished Fendi, which is like an art gallery of creativity.

Via Veneto   I know that every American in Rome has heard of the Via Veneto, if only from the movies. While I invariably stay at a hotel in this area, note that the shopping here is nothing to write home about or to go out of your way to visit. The large bookstalls on the street corners are handy for a vast selection of magazines (all languages) and supplies from postcards to videos (yes, even dirty movies) to paperback bestsellers in English. There are some shoe shops and several glitzy cafes. It's a pleasant street to wander, but not exceptional. If you are staying in the area, you will probably enjoy the side streets more.

Trevi   From the Spanish Steps, you can walk to the Trevi Fountain and segue into several "real-people" Rome neighborhoods. First hit **Via del Tritone;** both sides of the street have good offerings. Then there's **Via Nazionale,** which is a cab ride away, and **Via del Corso,** which is back toward the Spanish Steps. If you can't get to all of these areas, try for one or two. The stores are not as fancy as the grand boutiques, but the prices are much, much better.

Via dei Coronari   You say you like to stroll down medieval streets and look at antiques shops? Hmm. Well, guys, have I got a street for you. This particular street takes you back to a previous century, and has the best antiques stores in Rome. Located right around the corner from the Piazza Navona, the Via dei Coronari is very small; study your map first.

Walk down one side of the street and back up the other, an area of maybe 2 or 3 blocks. Some of the shops are extremely fancy salons with priceless pieces; others are a little more funky. Almost all of the dealers take credit cards. Those who don't speak English may speak French if your Italian isn't too good. The shop numbers will go to the middle 200s before you've seen it all; there are possibly 100 dealers here.

The dealers are very community minded and have their own block association that has various parties and promotions for the public. They've organized a few nights in May when the stores stay open late, and a party in October, also for late-night strolling and shopping (officially called the local **Antiques Fair**). Candles and torches light the way.

If you are looking for some place super to eat in the midst of the antiques stores, try **Osteria dell'Antiquario,** Piazzetta di San Simeone (☎ **06/68-79-694**). You can eat outdoors or in at this simple but elegant place that's also quite "in." Lunch for two costs about $80. Don't let the address throw you; it's right on the Via dei Coronari.

Via del Corso   Via del Corso is a very long street; the part that you will be most interested in begins where Via del Tritone intersects it and extends all the way to Piazza del Popolo. Both sides of the street are lined with stores; many are branches of famous names, such as Frette or even Benetton, and many are stores that I just like for local color.

The really hot part of Via del Corso is right below the Spanish Steps in the area from Via Condotti to Piazza del Popolo, where you'll find all the fancy designer shops, a zillion teen shops (rock music blaring), and the new version of neon rock fashions for 14-year-olds, like **Onyx.**

Via del Tritone   This is a big real-people shopping street that connects the Via del Corso and Spanish Steps area to the Via Veneto and Piazza Barberini area; it is also an extension of the Trevi neighborhood. At the top is the **Piazza Barberini,** with the Bernini Bristol Hotel and a metro stop. As you move down the street until it dead-ends into Via del Corso, you have a lot of regular shops with more moderate prices than the big-name designer shops 3 blocks away.

Via dei Coronari

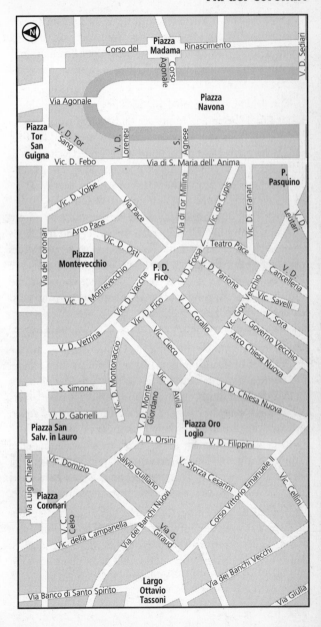

There is a large **La Rinascente** department store on the corner. If you walk a few blocks away from the Spanish Steps, you'll be at the Trevi Fountain, so to get your bearings, look at a map, and see that Via del Tritone is between Trevi and the Spanish Steps.

Campo dei Fiori Campo dei Fiori is one of those neighborhoods that is beginning to attract tourists and will certainly be ruined in no time at all; right now it is a genuine daily fruit and flower market that packs up by about 1pm. Get there mid-morning, browse the stalls and photograph the fruits, and then plop down at any of the dozen or so cafes nearby. There are also pizza places, if you don't want a $60 lunch.

Aside from the market, you are in the midst of an old Roman neighborhood, where rents are lower and fun shops are opening up. There are a number of food and cookware stores surrounding the Campo dei Fiori; the Piazza Navona is just a few blocks away . . . this gets you to the **Rancè** soap shop and a stroll around the piazza, of course. Note—there is no market at Campo dei Fiori on Sunday.

Via del Governo Vecchio This is sort of a hidden street, between the Piazza Navona and the Campo dei Fiori. Before you attempt to find it on foot, first try to locate it on a map. The street is dark, narrow, medieval, and blessed with a few vintage clothing shops. Some are the Army-Navy type; others sell serious vintage—I had my $50 Pucci triumph on this street, although the actual store where I got lucky is now gone.

Aside from the vintage stores, there are some cutting-edge fashion boutiques. I like **Morgana** (no. 27) and **Arsenale;** both are hot and happening. This neighborhood is easy to reach, is fun to shop, and gives you a less touristy perspective on Rome.

Via Fontanella Borghese Right now, this is still coming into its own as an extension of the Via Condotti on the other side of the Via del Corso. This street is quiet, unvisited by tourists, and home to several new branches of big-name designer shops, such as **Fendi** (no. 57) and **Fendissme,** their bridge line.

Via del Babuino Remember when I told you that Spanish Steps/Condotti had another part to it that was the same but different? Well, this is it. This is one of the antiques neighborhoods of Rome, and boasts some snazzy designer shops, too. It's a fun neighborhood, especially if you're just looking for furniture, paintings, or the hottest items in Europe these days: art-deco tabletop accessories.

I take it back—this is more than a fun neighborhood. This is a must-do.

Via del Babuino stretches from the Spanish Steps to Piazza del Popolo, and is filled with interior-design experts, antiques shops, and fabric and lighting showrooms, as well as a few leather-goods hot shots and designer somebodies. **Oliver** (no. 60) is the less expensive line produced by Valentino; **Emporio Armani** (no. 13) begins the parade—although it is almost directly across the street from **Etro** (no. 102) at the beginning of the shopping windfall. Further along you'll get to the new AJ, which is Armani Jeans, the Italian version of AX, although not identical (no. 70A).

Don't forget that right off this street, where you least expect it, is one of the better designer discount stores of Rome, **Discount Dell Alta Moda** (Via di Gesù e Maria 16). If you stay on Baboon Street, it dead-ends at the Piazza di Popola and the Hotel Russie, which you must wander through.

The Ghetto This is a far cry from the Grand Hotel, but for those of you who want to stay in a fabulous hotel but then travel to the grittier parts of the city, you are off on a crazy adventure. Take a bus from the train station to the Vittorio Emanuele monument and walk, or just taxi, right to the oldest part of Rome, where the ghetto was.

Take the **Via delle Botteghe Oscure** for 2 short blocks, note all the fabric jobbers (wholesalers), then turn left at the **Piazza Paganica.** You'll now enter a small neighborhood that seems very residential. Wander the weaving streets looking for the shops that interest you. This is the kind of adventure that is welcomed by a true *garmento*, someone who likes to see bolts of fabric piled up in store windows and doesn't care about fancy architecture or salespeople in matching uniforms. The area is charming, very old, crumbling, and undiscovered by tourists. All of these stores are jobbers; you'll find jeans and underwear and sweats and even a few jewelry stores. *Don't miss:* **Leone Limentani,** Via Portico d'Ottavia 47, a discounter with mounds of dishes and china—even Richard Ginori patterns.

Via dei Cestari   If you're looking for a unique shopping experience, a unique gift, or just something special and different, after you visit the Pantheon (bad gift stalls), check out the Via dei Cestari, which is filled with ecclesiastical shops selling ribbons, robes, socks, and all sorts of fascinating supplies. Start at De Ritis (no. 48) and check out all the surrounding stores. Many also sell chalices and religious souvenirs.

ROME RESOURCES FROM A TO Z

Antiques

While I can't go so far as to suggest you actually buy antiques in Rome, this is the Italian center of fancy antiques shops. There are several streets where stores abound, including **Via del Babuino** and **Via dei Coronari** (see above). If you're shopping for serious antiques and looking for a dealer to trust, look for the gold seal representing the Associazione Romana Antiquari. Note that each fall, for 1 week, there's an antiques market at Pala Parioli, and the shops on Via dei Coronari are usually open at night.

Beauty

AVEDA
Rampa Mignanelli 9

Although this address sounds screwy, actually "rampa" very well describes the fact that the shop is on a ramp to the Spanish Steps. This is an American brand, and prices are slightly higher in Rome than in the U.S., but it's a high-quality brand and good for travel sizes if you need products.

BEAUTY PLANET
Grand Hotel Palace
Via Veneto 66–70

Full-service spa and beauty center. Closed Sunday.

SERGIO VALENTE
Via Condotti 11

Logan says this is the must-do salon if you need your hair done. It has been the "in" fashion hair-stylist salon for 3 decades. Closed Monday. *Note:* Cash only; credit cards are not accepted.

Books

The large news kiosks on the Via Veneto sell paperback books in many languages, including English.

LION BOOKSHOP & CAFÉ
Via dei Greci 33

Located in the Spanish Steps shopping district, this store specializes in English-language books; they also have great stuff for kids. Closed Sunday and Monday.

RIZZOLI ROMA
Largo Chigi 15; Via Tomacelli 156

Tomacelli is the larger of the two shops; both are open on Sunday at 10:30am until 1:30pm and then 4 to 8pm. During the week, hours are nonstop. Italy's best bookstore with books in all languages.

Cashmere

AMINA RUBINACCI
Via Bocca dei Leone 51

Visitors to Capri will know the name of this famed Neopolitan source that has recently opened a small shop in Rome specializing in cashmeres, but there are also cottons and cash-mere blends. To die for.

SOLO CASHMERE
Via del Babuino 55a

This is a small shop selling garments made of 100% Italian cashmere, which is of very high quality with very high price tags. Still, check out the sales and the selection of styles, which are both sublime.

A Cooking Class

FROM MARKET TO TABLE
Via Due Macelli 106

Jon Eldan (a baker) and Carla Lionello (a cook) offer assorted tours and cooking classes and workshops for food lovers, including a market-day workshop that runs from 9am to 2pm and costs $175 for two people, with lunch included. You can e-mail this young team for more information at j.eldan@ agora.stm.it or call ☎ 06/69-92-04-35 for information and reservations. While I haven't done their class, I did a similar one in France and loved it. I'd consider this a must-do for any foodie. Yes, of course, it's all done in English.

Costume Jewelry

CASTELLI
Via Condotti 22 and 61; Via Frattina 18 and 54

This small, wood-paneled shop is crammed with perfume, beauty supplies, and a wonderful collection of costume jewelry. Don't miss the variety of evening bags. I saw this fabulous hair contraption in chenille (sort of a chignon catcher), but it cost $100—and that was with the new improved dollar. The store at Via Condotti 22 is open nonstop (through lunch, that is).

CONSUELO BOZART
Via Bocca di Leone 4

You can leave here with a collection of fake art deco and other costume jewelry. The styles and selection are great; this place is definitely worth the stop if you didn't get what you wanted in Florence. It's famous in designer circles.

D'AVOSSA GIOIELLI
Via dei Due Macelli 72

This shop offers the most exciting costume and real jewelry I've seen in ages, with inspiration from ethnic and Etruscan sources. Not for the shy.

Department Stores

Italy doesn't have great department stores, and I don't suggest you go out of your way to shop in one. There are two that are somewhat convenient to mainstream tourist shopping: a branch of **La Rinascente** at Via del Corso 189; and a branch of **Coin** at Piazzale Appio, which is across the street from the Via Sannio market and may possibly be on your itinerary (if you are spending a week in Rome and can't stand to look at another fountain).

Upim, the dime-store version of an Italian department store (which may be a contradiction in terms), has stores at Via del Tritone 172 and Via Nazionale 211. The **Standa** on Viale Trastevere 60 has a supermarket downstairs.

Designer Boutiques

CONTINENTAL BIG NAMES

CARTIER
Via Condotti 83

CÈLINE
Via Condotti 20

CHANEL
Via del Babuino 98a

ESCADA
Salita San Sebasstianello 8

FOGAL
Via Condotti 55

HERMÈS
Via Condotti 60

KENZO
Via del Babuino 124

KOOKAI
Via Bocca di Leone 5

LOUIS VUITTON
Via Condotti 15

MONDI
Piazza di Spagna 98

SWATCH
Via Condotti 33

UNGARO
Via Bocca di Leone 24

YVES SAINT LAURENT RIVE GAUCHE
Via Bocca di Leone 35

ITALIAN BIG NAMES

BELTRAMI
Via Condotti 84

BENETTON
Piazza di Spagna 94

BOTTEGA VENETA
Piazza San Lorenzo 9

BYBLOS
Via Borgognona 7

DOLCE & GABBANA
Piazza di Spagna 82–83; Via Borgognona 7d

EMPORIO ARMANI
Via del Babuino 140

ETRO
Via del Babuino 102

FENDI
Via Borgognona 36–49; Via Fontanella di Borghese 57

FENDISSIME
Via Fontanella di Borghese 56a

FERRAGAMO
Via Condotti 73

GIANFRANCO FERRÈ
Via Borgognona 42

EGON VON FURSTENBERG
Via Belsiana 5/6

GIANNI VERSACE (MEN)
Via Borgognona 24

GIANNI VERSACE (WOMEN)
Via Bocca di Leone 26

GIORGIO ARMANI
Via Condotti 77

GUCCI
Via Condotti 8

ICEBERG
Via Condotti 6

LA PERLA
Via Condotti 79

LAURA BIAGIOTTI
Via Borgognona 43

LES COPAINS
Piazza di Spagna 32–35

MAX & CO.
Via Condotti 46

MAX MARA
Via Condotti 17–19; Via Frattina 28

MIMMINA
Via Borgognona 22

MISSONI
Piazza di Spagna 78

MISSONI SPORT
Via del Babuino 96a

PRADA
Via Condotti 92/95

TRUSSARDI
Via Condotti 49

VALENTINO
Via Condotti 13

VALENTINO MISS V
Via Bocca di Leone 15

ZEGNA
Via Borgognona 7

Discounters

DISCOUNT SYSTEM
Via Viminale 35

This store is possibly owned by the same people who own Il Discount Dell Alta Moda, or else it is just patterned after it. They have a very similar brochure and the same price system—that means to get the accurate price, you must deduct 50% from the marked price on the tag. So don't let the price tags throw you.

In terms of selection, Discount System is a larger store and has a much, much, much greater selection. I spent an hour here touching everything and trying to buy something but left empty-handed. But Barbara has bought tons of Prada here.

There's menswear, women's wear, shoes, handbags, luggage, belts, ties, dressy dresses, and every big-name Italian designer in some form or another. The clothes are at least a year old.

The location is convenient enough to make this a thought-provoking choice for bargain shoppers. It's around the corner from the Grand Hotel and down the street from the main train station; you can take the metro to Repubblica and walk. The same metro will also take you to Piazza di Spagna and the Spanish Steps.

I once began my morning here (the store does not open promptly at 9:30am, so take your time) then walked the few blocks to the metro and went on to Piazza di Spagna, where I shopped the Baboon Street and ended up at Via di Gesù e Maria for the other discount store. Seeing both discount stores in 1 day made it a brilliant experience.

IL DISCOUNT DELL ALTA MODA
Via di Gesù e Maria 16

This discount resource advertises like mad, so you may have already read about it. The best news is that it is so close to the designer stores in the Spanish Steps area that you have nothing to lose by stopping in. The bad news is that you might be wasting your time, as is possible at any discount outlet. I am large and have a size problem, but there's no question that these guys carry big-name stuff.

Both designer clothes and accessories are at discounted prices—the problem is lack of range, lack of sizes, and sometimes high prices (even at a discount some of these prices will make you wince). *Important note:* The price is one-half of the marked price on the ticket. So if you are going to wince, do so accurately.

The help may not speak English, and you may not feel comfortable with the system until you figure out how to read the price tags properly. The house does offer a free color brochure with text in various languages that describes its retail system. The text is so breathless (the English text, anyway) that it doesn't give you the hard facts.

The handbags are probably the best deal. There's a little bit of menswear, though the ties are awful. Yes, I have seen Gucci here.

SHOCK STOCK
Via della Farnesina 99–101

This is one of Barbara's finds. It's not far from Campo dei Fiori and carries brand-name clothes and cashmeres. It is open in August but closed Saturday afternoon of every August weekend.

Home Style

C.U.C.I.N.A.
Via del Babuino 118

This store is actually similar to Pottery Barn or Crate and Barrel in the U.S. or even Conran's in London, but this is the Italian version. It's a must for foodies and those seeking gifts for cooks and gourmands; lots of little doodads. They also have a small store farther up the street for storage items.

FRETTE
Piazza di Spagna 11

This is a branch of the famous Italian linen house that sells both luxury linen and a hotel line, which is high quality but less expensive.

RICHARD GINORI
Via Cola di Rienzo 223

Ginori gave up its Condotti address years ago; this is the Roman branch of the Florentine porcelain maker.

Jean-Louis Ginibre's Secret List of Jazzy Record Dealers

Jean-Louis Ginibre, the editorial director of Hachette Filipacchi Magazines in New York, has passed along his favorite Roman picks for second-hand jazz LPs:

DOCTOR MUSIC   *Via dei Gracchi 41–43*

MILLERECORDS   *Via dei Mille 41*

ROUND MIDNIGHT DISCHI   *Via P. Antonio Micheli 30*

Malls

CINECITTA'DUE SHOPPING CENTER
Via Togliatti 2

My God, what is Rome coming to? It's an American-style shopping mall with more than 100 stores; open "nonstop." Metro stop: Subaugusta-Cinecitta. This mall is for locals; I cannot imagine why a tourist would visit this one.

ROMA DOWNTOWN
Via di Propaganda 7a

This is a store with the concept of a mall—major brands and goodies all located under one roof. At least it's conveniently located near the Spanish Steps. It's for tourists and it is open on Sunday. Hours are unusual, so please note: Monday, Tuesday, and Thursday to Sunday 10am to 8pm, Wednesday 3 to 8pm. Popular with Japanese visitors.

Markets

Although Rome's main flea market at Porta Portese is famous, I've never found it that good—except when I needed to buy extra luggage because I'd gone wild at Fendi. The biggie is held on Sunday from 6am to 2pm. You can get there at 8am and do fine; this is not like the Bermondsey Market in London, where you must be there in the dark with a flashlight in your hand. In fact, in Rome, please go to flea markets only in daylight.

The big flea market is officially called the **Mercato Di Porta Portese;** it stretches for about a mile along the Tiber River, where about 1,000 vendors are selling everything imaginable—a lot of which is fake or hot (or both). Enter the market about halfway down Viale Trastevere, where the old clothes are. This way you avoid miles of auto accessories. You can give it a miss as far as I am concerned.

The big news in Rome, though, is that "private" flea markets are popping up—real people just rent a table and sell off last year's fashions or whatever turns up in grandma's palazzo. Often the sellers are aristos or celebs. Check the Friday edition of the local newspaper *La Repubblica* for the weekend market schedule, listed under a heading called Mercatini (Markets) on the weekend what's happening page.

Typically these events are held on Sunday, may cost 3,000 to 15,000 lire to attend, and have a few hundred vendors. They do not open super early but struggle to open around 10am and are hottest from noon to 1pm; most are in areas off the beaten track and may require a bit of a taxi ride.

Via Sannio is a busy "real people" market area with all kinds of fabulous junk. Everything is cheap in price and quality. The goods are all new, no antiques. Many of the vendors who sell on Sunday at Porta Portese end up here during the week, so if you miss Sunday in Rome, don't fret. Just c'mon over here. The crime problem (pickpockets) seems to be less during the week, also. There's a **Coin** department store on the corner. You can get here by bus or metro; because it's in a corner of central Rome, the taxi fare can be steep.

Piazza Fontanella Borghese, not far from the Spanish Steps, has 24 stalls selling prints, maps, books, coins, and some antiques. Good fun; a class act. Open Monday to Saturday 9am to 6pm, possibly later on summer evenings.

Pharmacies & Soap Sellers

RANCÈ
Piazza Navona 53

This firm was from the south of France, where its ingredients originate, but it has since become Italian. They are most famous for their soap, although now there is a full line of bath and beauty products as well as scents. The brand is sold mostly through catalogs in the U.S. but costs half the U.S. price when bought in the new shop in Rome. You'll have a wonderful time with the assortment and with making up gift baskets and packs. There is a booklet in English that explains the French origins of the goodies as well as all the properties of the line.

SANTA MARIA NOVELLA
Corso Rinascimento 47

Hmm, this isn't a traditional pharmacy even though it calls itself a pharmacy. Yes, this is a branch of the famous Florentine address. They have expanded enormously in the last few years with stores in many European capital cities. This one, small and new, is a block from Piazza Navona. The salespeople do not speak English, but if you give it some time and some mime, you'll sample everything and figure it all out. Weekend soap, for $10, is one of my favorite gifts.

Plus Sizes

ELENA MIRO/SORRISO
Via Frattina 11

Designed by Spanish maven Elena Miro, this line begins at size 46 (about a size 16, although I wear a size 46 and am a 12–14 in U.S. sizes). The store is a chain with stores popping up all over Europe selling chic and stylish work and play fashions for less money than Marina Rinaldi. Sort of in the Ann Taylor look and league.

Marina Rinaldi
Largo Goldoni 43

A division of the design firm Max Mara, Marina Rinaldi is now a global brand with chic fashions for the large-sized woman. Its first store has just opened in America.

Shoes & Handbags

There are scads of little shops selling leather goods all over Rome, and all over every other major Italian city, for that matter.

Bottega Veneta
Piazza San Lorenzo 9

This gorgeous Bottega shop is new, it's across the way from the newer Louis Vuitton that has newly become luxe headquarter off of the Spanish Steps shopping district; it is hard to find unless you know where to look. Is the store worth finding? Well, yes. Prices are less than in the U.S., but there are no bargains here. That won't shock anyone, as Bottega has never had inexpensive merchandise anyway. The store has two levels, many collections, and is to drool for.

Fragiacomo
Via Condotti 35

This store has goods for him and her, and high-quality goods at that, with prices closer to $100 than $200, which is more the average for this kind of quality. Many of the looks are adaptations of the current faves—a Chanel-style pump, etc. There are many low-heeled fashionable styles as well as ballet flats for $100, which isn't the lowest price in Rome but is pretty good. This is one of those bread-and-butter resources.

Tod's/Hogan
Via Borgognona 45

Tod's is significantly less expensive in Italy than the U.S. Although the scene started with the driving shoe, the cult is

Papal Shopping

If you are on a quest for religious items (nonantique variety), a dozen shops surrounding St. Peter's Square offer everything you've been looking for. Most of the shops will send out your purchase to be blessed by the pope. Allow 24 hours for this service. Some of the stores will then deliver the items to your hotel; others ask you to return for them. If you are having items blessed, make sure you understand how you will be getting your merchandise back.

Merchandise ranges from the serious to the kitsch. Papal shopping falls into three categories: There are a number of gift stands and shops scattered throughout the Vatican; there is a string of stores in Vatican City; and there are vendors who sell from card tables on the sidewalks as you walk from the entrance/exit of the Vatican Museum (this way to the Sistine Chapel) to the front of St. Peter's.

Buy everything from the sublime to the ridiculous: Bart Simpson meets the pope T-shirts, rosaries, medals, glow-in-the-dark 3-D postcards—all tastes, all price ranges.

If you are a postcard freak, remember that Vatican City is an independent state; it has its own post office and its own stamps.

so well established that now there's the Hogan line of sports shoes, high heels in the Tod's line, and very fancy (and expensive) leather handbags. Shoes begin at around $200. Note that this brand used to be called jpTod's but has now streamlined to simply Tod's.

FRATELLI ROSSETTI
Via Borgognona 69

The Rossetti brothers are at it again—shoes, shoes, shoes, and now at affordable prices with the wonder dollar making a pair of gorgeous shoes come in under $200. That happens to be a major breakthrough. There are men's and women's shoes as well as belts and even some clothes.

LILY OF FLORENCE
Via Lombardia 38

With shops in Florence and in Rome, Lily comes to me via a letter from Dr. Rocco DeMasi, who wrote to tell me all about his wife's purchases. Anytime a husband writes I've got to take notice. It seems that Mrs. DeMasi has narrow feet (hard to fit in Italy) but bought several pairs of fabulous shoes at 30 to 40% less than American prices. The Rome shop is right off the Via Veneto, in the rich area I described in "Shopping Neighborhoods" above. I must say I was not knocked out, but I don't have narrow feet either.

TESTONI
Via Condotti 80

A source for normal looks for men and women and a few out-rageously hip designs, found in the Duck Shoe collection.

Teens

DIESEL
Via del Corso 184

The Italian jeans firm with jeans and other casual clothing items, a must-do for the local scene and the perfect gift for any blue jeans snob. The Style Lab is upstairs.

ONYX
Via del Corso

There's another Onyx on the Via Frattina and stores all over the world; this Roman flagship is a block deep and lined with video screens, blue neon lights, teenage girls, and copies of the latest looks re-created into inexpensive clothing and trends. Even if you buy nothing and know no teens, come by just to wander around and marvel at what has happened to civilization.

ROME ON A SCHEDULE

....

TOUR 1: ROMAN HOLIDAY

Knowing your way around Rome is great; browsing all the stores between the Grand Hotel and the Piazza Navona is fun. But let's get small.

The best shopping in Rome is in the Spanish Steps area, and what you really need is a good understanding of how to tackle that area. Essentially, what you should do is walk up and down every street from the Via Frattina to the Via Vittoria, between Via del Corso and Piazza di Spagna, including the fabulous Via del Babuino, which shoots off beside the Piazza di Spagna heading to the Piazza del Popolo.

If you are thorough and really enjoy each of the shops, you can probably do this in a week. If you are swift, you'll do it in a day. If you are desperate, you can manage in a half day. Obviously, you'll just go into those stores that beckon you.

Once you reach Piazza del Popolo, make sure you walk back toward the Spanish Steps on Via del Corso. That's after you have peeked at the new **Hotel de Russie,** of course.

Via del Corso   Forgive me for raving, but I think this is tons of fun. It's a "real people" shopping street with normal stores, lots of locals, and a lot of teenage shops. You may even find the Via del Corso refreshing, after you've seen the high prices in the tony shops along the Via Condotti.

Via dei Due Macelli   This one runs parallel to Via del Corso, but at the top of the shopping trapezoid, so it bumps into the Spanish Steps. This is a more upscale street than Via del Corso. It is considered a fine address, harking back to the immediate post–World War II years. **Pineider** has a shop here (no. 68), one of their nicest shops in all of Italy for paper goods, office items, and stationery chic. The Via dei Due Macelli runs right into the **Piazza di Spagna,** so it's a good path to walk if you are coming from Via del Tritone. If you're hungry for home, don't miss **McDonald's** (no. 46), which is hard to find because it does not have a big sign and is hidden in a pseudo-villa.

Via Frattina   This is the first serious shopping street, as you approach from the Via del Tritone area. It is very different from the rest of the Spanish Steps streets, because it still has reasonably priced stores on it and is by no means as hoity-toity as the rest of the neighborhood. Among the finds are two identical Castelli shops—a perfume shop that sells lots of hair clips, earrings, costume jewelry, and fun doodads.

Via Borgognona   Pure heaven! This is now the fanciest of the Spanish Steps streets, although those with shops on Via Condotti may argue otherwise. Look for **Laura Biagiotti's** high-tech mini–department store (no. 43), **Gianfranco Ferrè** (no. 42), and **Gianni Versace** (no. 41). **Fratelli Rossetti** is at no. 5a, and Fendi is at nos. 39 and 40. And, of course, my favorite restaurant, **Nino,** is here (no. 11). You must stop into the Fendi shops because they have done major renovations. Much fun.

Via Condotti   This is the best-known shopping street of Rome with the most famous names on it. It is an old-fashioned area and still has many of the big-time shops, where you should at least check the windows. **Fogal** (no. 55) has no bargains compared with U.S. prices; **Prada, Cèline,** even **Valentino.**

TOUR 2: BACK STREETS SHOPPING TOUR

This tour assumes you have already done Tour 1 and shopped your heart out in the nirvana of Italian big-name retail around the Spanish Steps area. If you didn't finish that tour, you can piggyback it onto this tour as the first part, or you can start at the Via del Babuino and walk toward Piazza de Popolo and then come back in the other direction on the Via del Corso. I'm starting you out on the Via del Corso; how you get there is your business.

1. Walk along the Via del Corso from where it begins at the Piazza del Popolo. Things may begin a little bit slowly, but within a

block you'll be surrounded by teenybopper shops that specialize in the Italian version of the American look. If you have teens with you, be prepared to spend. If this kind of fashion bores you to tears and you haven't had a shot at the Italian version of Loehmann's yet, then make a quick detour on Via di Gesù e Maria and pop into the discount designer shop at no. 16. Then hop right back onto the Corso and continue walking.

2. When you get to the Piazza San Lorenzo, which is right near the Plaza Hotel, hang a right. You'll see a cinema, but since you are on a shopping tour, instead head for **Deco,** a knick-knack designer store where even if you don't smoke you'll have to marvel at the ashtrays and other objects (Piazza San Lorenzo in Lucina 2).

3. At the end of this piazza, tuck into the left on Via Campo Marzio and enjoy the tiny shops and workshops that make Italy what it is.

4. Curve around the little streets, shopping wherever you please until you hit the Piazza Navona. Should you get lost in this area of old-fashioned cobblestones, just ask for the Piazza Navona. If you do not mind paying 22,000L (ouch!) for an ice cream, you can sit down at one of the cafes on the piazza for a break. You can shop the tourist stalls, have your caricature painted, or keep on moving right through to the end of the piazza to cross the Corso Vittorio Emanuele II.

5. Once across the street, you are walking straight, but the street is now named Via Baullari; this will lead you directly to the Campo dei Fiori. Ready for lunch? *Si!*

Chapter Six

·················

FLORENCE

WELCOME TO FLORENCE

··

Putting the Hannibal Lecter School of Tourism on behalf of
the city of Florence aside, Florence is indeed a terrific city. Travel
agents will tell you that Florence is as popular as it is because
of all the art treasures housed there, all the palaces and statues and masterpieces and fountains and churches and culture.
They remind you of the magnificent light and of the Arno River
gracefully winding its way under medieval bridges.

Rarely do they tell you that on top of all that, there are so
many tourists that you could die; that the shopping in the city
center is expensive and touristy; or, that the real fun is nearby,
but out of town . . . or hidden in secret sources. I guess that's
my job.

Oh, plenty of people will rave about Florence as a fabulous city, and it is. But I speak from a jaded point of view. And
I feel compelled to tell you everything. It's not that I'm down
on Florence or want to rain on your parade, I just consider
myself honest. Hmmmm, let's call that sophisticated.

In terms of shopping, Florence does not offer as much of
the classic, big-name, big-ticket Italian designer shopping as
in Rome or Milan, although Florence does have a street of dream
shops and fashionable big names. And every shoe maven
knows by heart the address of the flagship Ferragamo store,
located in the sole of the best shopping. Sorry. I lose myself.

Florence does indeed offer a charming, country-elegant shopping paradise that combines every element of retail: boutiques representing many of the hottest designers in the world, trendy local shops offering the best of finely crafted gift items, several flea markets, and a fabulous old bridge jammed with jewelry shops. It's also got two competing department stores a block from each other, so you have more shopping ops right there; there's also a good dime store unless they change it into a FNAC, selling CDs, by the time you get there, some nice flea markets, and best of all, Florence serves as the gateway to some superlative factory outlets.

The city reverberates with a total feeling of Old World delight that makes every minute you spend in Florence an added value to the price of your purchase. It also reverberates with tourists, so don't be shocked if the crass gets mingled with the charm. My suggestion? Spend some time getting culture; spend a few hours on the prowl; book a day with Faith Heller Willinger, the *Gourmet* editor and American food maven living in Florence, who now takes on visitors; and then book a day to hit the outlets to shop your heart out; and perhaps another day to drive in the countryside, to taste wine and olive oil and find a few artisans.

ARRIVING IN FLORENCE

By Train

If you are coming to town by train, do pay attention: There are about three train stations in Florence, and while you probably won't get off at the wrong one, you may have a few very nervous moments. You want the **Santa Maria Novella** (often written as S.M.N.) rail station. If you're arriving by plane from Pisa, you can take the train directly from the Pisa airport to Florence.

The train station is smaller than the one in Milan and less intimidating—porters (for a fixed price, currently 1,500L per suitcase) will help you to a taxi, or you can simply follow signs to the left side of the station (left if you are arriving and walking toward the front of the station).

The train ride from Rome takes about 2 hours; from Milan about 3 hours. Note that there are Eurostar trains and IC (Inter-City) trains; the IC takes a half hour longer to Rome but may be less expensive or included without a supplement in your travel pass. Ask.

By Plane

Before small intra-European airlines were fashionable, you had to fly into Pisa to fly to Florence. While you still have that option and the Pisa airport is larger, you can now fly directly into Florence.

Please note that the airport is lovely (good shopping for such a small airport), but there are often weather problems, and you can't count on a timely arrival or departure. But then, this is Italy after all.

Most people still use the Rome airport because you get your long-haul flights there and can easily connect to Florence by train from Rome, although there is no longer a train from the Rome airport straight to Florence. Still, you can connect through the Central station quite easily.

Getting Around

It's a good thing you can walk just about everywhere in central Florence, because more and more bans are being put on vehicular traffic. You can get a taxi at the train station, but this is a city for walkers. There are very few taxi ranks, and taxis do not cruise; be prepared to call a taxi if you want one.

For your day trip to Siena (see below), you'll want to take the **SITA bus.** The SITA station (☎ 055/48-36-51) is across the street from the Santa Maria Novella train station, and it's an easy walk from most hotels. For your day trip to **Forte dei Marmi,** you'll need the **LAZZI line** (☎ 055/21-51-54), also located near the Santa Maria Novella station.

If you need a taxi to pick you up somewhere, call ☎ 055/43-90 or 055/42-42.

Florence

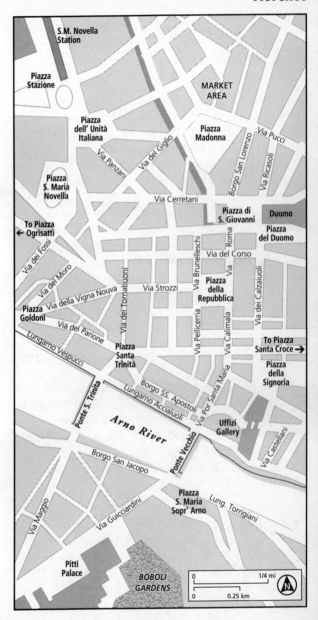

SLEEPING IN FLORENCE

....

GRAND HOTEL VILLA MEDICI
Via il Prato 42

I have been hanging out at this hotel for years and while the
location at first seems slightly off, it's actually great—you are
walking distance to the train station, the bus station and city
center, and also not far from the *autostrada* if you are headed
to the outlets or to Siena or the countryside. It's also one block
from the Tuesday flea market and a 10-minute taxi ride from
the airport.

Meanwhile, the charm of the hotel is the property itself—
it has a garden, and you can see mountains out your window.
The furnishings fall into the shabby-chic mode, which means
that while the hotel is a palace, it's a comfortable palace and
the kind of palace you would want to have for your own; it's
not stiff and formal or forbidding.

On my last visit I had what they call an apartment, which
is sort of a suite, but it has two bathrooms, and the living room
has a sofa bed; this is great for those traveling with kids. It has
numerous rates and promotions based on the season; doubles
are about $300 without a promotion.

Member, Leading Hotels of the World, in the U.S. book
through ☎ **800/233-6800**. Local phone ☎ 055/238-13-31;
fax 055/238-13-36; www.villa.medici@fi.flashnet.it.

Note: Do not confuse this hotel with the Grand Hotel.

HOTEL HELVETIA & BRISTOL
Via dei Pescioni 2

Location, location, location: charm, charm, charm. This is a
small hotel, that just added about 20 rooms and is right smack
in the heart of downtown. A double room will cost about $300
(including tax). Book in the U.S. through **Relais & Chateaux,**
☎ **212/856-0115**. Local phone ☎ 055/28-78-14; fax 055/
28-83-53.

HOTEL LUNGARNO
Borgo San Jacopo 14

This hotel was a great secret find of mine when it was a dump—it overlooks the Arno, it's on the Pitti side of the river, and it's right in the heart of some fabulous boutiques. Now the Ferragamo family has bought it, totally renovated it, and turned it into a post-moderne layout from a design magazine. Local phone ☎ 055/272-61.

SAVOY HOTEL
Piazza della Repubblica 7

If I hadn't seen it, I wouldn't believe it. This dumpy old grande dame was bought by Sir Rocco Forte and totally redone. It's now similar to the Hotel Russie in Rome and a must-do, if only you pop in for a drink or to sit in the library of the lobby. The style is neo-classical Miami Beach super chic and oh so moderne, elegant, and plush. It's the center of the city and a fabulous shopping location as well. Doubles begin around $400. Book through Leading Hotels in the U.S., ☎ 800/233-6800. Local phone ☎ 055/273-51; fax 055/273-58-88; www.rfhotels.com.

THE SHOPPING SCENE

If you're in Florence for the first time, you may be overwhelmed. If you are combining art, culture, and shopping on a short time schedule, you will most certainly be overwhelmed. If this is a repeat trip and you have a discerning eye, you may want to take a few shortcuts. Certainly the shopping scene is changing quickly, and sophisticated travelers may not be pleased.

The department store **La Rinascente** has brought some energy to the heart of town, but the lack of a dime store or real people store is felt. (Although I will point you to Standa, stand by.) Many designer big names keep coming to town or renovating. However, you can do your serious shopping in other cities and save Florence for specialty shopping, unique items, and shopping experiences you simply can't get elsewhere. In fact, if you ask me, Florence is for having some experiences that make for memories, not for buying junk. Come to think of it, I love junk.

You will undoubtedly have to make lists of priorities so you can work in as much as possible. (Save the rest for the return trip you will be committed to making.) If your time for shopping is truly limited to perhaps 2 or 3 hours, here's a quick plan for first timers:

- Spend an hour at either the **San Lorenzo flea market**—the area from Piazza Madonna around to San Lorenzo Church, where goods are heaped on carts, and faux designer scarves and handbags commingle with pottery, T-shirts, traditional paper goods, and blue jeans—or the **Straw Market,** where you'll find a similar scene. You don't need to do both markets, and the Straw Market is more centrally located, 2 blocks south of the Piazza della Repubblica.
- Walk across the **Ponte Vecchio,** if only for the experience, and head toward the Pitti Palace—there are a few other shops here that you just have to see before you return to your schedule or tour. You will have only sampled the Florentine wonders, but you'll go home with more than enough gifts and souvenirs.
- Try my "back alley walk," which will get you to the San Croce Leather School and past a million so-called leather factory outlets. Along the way you'll find many cheapie handbags. (Try **Eusebio,** Via del Corso, where I bought my $30 plastic/reptile Birkin bag!)

Here are some other thoughts on how to organize your shopping time:

- If you are going on to Rome, you may want to do your designer shopping there and concentrate on handcrafted items in Florence. The very fact that several big-name design houses, including **Chanel** and **Missoni,** have stores in other Italian cities, but not in Florence, tells you right off the bat that Rome and Milan are better designer sprees.

- If you plan to take home gifts, have a list of the recipients and how much you want to spend on them—yes, we all have $5 friends. Take the list with you so that you can buy all the gifts in one market or at one TT (tourist trap). Bargain like mad for the multiple units at one time.

- The Straw Market and the San Lorenzo market are both wonderful fun, but they now have very, very similar merchandise, and, let's face it, it's mostly junky and touristy. If time is truly limited, choose one. Ties at San Lorenzo cost 10,000L and 12,000L at the Straw Market. More fun is the monthly flea market, although they don't sell ties there.

- If you are making day trips from Florence but have limited time in Florence, consider doing your souvenir shopping during your day trips rather than in town. Gucci makes excellent souvenirs, especially when purchased from the Gucci outlet. Florence's shopping is a dream, but prices are often lower out of town. If your shopping list only adds up to a few souvenirs, you can get them quickly and with much joy in Siena, Deruta, or at an olive oil mill.

The Best Buys in Florence

Junk   Okay, you already know this about me, it's not a secret. I love junk; I love $5 to $25 gift items. The markets are crammed with them. Florence provides better quality, easier-to-get-to junk than any other major Italian city. Choose marbleized paper goods, renaissance-style printed letter papers, mosaic picture frames, gilt wooden trays, and so on.

Olive Oil   Olive oil is much like wine, with olives very much like grapes. Often, especially in this part of Italy, vineyards that make wine also make olive oil, and have wine shops (*entoca*) that sell it. The airport in Florence has an excellent selection; otherwise you can try a wine shop, a grocery store, or even some of the specialty sources directly. There are many tours and tastings that help educate your palate; see p. 17 for Faith Willinger's list of the best brands. Remember, the good stuff isn't cheap; it usually comes in a glass bottle and is heavy and fragile.

Shawls   This category reflects my need to feel chic and wrap myself in warmth. Not found too easily in the summer months, shawls are prominently displayed in Florence markets throughout fall, winter, and spring because they are a must-have accessory for locals who wear them over their coats to keep out the winter chill. Shawls come in a variety of styles, and there's plenty of fake pashmina as well. Expect to pay 55,000L for a shawl, 35,000L for a stole, 20,000L for a fake pashmina.

One tip: To dress up my black shawl, because I bought it for evening events when a coat would be all wrong, I bought some black trim and hand-stitched it along the seam between the shawl and the ruffle. This improves the image and the viewer's perception of the quality.

Ceramics & Faience   If you get into the hill towns and pottery towns, you will save 40% to 50% off Florence prices for ceramics and faience. If you don't have the opportunity to get out of town, you'll find plenty to choose from in Florence— from the huge jardinières to the little rooster jugs. Some items are sold in the two town markets; better-quality (and more expensive) items are sold in specialty shops around town. Prices for ceramics are even lower in Siena, just an hour away.

Paper   If you didn't get your fill of Italian-style papers in Venice, you can buy more in Florence. The assorted merchandise is so classy looking that it makes a marvelous gift; pencils cost less than $1 each. There are about half a dozen stores in central Florence that specialize in Florentine paper works; items of less quality are sold at souvenir stands and in the markets.

Sweaters   This possibly should have come under the same heading as shawls, because the basic idea is the same. Yet to me, they are two very different categories. You buy the shawl because it's incredibly chic and you add class to your outfit;

you buy sweaters in Florence because they are boring, classic, and cheap. The average sweater costs $15! How can you resist?

Gilt Wood   My friend Sam Gerson, just retired from Filene's Basement, used to say his store offered "guilt-free shopping." In Florence, you get gilt-laden shopping: Renaissance-style rubbed gold is slathered onto picture frames, serving trays, knickknacks, and even religious souvenirs. Know what? I love it.

Mosaic Inlay   Just as Venice has its own Murano-style beads, Florence has its own mosaic works made from teeny tiny beads inlaid in a rather Victorian, old-lady style. Brooches, rings, and miniature picture frames make fabulous gifts. You'll pay all of 5,000L for a ring (less than $3). Picture frames can get pricey (up to $30), but they make stunning gifts and are easy to bring home because they range in size from small to very tiny. I have also seen the smallest size priced in the $15 range in the markets.

There is another type of mosaic inlay found in Florence, done with semi-precious stones, that some laypeople refer to as "Florentine mosaic," which is not what I am talking about and is not sold in markets or at reasonable prices. Try Pitti Mosaici, Piazza de Pitti 23a.

Cheap Handbags   I am only slightly ashamed to tell you this: The triumph of one recent shopping trip to Florence was a faux, reptile-printed plastic Birkin-style handbag for $30 that is so stunning you could faint. Because it is textured, it's harder to detect that it's plastic, and it's absolutely fabulous with gray flannel. It's also great for travel because it's not too fragile.

Secret Dealings

To compensate for lack of sales in off periods, many store owners, especially those outside the deluxe brands, will make deals. I saved about $100 on a handbag once because I was able to go down the street to the cash machine and pay in cash. Yessss!

Hidden Finds in Florence

If you are offended by all the tourist junk in Florence, fear not. There are a handful of hidden places that are yummy and worth the slight trouble it takes to find them. There's more on outlets at the end of the chapter, because they are out of town.

ANTICO SETIFICIO FIORENTINO
Via Bartolini 4

Within easy walking distance of the center of downtown, this factory is truly hidden in an industrial neighborhood, behind a high fence. Once through the gate, you will step back in time to the 18th century. The compound includes a private house, a factory (hear the hum of the shuttles?), and a showroom laden with fabric and ribbons. The showroom is organized by price and by type of silk and cotton: Prices are not low. To visit this factory is an almost religious experience. If you don't intend to buy $100-a-yard (or more) goods, don't worry. You can afford a small bag of potpourri. You may want your concierge to phone ahead, as you need an appointment (☎ 055/21-38-61) and may be asked to pay for the right to visit.

LORENZO VILLORESI
Via dei Bardi 14

This place is as hidden and private as they get, and you must telephone for an appointment at least a day in advance (☎ 055/234-11-87). Mr. Villoresi is a young nose who has created some big-time scents for some big-time firms, but he will allow you a private workshop with him. It costs $200 and takes as long as it takes, because the two of you will create your own fragrance from scratch. Heaven scent.

CUCINA TOSCANA
(Faith Heller Willinger)
get address at time of booking

Every Wednesday Faith Willinger, famous for her books and articles and importance in the world of Italian food and wine, gives a private cooking lesson in her home in the heart of town near the Pitti Palace. I do not give the address because, after all, this is Faith's home and the woman does deserve a little privacy.

Technicalities first: The class costs $450 for the day but will be discounted to $400 per day if you mention *Born to Shop* when you book. Yes, you get more than $450 worth of fun, and an excellent goody bag to take away with you.

The class begins with a lesson in making the perfect espresso, and then you're off to the market to pick out lunch. The class makes lunch together, gets a few life lessons from Faith, and then eats the lunch ensemble. Sometimes there is a guest chef at lunch.

I'm sure I don't need to tell you that Faith is warm, funny, fabulous, and lives in a dream apartment; very funky. To book, contact her by e-mail: fwillinger@dinonet.it.

FARMACEUTICA DI SANTA MARIA NOVELLA
Via della Scala 16r

This is by no means a new source or much of a secret, but it is a little hard to find and fits with the mood of most of the other shops on this list—it is a step back in time as you enter a former convent that looks like a museum. The usual soaps and skin creams are sold in the front rooms; in the rear, a newly opened room sells herbal cures.

ARTISAN JEWELS

Okay, this is a tad tricky, so here goes. Through Faith, I discovered a fabulous jewelry artisan who lives in the hills above Florence. He sells to major stores in town and in the U.S., and for this reason, I am not allowed to tell you his name. He does, however, have the right to sell to private clients in his home, and of course, the prices are less than in stores.

This is the right stuff; the jeweler has won many international awards. He works in silver, gold, and platinum. Serious shoppers who are interested can make an appointment to visit through his assistant in Florence. If you don't have your own car, there is a flat fee that will guarantee you a ride back and forth in comfort. E-mail to jelcora@dinonet.it.

Shoppers Beware

Be careful when buying:

Leather goods   I know Italy, especially Florence, is famous for its leather goods; I know, I know. I'm not telling you to refrain from a leather purchase. I merely ask that you purchase slowly and carefully. There are so many fake leather factories in Florence and so many handbags for sale in markets and on the street that you will lose your mind in short order. More important, leather goods in Italy are well-made but expensive. If it's not expensive, it might not have been made in Italy.

For real value in leather goods, you'll do far better spending a little more money and buying from a big-name leather-goods house with a reputation to back up the goods. And forget about those so-called outlets.

Do note that there is a huge territory of no-man's land: no name, no brand handbags and leather goods that are not inexpensive ($250 and up) but offer great value if bought properly. Buying and bargaining for them is tricky.

Gold   There are plenty of jewelers on the Ponte Vecchio, but I can't give you one good reason why you should buy from them unless you have romance in mind and are willing to pay for it.

Silk   I have to steer you away from the silk scarves and the silk ties in Florence; to me, the patterns are all cheap copies of famous works that simply miss. Years ago you could buy marvelous fake scarves in the San Lorenzo market; no more.

Check edges to see if they are hand-stitched; make sure it's silk and not polyester—unless you want polyester, which is less expensive.

Shopping Hours

Like all Italy, Florence is celebrating a new world in shopping hours. The two big department stores are open on Sunday, and there's a lot going on that didn't used to be happening. Many stores still close at lunchtime during the week, but Florence doesn't close tight for lunch. You can find some life if you look for it.

Shops are basically closed Sunday and Monday, or at least on Monday until 3:30pm. In summer, they also close on Saturday afternoon at 1pm. Remember though, Sunday (even Sunday morning) is surprising in Florence, so don't stay home making false assumptions—get out there and shop. Sunday hours for those stores that are open are 10am to 4pm or 11am to 5pm.

Also note that the last Sunday of the month is a special day in retail so more stores are open than (there's also a cute flea market that day) the first Sunday of the month; the suburban American-style shopping mall is open. Most of the big factory outlets are also open on Sunday, but check before you make the trek.

Markets always close for holidays but do not necessarily close for lunch. The San Lorenzo market is closed on Sunday and Monday, but is open during lunch on other days. The Straw Market is open but not in full bloom on Monday; it is open during lunch every day—except Sunday.

Food stores are open Monday morning. In winter, food stores are also open on Saturday afternoon but are closed on Wednesday afternoon. In June, the pattern switches, and the food stores close on Saturday afternoon and stay open on Wednesday afternoon.

Speaking of summer hours, everything except major TTs is closed from mid-August through the rest of the month.

Sunday is now livelier than Monday morning.

Sunday Shopping

While Sunday isn't a big shopping day in most of Italy, if the weather is nice, or if the tourists are in season, you'd be surprised at just how much business goes on. The Straw Market has sellers who open up their carts. It's not as hot and happening as Venice, but Sunday is beginning to catch on. The last Sunday of each month, stores do open. Every Sunday, there's a big bookstore open (see "Florence Resources from A to Z," below).

The real action is on the **Ponte Vecchio.** The usual shops are indeed shuttered, but on the walkway over the bridge, standing shoulder to shoulder on both sides of the walk, is an incredible array of vendors—from boys with imitation Louis Vuitton tote bags, to hippies with poorly made jewelry, to real artisans with craft pieces. Much of what you will see here is delightful junk—the exact kind of thing you want to see on a Sunday. But there are a few buys.

There's also a vast amount of Sunday shopping available in the so-called factory outlets and TTs that stretch from the Duomo to Santa Croce. I think the single best store for Sunday shopping (if you have to pick one) is a dressed-up version of a TT that's more like an art gallery called **Ducci** (Lungarno Corsini 24r).

One last thought: If you like upscale, tony shopping rather than touristy stuff, there's magnificent shopping in **Forte dei Marmi** on Sunday. It's just an hour from Florence. Alternatively you can go to Montecatini where stores are also open; this is a town famous for its spa.

Also, please know your local prices before you jump at a "good deal" on a Sunday shopping spree. If anything, prices on Sunday will be higher than regular retail because you are a lame duck, especially at street markets and with independent vendors. If you can hold out, consider doing so, unless you are certain you have found something unusual, or you are shopping in a store with fixed prices.

About Addresses

Florence is more strict than many other Italian cities about its numbering system; stores (to differentiate them from residences) are zoned red, or rosa, and therefore usually have an "r" after their street number. The same number in black (to depict a residence) is somewhere else entirely on the street. Go figure.

Sending It Home

If you don't feel like schlepping your purchases with you, there's a giant post office in the heart of town—right near the Straw Market—that offers what's called **Express Mail.** Italian mail makes me nervous; you can use Federal Express if you prefer or if cost is no object.

Scams & Rip-Offs

While Florence is not a high-crime city by any means, it is a very sophisticated city where many people come to shop and trade goods. As a result, expect the usual international deals and scams:

- Pickpockets abound (especially in San Lorenzo market).
- Be wary of Etruscan art that's too good to be true—it is the most highly imitated art form sold in Italy.
- If a store says it has a factory on the premises, don't assume the store is a factory outlet and therefore cheaper; many of those factories are just for show. If you are taken to a factory or a resource by your tour director, expect that he or she is getting a kickback. Ask for free time to do your own exploring. On the other hand, maybe the tour director is taking you to a great place.
- Prices on similar goods are the same all over town, but the quality may be better at certain vendors; not all cheap sweaters were created equal.

Scams & Rip-offs: The Revenge

This is a terrifying piece of news, but I got it from the *International Herald Tribune* and many journalists as well, so I am taking it as true. The word is that all those fake Prada handbags sold on the streets in Italy and all over the world are actually real and come directly from Prada! Prada makes them and supplies them to the street dealers. In short, business is business in Florence as elsewhere. Life is pretty hard when you can't tell the good guys from the bad guys. Buy with care and maybe a giggle.

SHOPPING NEIGHBORHOODS

Tornabuoni   The Via dei Tornabuoni is the main whoop-dee-doo, big-time street for the mainline tourist shopping of the gold coast kind. This is where most of the big-name designers have their shops, and where the cute little specialty stores and leather-goods makers cluster. This is where you'll find everyone from **Gucci** (Via dei Tornabuoni 73r) to **Ferragamo** (Via dei Tornabuoni 16r), but, alas, no Chanel. Who needs Chanel with the Ferragamo museum to keep you busy? If you have only an hour for seeing the best shopping in Florence, perhaps you just want to stroll this street. Although most of the hotsy-totsy names are on Tornabuoni, some of them are on nearby side streets, especially on **Via della Vigna Nuova,** which you will recognize because it has the **Enrico Coveri** shop on the corner (Via della Vigna Nuova 27–29r).

The Tornabuoni area begins (or ends) at the Piazza di San Trinita, which is a small *piazza* (plaza) with a very tall, skinny obelisk. The Via dei Tornabuoni itself leads easily into Via della Vigna Nuova, but don't think it ends there. Stay with the street as the numbers climb because **Profumeria Inglese** (no. 97r) is well past the thick of things, but it's a great place for perfumes and beauty supplies (assuming you are not going to France).

Also check out **Via degli Strozzi,** the connector between Tornabuoni and the Piazza della Repubblica. **Emporio Armani** (Piazza Strozzi) is here.

Excelsior/Grand   The Westin Excelsior/Grand neighborhood backs up to Tornabuoni, where the famed hotels are located. Many good stores are actually on **Piazza Ognissanti;** the rest line **Borgo Ognissanti** until it hits Piazza Goldini and becomes Via della Vigna Nuova. If all this sounds confusing, don't panic.

The neighborhoods are close to each other and could even be considered one neighborhood, which is why staying at either of these hotels makes good sense if you love shopping, want to walk, and need a luxury property.

The shops in the Excelsior/Grand area are less touristy and more mom-and-pop than the big names in Tornabuoni, but the area does include a big name or two, such as **Bottega Veneta** (Piazza Ognissanti 3).

Grand/Medici   You can walk from the luxury hotels at Borgo Ognissanti all the way to the Grand Hotel Villa Medici, another luxury hotel only 2 blocks away. In doing so you will pass several local resources and a discount shop as well as two major American car rental agencies, Avis and Europcar (National). If you want a discount shop, check out **One Price** (Borgo Ognissanti 74r), where the sweaters come in dreamy colors (all lamb's wool) and sell for about $25. Then there's **Porta del Tartufo** (Borgo Ognissanti 133r), a gourmet food shop that specializes in truffles but has other food products as well.

Excelsior/Grand Antiques   There are two main antiques areas in Florence, one near the Pitti Palace and the other right beside the Excelsior/Grand area at **Piazza Ognissanti.** If you're facing the Excelsior Hotel (with the Grand Hotel to your rear, the Arno River to your right, and a church to your left) and start walking, you'll pass a small street called Via del Porcellana. From there, look across Borgo Ognissanti to **Fioretto Giampaolo** (no. 43r). Stop in, and then walk a block toward Tornabuoni until you get to the Piazza Goldini.

At the Piazza Goldini, you'll discover **Via dei Fossi,** which is crammed with antiques dealers. In fact, the area between the two streets and including the **Via del Moro,** which runs next to Via dei Fossi, is host to almost 2 dozen dealers. Most of these stores sell larger pieces of furniture and medium-to-important antiques; there's not too much junk. There are some businesses that are geared to the design trade without being in the antiques business—like **Riccardo Barthel** (Via dei Forri 11r), which does tiles. One Sunday each fall (ask your concierge for the exact day because it varies from year to year) all the dealers in the area have open houses.

Arno Alley   The Arno is a river, not a neighborhood; the main street along each bank of the river changes its name every few blocks. On the Duomo side of the river, the portion of street named **Lungarno Amerigo Vespucci,** which becomes **Lungarno Corsini,** is crammed with shops, hotels, and even the famous Harry's Bar.

Some of these shops sell antiques; several of them sell statues and reproductions of major works; some sell shoes, clothes, and/or handbags; and one or two are just fancy TTs.

Note: Several of these shops are open on Sunday.

The Duomo   As in Milan, there is excellent shopping around the Duomo. Naturally, this is an older, more traditional area. Most of these stores are in older buildings. Locals as well as tourists shop here.

Stores are situated around all four sides of the church. (There's even shopping in the church, in the little museum store downstairs.)

The main shopping street of this part of town is called **Via dei Calzaiuoli,** and it's directly behind the Duomo and runs right smack into the Uffizi. It is closed to street traffic so pedestrians can wander freely from the Duomo to Piazza della Signoria, another large piazza filled with pigeons, postcards, incredible fountains and statues, tourists and locals, charm and glamour, and everything you think Florence should have. You can't rave about an area too much more than that, can you?

A second main shopping street, **Via Roma,** connects the Duomo and the Ponte Vecchio and runs past Piazza della Repubblica, where many traditional stores are located. This street runs parallel to Via dei Calzaiuoli, and you could mistake it for the main shopping street of town unless you knew better. The Savoy Hotel is on Via Roma.

Just before it reaches the Ponte Vecchio, Via Roma becomes Via por Santa Maria. Don't miss **Luisa Via Roma,** at Via Roma 21r, which is sort of the local version of Barney's, and then the Straw Market and the Ponte Vecchio, which are at the other end of the spectrum from Luisa.

Ponte Vecchio]If you keep walking a few hundred meters from Piazza della Signoria right to the banks of the Arno River, you will see the Ponte Vecchio. You'll zig to the right a few yards, and then walk left to get across the bridge. Or you can connect by continuing straight along Via Roma, which will change its name each block and become the Ponte Vecchio 3 blocks after you pass the Duomo.

By my definition, the Ponte Vecchio neighborhood includes the bridge and the retailers on the Duomo side of the bridge. Once you cross over the bridge, you are in another neighborhood: Pitti.

I consider Ponte Vecchio a distinct area, however, because the entire bridge is populated by jewelry shops. They are tiny little shops that have been there for centuries in one form or other. The ones on the Duomo side of the bridge are fancier than the others, and prices are cheaper as you move across the bridge. If you are standing on the Duomo side, about to cross over the bridge, the shops on the right-hand side are nicer than the shops on the left-hand side. The shops sell a little of everything, but you can find nice gift items and trinkets. You needn't be looking for a diamond to match Elizabeth Taylor's. On Sunday, when shopping opportunities in Florence are limited, the bridge is crammed with vendors who sell everything from handcrafted jewelry to brand-name imitation leather goods.

Over the Bridge (Pitti & Santo Spirito)   Once you cross over the Ponte Vecchio, you reach a different retailing climate. You are now on the Pitti side of the bridge. The stores are smaller but no less touristy; you get the feeling that real people also shop here. You can wander, discovering your own personal finds; you can stop and get the makings of a picnic or grab a piece of pizza. The shopping goes in two directions: toward the Pitti Palace or uptown along the Arno. (If your back is to the Duomo, turn left along the Arno to head uptown.) See both areas, looking at shops on **Borgo San Jacopo** and on **Via Guicciardini**.

If you are headed to the once-a-month flea market or looking for antiques shops and crafts vendors, the Santo Spirito neighborhood—actually part of Pitti—is where you want to be. Santo Spirito may not be on the tiny freebie maps handed out all over town, but it is truly convenient and easy to find: If you are standing in front of the Pitti with the Pitti behind you, walk straight 1 block.

Santa Croce & Back Alley   Shoppers know this area mostly because of the famous Leather School located inside the Santa Croce church. It's nice to wander around this area because it *feels* like it's a little off the beaten track and seems more natural than the parts of town where tourists swarm (yet this is a major tourist area with many, many TTs). Face it, it's all tourist shops.

There are also some cafes and pizza eats, more so-called leather factory outlets than you ever care to see in your lifetime, one or two fun antiques-cum-junk stores (the best kind), and a good bit of Sunday retail.

I like to get here via my "back alley"—the Via del Corso—which you pick up right near Coin department store. Walk away from the center of town toward Santa Croce and you can't go wrong.

Out of Town   If head-for-the-hills is your choice of neighborhood, you've picked a great part of Italy to explore. Yes, you can rent a car and drive; but, if you want someone else to drive you then you need only call my friend Maria Teresa, who has a private tour service and will arrange anything you want, from olive oil tastings to private tours to trips to the outlets.

Prices are based on whether or not you have an English-speaking escort with you and how far you go. Prices include departure and return to any hotel in Florence:

1. Half-day shopping tour (5 hours) with car and driver— Gucci and Prada outlets: 400,000L.
2. Full-day tour with car and driver (6 hours)—Gucci, Prada, and Malo outlets: 500,000L.
3. Full day with car and driver (7 hours)—Gucci, Prada, Malo, Pratesi, and Ralph Lauren: 600,000L.
4. Full day (6 hours) as above in no.2, plus English-speaking guide and a visit to olive oil mill and castle: 900,000L.
5. Full day as above in no. 3, with escort and visit to a local winery or to Montecatini: 1,000,000L.

To contact Maria Teresa, e-mail her at tuscany@italway.it.

FLORENCE RESOURCES FROM A TO Z

··

Antiques

As an antiques center, Florence gets pieces from the entire Tuscan area. The problem of fakes, which is so severe in Rome, is not as great here. Anyone can get taken, that's well known, but the chances are less in Florence than in Rome.

• Antiques are available at a flea market at the **Piazza dei Ciompi**, but this is really grandmother's attic, fun stuff. We're talking car-boot or tag-sale quality here, but you may uncover a find every now and then (or absolutely nothing). Note that there are two parts to this market, the regulars who are open every day in the center aisles in little huts, and the people who set up on tables in the open air on the last Sunday of each month.

- For more serious stuff, check out any of the following streets: Via Guicciardini, Via Maggio, Via dei Tornabuoni, Via della Vigna Nuova, Via del Porcellana, Borgo Santi Apostoli, Via dei Fossi, Via del Moro, Via di Santo Spirito, or Via della Spada. There's a string of fun shops for everything from old postcards to 1950s jewelry on the Borgo San Jacopo right over the bridge. I happen to like Via dei Fossi for medium-range antiques—possibly affordable.
- Affordable antiques are best bought at flea markets that are regular events, most often held once a month.
- Many locals like to go to **Viterbo,** a city about 45 minutes away, because it has a fairly decent Sunday flea market for antiques. Viterbo also gets a less touristy crowd.
- The best flea market in Florence proper is the monthly event held at **Santo Spirito** every second Sunday.
- There's an antiques fair in Pistoia, a half-hour away, on the second Saturday and Sunday of each month; the market is covered, and houses about 150 stalls. There is no market in July and August. Head for the **Via Ciglliegiale.**
- There's a market in Pisa on the second Sunday of each month and the Saturday that precedes it. This market, which also has about 150 dealers, is known for its furniture, which can be bought at a low price and then restored. The market is not held in July and August. It's located on **Via XX Settembre.**
- The town of Siena has a flea market on the third Sunday of each month. There are only about 60 dealers, but the market does get a lot of "smalls" (the trade term for small objets d'art) and locals selling off estate pieces, so buyers can hope to get lucky here. There's no market in August. Head for the **Piazza del Mercato.**
- The biggest (and best) antiques fair in Italy is held in **Arezzo,** about an hour south of Florence by train: It's held the first Sunday of each month and the Saturday that precedes it. There are over 600 dealers at this event, and it does not close in the summer months. Head to the **Piazza Vasari** and work the area to the **Piazza San Francesco.**

Please note that the laws defining what is and is not an antique are different in Italy than in many other countries, so that items made from old wood or from older items may be classified as antiques even if they were made yesterday! The craftspeople in the area are gifted at making repros that are so good you can't tell how old they are.

Books

BM BOOK SHOP
Borgo Ognissanti 4r

This English-language book shop, right smack in the heart of everything, specializes in American and British books; it's a great place to hang out and ask questions or touch base with the owners.

LIBRERIA EDISON
Piazza della Repubblica 27r

This is sort of the local Barnes & Noble. Although most of the books are in Italian, there are also foreign-language books, which means you will pay $11 for a paperback. The store is large, continues on the lower and upper levels, and sells everything in book- and communications-related media, from postcards to CDs. The shop is open on Sunday from 10am to 1:30pm and 3:30pm until 8pm. Other days of the week, (including Monday!), it's open nonstop from 9am to 8pm.

Costume Jewelry

ANGELA CAPUTI
Borgo San Jacopo 82

This place serves up dynamite, creative costume jewelry with bright-colored plastics and lots of inventive twists and turns. Prices range from $10 to $100. Caputi is well known in designer circles as a hot talent, and now has young, modern clothes to go with her jewelry. She should stick to jewelry. This is on the Pitti side of the Ponte Vecchio.

BIJOUX CASCIO
Via por Santa Maria 1

Bijoux Cascio is an old name in fancy fakes—they have been making classy versions of the real McCoy (e.g., Bulgari) for ages . . . but the product has really gone downhill. I am brokenhearted. The store is small (jewels are small, after all) and is right across from the Ponte Vecchio on the Duomo side of the river.

Department Stores

COIN
Via dei Calzaiuoli 56r

A small department store concentrating on ready-to-wear. It features quasi-modern architecture in a multilevel space that exhibits a little of everything for men, women, and children. It's a good place to sniff out next season's fashion direction. Prices aren't at the bargain level, but they are moderate for Italy. Remember: When the elevator says T you are at street level; S stands for second floor. The biggest news here is that they have totally eliminated makeup and perfume and have only a MAC boutique on the ground floor right at the front door.

LA RINASCENTE
Piazza Repubblica

La Rinascente is right in the heart of town, obviously put there to compete with the lovely Coin. The store is moderately priced, light, modern, fun to shop, and open on Sunday. It is not a great store, so don't be too hurt.

STANDA
Via Panzani 31r

Standa is sort of the local dime store, although it's getting more and more upmarket—I like it better as a dime store than a department store. Now then, here's the catch: Standa has been bought by PPR Groupe from France, and most Standa stores are being turned into branches of FNAC, selling CDs. Watch this space.

As we go to press, this Standa is a Standa. There is another Standa, just a grocery store, right near Piazza dei Chiompi (via Pietrapiana 4r), which is open on the last Sunday of each month to serve the flea-market crowd. Great fun, plus ready-made foods and rotisserie chickens.

Designer Boutiques

CONTINENTAL BIG NAMES

CARTIER
Via Tornabuoni 40r

ESCADA
Via Strozzi 30/36

HERMÈS
Piazza degli Antinori 6r

LACOSTE
Via della Vigna Nuova 33r

LAUREL
Via della Vigna Nuova 67/69r

LOUIS VUITTON
Via dei Tornabuoni 2

WOLFORD
Via della Vigna Nuova 93/95r

ITALIAN BIG NAMES

ACCESSORIES OF BENETTON
Via Degli Speziali 6/8r

BENETTON
Via por Santa Maria 68r Bottega Veneta

BRIONI
Via Calimala 22r

EMPORIO ARMANI
Piazza Strozzi

ENRICO COVERI
Via della Vigna Nuova 27/29r

ERMENEGILDO ZEGNA
Piazza dei Rucellai 4/7r

FERRAGAMO
Via dei Tornabuoni 16

FRETTE
Via Cavour 2

GENNY
Via dei Tornabuoni 35

GIANFRANCO FERRÉ
Via dei Tosinghi 52r

GIORGIO ARMANI
Via della Vigna Nuova 51r

GUCCI
Via dei Tornabuoni 73r

LORO PIANO
Via della Vigna Nuova 37r

MARINA RINALDI
Via Panzani 1

MASKA
Via Roma 32r

MAX & CO.
Via de Calzaiuoli 89r

MAX MARA
Via dei Pecori 23r

PUCCI
Via della Vigna Nuova 97–99r

TRUSSARDI
Via dei Tornabuoni 34–36r

VERSACE
Via dei Tornabuoni 13r

VERSUS
Via della Vigna Nuova 36–38r

ZEGNA SPORT
Via della Vigne Nuovo 62r

Home Style

DITTA LUCA DELLA ROBBIA
Via del Proconsolo 19r

This place is a little bit off the beaten path (but not enough to count) and is one of the best pottery shops in town. I dare you not to buy. They ships—although it may double the price of your goods. They carry plates, tiles, religious souvenirs, and more. The shop is located between Piazza della Signoria and Santa Croce.

GALLERIA MACHIAVELLI
Via por Santa Maria 39

Despite the stupid name for a shop, this is one of the best resources in town for country wares and ceramics. It's located right in the center of downtown, so you can easily pop in. They ship.

PASSAMANERIA TOSCANA
Piazza San Lorenzo 12r; Via della Vigna Nuova corner of Via dei Federighi

Maybe you don't plan your travels around your ability to find trim or tassels, but when you luck into a source that makes the best in the world and is affordable, it's time to celebrate.

This firm actually has two shops—both in neighborhoods that you will be visiting anyway. I've been buying my cotton multicolor tassels in Paris for about $5 each (at the flea market, no less)—in Florence, they are $6 each! You'll also find pillowcases, embroideries, brocades, assorted trims, and fabrics. The San Lorenzo shop is larger. Chic, but expensive.

PASSAMANERIA VALMAR
Via Porta Rossa 53r

This shop is right in the heart of town; just look at your map for easy access to one of the best sources in town for tassels, tie backs, trims, cushions, and more.

RICHARD GINORI
Via Rondinelli 17

RICHARD GINORI OUTLET STORE
Sesto Fiorentino ☎ *055/421-04-72*

Richard Ginori is one of the most famous international names in bone china; Ginori's fruit pattern (and the price per plate) has been known to make brides faint. While the firm is in fine shape, it has lost its luster as a retail resource—the Via Condotti (Rome) store has closed, and the shop in Florence is less than memorable and carries other brands besides Ginori.

Your best bet, if you believe in the tooth fairy or have the time and the adventuresome spirit of a true shopper, is to stop by the factory outlet shop in Sesto, a small village about 20 minutes outside Florence. Give it a try if you have a car, don't mind splurging on a taxi (have your driver wait), or if you can hire a car and driver. The factory shop is open Monday to Friday 9am to 1pm and 3:30pm to 7pm. It does not take credit cards.

Linens & Lace

BRUNNETO PRATESI
Via Montalbano 41, Pistoia

See "Day Trip 1: Pistoia," later in this chapter, for how to visit this factory store, which is just a half hour outside of Florence in the town of Pistoia.

LORETTA CAPONI
Piazza Antinori 4r

If you've ever dreamed of being either a Lady Who Lunches or a Lady Who Sleeps Late, this lingerie store is for you. Here you'll find the dreamiest silks in underwear, linen, negligees, and more, as well as some cottons and table linens. This is what having money is all about.

GIUSEPPE PALOMBELLA
Piazza Duomo 62r

My friend Maria Teresa took me here; as she herself said, it's the kind of store you would walk by and think it was for old ladies. Inside is a wide range of sheets and table tops, a few contemporary things (such as Burberry sheets), but mostly the old fashioned, classical, and simple work that is pretty hard to find, including all-linen sheets. Prices are not low, but they are a lot less than Pratesi.

Makeup & Perfume

If you can help it, don't buy makeup in Florence—it's expensive, and the choices are pretty average. If you're desperate, you can get dime-store brands at **Standa** or a handful of big-name brands at **La Rinascente**. The **Profumeria Inglese** (Via dei Tornabuoni 97r) is a temple to good taste, fine goods, and every imaginable brand, right in the heart of the shopping district. There are no bargains here. For beauty cures and treatments, check the pharmacy listings below.

Markets

MERCATO DELLE CASCINE
Piazzale Vittorio Veneto

Held once a week (Tuesday only), this market is famous with locals because it serves them in the same way a department store might. The various vendors are regulars, so everyone gets to know everyone, and some of the vendors even have famous reputations. I found the market fabulous from an academic standpoint but not actually the kind of place with much to buy.

Granted, a lot of that depends on luck and taste, but I just didn't need new pots, pans, dishes, tires, or baby clothes. I was wildly interested in the heap of designer handbags that Faith and I have decided must have been fake (just too good to be true—various big names selling for 50,000L each). I liked the local fabrics, tablecloths, and dish towels; I loved the food vendors. I did work my way through mounds of used clothes and linens in hopes of finding something I had to have.

The market opens at 7am; I got there at 8am, and vendors were still setting up. If your time in Florence is very tight, this probably isn't the market for you.

To get there, take a bus to the Jolly Hotel or walk along the Arno—it's a bit of a walk from the center of town, considering that once you get to the market you are going to walk even more, but you can do it.

Mercato delle Pulci
Piazza dei Ciompi

This is the local flea market that sells everything from furniture to pictures, coins, and jewelry; it's great fun especially if the weather is fair. Held the last Sunday of each month. Meanwhile, every week, Tuesday to Saturday (not at all the same as the once-a-month affair) the regular dealers in a small strip of stalls are open. Possibly not worth the trip.

The Sunday market is an all-day job beginning around 9am; the daily market closes for lunch and follows more traditional business hours. To get there, walk out the back end of the Duomo onto via dell Oriuolo, pass the Piazza Salvemini and hit Via Popolo, which in 1 block takes you to the flea market. It's an easy walk. On Sunday, the nearby Standa is open.

SAN LORENZO
Piazza del Mercato Centrale

I'm sad to report that San Lorenzo does not offer the thrills of years gone by. Either I can't stand a bad fake anymore, or the fakes are going downhill. But wait, all is not lost—the gorgeous sweater for $15 brightened me right up. I'm also pleased with the dealer who sells pottery and faience; I found shawls and a few pieces of ready-to-wear I just couldn't live without. And the food market, hidden beyond all the junky stalls, is heaven on earth.

You name it, and San Lorenzo has it. Specifically, San Lorenzo is good for cheapie ties and scarves and gifts galore, cheap clothing for kids or teens, T-shirts, and souvenirs. The selection of leather jackets doesn't cut the mustard with me— I think you can do better in the U.S. I didn't see any handbags that even looked kosher to me.

The market has a few pushcart dealers, and then several rows of stalls that lead around a bend. The stalls are very well organized; this is a legal fair, and stallholders pay tax to the city. Many of the stalls give you shopping bags with their numbers printed on them. Now, there's class.

With the recent crackdown on phony big-name merchandise, few of the pushcarts have imitations. *A word of caution:* Do not get so excited with the bargains that you don't cast an eagle eye over the goods or, in your haste, think that these are real designer goods. Look for defects; look for details. I have yet to find a faux designer scarf here that really looks good enough to pass as the evil twin sister.

Most stall owners take plastic.

The market is open Tuesday to Saturday from 9am to 7pm. Closed Sunday and Monday.

STRAW MARKET
Via por Santa Maria

The best thing about the Straw Market is that it doesn't close during lunchtime. It's also within walking distance of the

Ponte Vecchio, the Duomo, and all the other parts of Florence you want to see, so you can make your day's itinerary and get it all in. Locals call this market *Porcellino,* in honor of the boar statue that stands here.

This market sells far more junk and much more in the way of souvenirs than the other markets. It also gets more crowded than other markets. Still, it's a marvelous TT and worth a visit, if only to fill a lunch void. The merchandise varies with the season, as it should.

I bargained on several cheapie ties, priced at 12,000L each, and finally got the vendor to knock off a grand total of 1,000L because I was making a multiple purchase. When I whipped out my credit card to pay, he said, "No discount on credit card." (For a difference of about 50¢, I was happy to use my credit card and earn mileage in my frequent flyer plan.)

The market is open daily, from 9am to 5pm in winter, and 9am to 7pm in summer. Closed tight on Sunday.

THE TRAIN STATION
Santa Maria Novella

Technically speaking, the main train station is a train station and not a market. But it functions as a marketplace. There's a McDonald's, stores, and plenty of people and action. All the shops are open on Sunday. It's a good place.

Paper Goods

Florentine papers are one of Florence's greatest contributions to bookbinding and gift giving. There are two styles, marbleized and block printed. The marbleized style is readily found in Venice; neither style is handily found in Milan and/or Rome.

In Florence, there are scads of stores selling papered gift items; such items are even sold from souvenir stands, in markets, and at the train station. Prices are generally modest, although they can get up there with larger items.

BOTTEGA ARTIGIANA DEL LIBRO
Lungarno Corsini 38–40r

This is a small shop, next to the Arno, that has beautiful things and can solve many a gift quandary. Small address books are in the $8 range; pencils are stunning and inexpensive; picture frames range from $5 to $15, depending on the size. These frames have plastic fronts, not glass. There are photo albums, bound blank books, and all sorts of other items. Note the business cards printed on the back of marbleized paper swatches.

CARTOLERIA PARIONE
Via Parione 10r

I got a letter from a reader a few years ago, a professional photographer, who was looking for marbleized photo albums that she could use to show her work. She said she could find them in the U.S., but they cost about $100 and could I find some in Italy for less. Well, it took me a year, but yes, Virginia, here you go—this store, which sells many of the usual paper goods, also has the photo albums. They come in various sizes, and prices begin at $30! They will ship (fax your order to 055/21-56-84). The shop is located right in the heart of the Tornabuoni shopping district.

GIANNINI E FIGLIO
Piazza Pitti 37r

Historically well known for the marbleized type of Florentine paper, this shop has been in business for centuries. They also make bookplates, calling cards, and items for all other paper needs. I think several paper-wrapped pencils tied with a bow make a great gift; the price obviously depends on how many pencils you buy, but you can put together a beautiful $10 package. There are many good paper shops in Florence, but this is the single most famous.

IL PAPIRO
Lungarno Acciaioli 112r

This is the most commercially successful of the marbleized-paper stores, with branches all over Italy and in the U.S.

PINEIDER
Piazza della Signoria 13r

Do you love to send handwritten notes in the mail? Thick formal note cards that smell of old money and inseparable style? At this shop you'll find very conservative, old-time stationery as well as some gift items. Prices are steep. Prints are sold upstairs. This is a serious international status symbol.

Pharmacies

Not the kind of pharmacy you go to when you need an *aspirina,* these pharmacies seem to be a specialty of Florence—they are old-fashioned, fancy-dancy places where you can buy creams and goos and local brews and various homeopathic treatments as well as European brands or local homemade potions for all sorts of things. There are tons of these places in Florence. One or two will be all you need for great gifts and, possibly, dinner table conversation.

BIZARRE
Via della Condotta 32r

This is Logan Bentley's (my Italian correspondent's) secret resource for spices and essences.

ERBORISTERIA PALAZZO VECCHIO
Via Vacchereccia 9r

This is an herbalist, not a pharmacist—puh-lease! Buy hair tonic, bosom tonics, and much more. It's right in the thick of the shopping in central downtown.

FARMACEUTICA DI SANTA MARIA NOVELLA
Via della Scala 16r

Yep. This is the one—the one you've read about in every American and English fashion and beauty magazine; the one where you buy the almond cream. At least, that's what I buy here. Go nuts. (Almonds are nuts, so go nuts.) Fabulous gift items, fabulous fun. It's located near the train station and downtown—go out of your way to find it. I had to ask three times just to find it; I was even stumped when I was standing outside the front door. Never mind—walk in! It looks unusual because it's a convent, not a storefront. All the more yummy.

FARMACIA MOLTENI
Via Calzaiuoli 7r

Remember this one because it's open every day of the week, 24 hours a day. It's centrally located, and it's where you go in case of a medical emergency of the pharmaceutical kind. It's also gorgeous.

Shoes & Handbags

BAJOLA
Via Rondinelli 25r

If only Old World style will do for you, but you find Louis Vuitton too obvious, you probably want luggage from Bajola, which was founded in 1896. This is a very local kind of resource, one that the "in" society knows about, but the American tourist does not. It's not far from the Richard Ginori regular retail store, on your way to (or from) the main train station.

CASADEI
Via dei Tornabuoni 33r

This is a wild shop with wild shoes and a nice rep within Italy for good-quality creative work. The interior is rather

Greco-Roman, with taupe stone floors leading to a stone-and-tile fitting area. In front of the back wall, two bronze mermaids hold urns on their heads. The designs are very special; prices range from $150 to $250.

DESMO
Piazza del Rucellai 10r

Desmo is one of my best Italian secrets for reasons of pride and pocketbook—excuse the double entendre. They make a top-of-the-line, high-quality, equal-to-the-best-of-them hand-bag at a less than top-of-the-line price. Years ago they made their name as a maker of leather clothing, shoes, and accessories, copying Bottega Veneta creations; now they have their own style and plenty of winners. Colors are always fashionable and up-to-date; the prices are pretty good—few items in the house top $200, and you can get much for considerably less.

Now then, don't let the address throw you; Piazza del Rucellai is a little dip in the Via della Vigna Nuova—you can't miss the shop when you are in the thick of the designer stores. Outlet information can be found at the end of this chapter.

FURLA
Via dei Tosinghi 5r

This is a small shop, but it's stocked with Furla handbags and accessories. The styles are always ahead of their time and designed with a sense of humor. Prices are moderate to high. There are some two dozen stores all over Italy (and two in New York), but this one is most convenient to the high-traffic shopping areas. The street is a connector between the two main shopping streets of the Duomo area.

GHERARDINI
Via della Vigna Nuova 57r; Via degli Strozzi 25r

One of the biggest leather-goods names in Italy and Asia but little known otherwise, Gherardini offers a specific look in luggage, shoes for men and women, belts, and accessories. I find their conservative designs drop-dead elegant with old-money style. They also have some tote bags and a printed canvas/vinyl line that is status-y as well as practical. There are two stores in Florence, both in the heart of the central downtown shopping district.

HOUSE OF FLORENCE
Via dei Tornabuoni 6

House of Florence is the other Gucci shop. Roberto Gucci, who is Dr. Gucci's son, began—along with his wife, who does the designing—a leather-goods status firm called "House of Florence." While the prices are competitive with those of the old Gucci (pre-Tom Ford), the styles and colors are very different. I saw a pale blue handbag with medium blue trim that would simply make you weep for its beauty, finesse, and balance.

Right now men's ties and women's silk scarves are also offered. Oh yes, one more thing: The space is not well marked—no big flashing signs or anything like that—and is actually located within the courtyard of an old palace, so you have to peer into doorways and make sure that you don't miss out. It is on the Ferragamo side of the street, almost across the street from the original Gucci.

LA ANGELA ATTARDI PELLETERIE
Lungarno Acciaioli 44r

This is a tiny, rather ordinary leather shop that sells the best copy of the Hermès H-buckle belt.

THE LEATHER SCHOOL
Monastery of Santa Croce, Piazza Santa Croce

If you insist on shopping in one of the many leather factories in Florence, you may as well go to the best—it's actually inside the Santa Croce church and is a leather school with a factory on the premises. The school is open Monday through Saturday year-round, and on Sunday from April 15 to November

15. You enter through the church, except on Sunday, when you enter through the garden.

MADOVA
Via Guicciardini 1

Gloves are back in style, so stock up. I'll take the yellow, cashmere-lined, butter-soft leather ones . . . or should I think pink? Maybe both? Unlined gloves are about $30 and come in about a million colors. There's everything here, from the kind of white kid gloves we used to wear in the 1960s to men's driving gloves to very ornately designed, superbly made, high-button gloves.

MANTELASSI
Piazza della Repubblica 25r

If made-to-measure shoes are what you have in mind, step this way with your instep. Men and women can design their own, bring a shoe to be copied, or choose from the many styles displayed.

MONNALISA
Borgo SS Apostoli 46r

Although so-called leather factories make me extremely nervous, I wandered into this store and fell in love with the Birkin-style handbags, which come in many colors and hides and sizes and prices to match. I started using the Birkin-style bag, which is similar to a Kelly but much softer and more pliable, after buying two in Hong Kong. Once in this store I was faced with the same prices as Hong Kong (bags $250 to $350 mostly), and had a hard time getting it down to a very practical cognac leather bag. The street is more like an alley, behind Ferragamo.

SALVATORE FERRAGAMO
Via dei Tornabuoni 16r

Yes, there are Ferragamo shops all over Italy and all over the world. But none of them comes near the parent shop in

Florence, which is in a building erected in 1215, complete with vaulted ceilings, stained-glass windows, and enough ambience to bring out your camera. The shop has several connecting antechambers with an incredible selection of shoes, boots, and ready-to-wear . . . as well as a library and a kiddie play room.

Shoes are in American sizes; however, there is a limited selection in big sizes.

Upstairs is the museum, which is *fab-u-lous*. It is not open to the public all day, or open every day, so call to ask for the hours (☎ 055/29-21-23) and to make an appointment—they are strict on the appointment stuff. There is also a research library for designers and a small museum gift shop with great merchandise, but very high prices. The postcards cost three times what they should. Save up for shoes, instead.

Each January and July there's a clear-it-all-out sale, but I confess that I left brokenhearted last January. Clothing provided better deals than the shoes. Prices were not as good as the sale at Saks. The sale is held in the basement, which has an entrance at the side door; there are guards and usually lines to get in.

Tanino Crisci
Via dei Tornabuoni 43–45

Tanino Crisci is a big name in Italian shoes and leather goods with an international reputation, but there are not many stores in the U.S., so Americans may not be familiar with the brand. This is a chain of moderate-to-expensive shoes in sort of sporty, conservative styles. There's something a bit chunky about a lot of the styles, but the look wears forever and looks better every year. Very preppy. The quality is well known; prices range from $140 to over $200. This is a very specific look that is either your style or not.

They make men's and women's shoes, dress and sports models; and also have belts and small leather goods. Logan, my journalist friend who lives in Rome, found the outlet; see p. 144.

Wool & Yarn

FILATURA DI CROSA
Via Guicciardini 21r

This shop sells knitting yarn, including designer wools such as Missoni. To dye for.

FLORENCE ON A SCHEDULE

TOUR 1: FULL-DAY FLORENTINE DRAMA

1. Begin the tour at Ferragamo, at the Piazza di San Trinita, at 9:30am. Hopefully you also have an appointment at 10am to tour the shoe museum upstairs. Then, walk down Via dei Tornabuoni to see the designer boutiques.

2. The fancy shopping ends in time for you to turn right onto the Via degli Strozzi and be at the Strozzi Palace where Emporio is housed. Then walk another block to Piazza della Repubblica and head left on Via Roma, toward the Duomo. You are now passing some of the older, established shops as well as places like Luisa Via Roma for young looks, important designer clothes, and local pizzazz. When finished here, you can have a coffee in the rear of the store or go across the street to the Hotel Savoy to have a coffee in the library. Once back on the street, note that at the corner, Via Roma becomes a much smaller street called Borgo San Lorenzo. Follow it for 1 long block. You are still walking straight, but the sub-text of the street has changed. At the end of the block you will arrive at the back end of the San Lorenzo market, which you will know by the stalls in the street. If there are no stalls in the street, it must be Monday.

3. Explore the market area until you're exhausted or ready for lunch. You may want to return to your hotel to dump your packages. Most shops in Florence will close from 1 or 1:30pm to 3:30pm, so if you want, this is your chance for lunch and a foot soak.

4. Or stroll back the way you came, pass the Duomo, and head toward the Straw Market on the Via por Santa Maria. The Straw Market is open during lunchtime. There are also two pizza joints right around here, so you can grab a quick bite to eat. My regular one is called Piccadilly. Walk back to Ponte Vecchio so you are on the bridge when the shops open after lunch at around 3:30pm.

5. Walk across the bridge on the right side of the street, visiting any of the tiny jewelry shops that meet your fancy. *Tip:* The stores are more expensive on the near side of the bridge, and many of them sell the same merchandise. When you get to the other side of the Arno, turn right onto the Via San Jacopo; don't miss Angela Caputi and a look at Ferragamo's new family hotel.

6. At the end of that block, turn around and do the other side of San Jacopo. When you get back to Via Guicciardini, hang a right and walk toward the Pitti Palace, shopping as you go. Too bad, no time for the art. (What a Pitti!) After the paper goods store Giannini E Figlio, turn right around and head back toward the Arno, now walking the other side of Via Guicciardini.

7. Then walk back across the Arno on the right side of the bridge, which will be the side opposite the one you crossed on.

8. Once over the Arno, turn right immediately on Lungarno Generale Diaz. Please note that the main drag running along the Arno changes its name at every bridge, so while you've probably been on the street before and will be again later in the day, its name will change, and you may get confused. Walk to the Uffizi, only a few yards away. Take in the beautiful view of the river, the excellent postcard dealer, and then the museum.

9. After your tour of the Uffizi, turn left into the courtyard and walk across to the Piazza della Signoria, which has a fabulous fountain, some cute little horse-and-buggies, a zillion

tourists, and an even better postcard dealer. Cross the piazza to Via dei Calzaiuoli, a famous shopping street. No cars are allowed here. Walk toward the Duomo, making certain not to miss the Coin department store. Then round the corner to the main shopping street and La Rinascente, an even better Italian department store. Once you get to the Duomo, you may tour the catacombs for only 2,000L. Or you may want to simply light a candle in memory of your feet.

Lesser shoppers would call it a day, but you are just ready for tea and a short pit stop. From the Duomo, back track to Via dei Tornabuoni (only about 3 blocks) and head down to Via della Vigna Nuova, which is where Enrico Coveri is located. The store not the man. The man is dead. Shop this designer street of wonders until it ends at Piazza Ognissanti, the location of one of Florence's best-known landmarks, Hotel Excelsior.

10. Take a break at the Excelsior Hotel for tea.

Of course you're going on! Option A is to return to the flea market at San Lorenzo and buy whatever you wanted but didn't buy earlier in the morning. By now you know the lay of the land and have seen a tremendous amount of retail goods. If you choose to go back to the market, treat yourself to a taxi from the front of the Excelsior. If you have no reason to return to San Lorenzo, go for Option B: Turn right at the front of the hotel and explore all the little boutique-filled streets that form a web from the main bridge streets. The stores will be open until 7:30pm, the flea market until 8pm. Because you shouldn't consider dinner before 9pm, you'll have plenty of time. Or you can do what I do—order room service and collapse!

TOUR 2: QUICKIE FLORENCE HALF-DAY TOWN TOUR

1. Begin at the Excelsior Hotel with a nice breakfast, or even luncheon on the rooftop; treat yourself to something grand. Then head off along the Arno toward the Ponte Vecchio.

Window-shop as you walk, checking out the stores selling local treasures and delights—replicas of statues and fountains, marbleized papers, tables inlaid with mosaic designs, and more. About half of these stores are open on Sunday.

2. When you get to the **Ponte Vecchio,** hang a right and cross the bridge.

3. Window-shop along the bridge; if it's Sunday, the bridge will be lined with vendors.

4. Turn right after you cross the bridge and stick to the right-hand side of the street as you walk along the **Borgo San Jacopo,** darting in and out of the antiques stores and window-shopping the rest. You'll find a few restaurants and a deli or two along here, if you need a snack. After a block or two, cross back and walk along the other side of the street: You are now headed back to the Ponte Vecchio.

5. Do not turn left and cross the bridge but stay to your right, headed for the Pitti Palace. Window-shop (and more) and then take in the Pitti. As you walk, you'll note a few more cafes and pizza places if you are hungry. You can even buy a slice of pizza and take it with you as you stroll. But please, no pizza in the Pitti. Then, shop your way back into town as time permits.

BEYOND FLORENCE

Day Trip 1: Pistoia

Okay, okay, so you weren't planning on a side trip to Pistoia. In fact, you've never even heard of it and perhaps think you can survive without it. Wrong. Pistoia may not be the garden spot of Italy, but it is the home of the **Brunetto Pratesi** factory. At the Pratesi factory there is a little shop that sells—you guessed it—seconds. If you show your copy of this book, or say you are a friend of the family, you will be allowed to shop there.

Pratesi, as you probably know, is a family business that makes sheets for the royalty of Europe and the movie stars of Hollywood. They are sticklers for perfection: A computer counts the number of stitches in each quilt. If there are five stitches too many, the quilt is a reject! What do they do with this poor, unfortunate, deformed quilt? It will never see the light of day in Beverly Hills, Manhattan, Palm Beach, or even Rome. No, because it has all of five stitches too many, it will be considered a reject, a defect, a second. It will be sold, at a fraction of its *wholesale* price, in the company shop. It's your lucky day.

The store is in the factory, a low-lying modern building, set off the street on your left as you come off the highway, and distinguished only by the discreet signs that say BRUNETTO PRATESI. Not to worry—because it's the most famous factory in the area, everyone knows where it is. Show the printed address to anyone at a nearby gas station or inn, and you will get directions. Don't be intimidated, it's not that hard.

If all this truly makes you nervous, ask your concierge to call ahead and get very specific directions for you: He or she can even arrange a person for you to call in case you get lost. The factory is located at Via Montalbano 41r (☎ 0573/52-68-68). Store hours are Monday 2 to 7pm; Tuesday to Friday 9am to noon and 2 to 7pm; Saturday 9am to 1pm.

Like all factory outlets, the store sells what it has; you may be lucky or you may not. Last time I was there, the showroom was filled with quilts, nightgowns, and gift items, but low on matched sets. There were blanket covers in various sizes, but you could not put together a whole queen-size bed set. The one total set I priced was no bargain. But, I ended up spending about $200 on baby-size pillowcases that were a dream. You just never know.

Not everything here is rock-bottom cheap! Price on an item varies depending on the defect; some items are visibly damaged, some are not. Prices are essentially half of what you would pay at regular retail—a blanket cover that retails for $900 costs $400 here. If you were expecting giveaway prices, think twice.

Pratesi is one of the leading linen makers in the world, and their goods compete with Porthault as the most sought-after by the rich and famous. Considering the quality, these are bargain prices. Do note, however, that Pratesi has sales once a year (in January) in their stores in Italy and twice a year in some other cities around the world. In January in Italy, the prices are marked down 30% off retail, and you have the whole store to choose from.

Pistoia is not quite an hour away from Florence, and is only about 10 minutes from Montecatini Terme, the famous spa area, so you may want to combine both stops on an afternoon jaunt. Or you can book to stay at the **Grand Hotel Croce di Malta,** a four-star establishment in Montecatini Terme, ☎ 05/727-58-71; fax 0572/76-75-16. It may indeed be worthwhile to spend a night or a weekend, as the entire area is known for its outlet stores (shoes, too), antiques shops, and auctions, which are held in the afternoon.

The scenery on the way to Pistoia is not gorgeous, but you drive on a freeway, so you don't need to worry about getting lost on winding country roads.

The town of Pistoia itself has a good bit of medieval charm, and there's a wonderful country inn–type family restaurant that I adore. So, all in all, you'll have a wonderful time. You can also go by train—get the train at Santa Maria Novella (S.M.N.) in Florence for Pistoia; you can catch a taxi at the station in Pistoia.

Day Trip 2: Siena

Siena is not very far from Florence, but it takes some thinking about should you decide to go, unless you have your trusty rent-a-car and are totally free and independent. It's a very pleasant day trip, especially nice for a Monday morning when most of the stores in Florence are closed.

There are prepackaged day trips just to Siena or to Siena and medieval San Gimignano, which is not a shopping town but rather one of those incredible hilltop villages. Do note that if you buy a tour you will pay about $50 per person for the day trip, whereas if you do it all yourself, it will cost less than $20.

The train ride, which is free if you have a railroad pass, is very long (over 2 hours) and often involves changing trains. It's a better use of your time to pay an additional $12 or $15 (round-trip) and buy a bus ticket via SITA; you want the *corse rapide* to Siena, which is direct. The bus takes 1 hour and 20 minutes.

There is basically a bus every hour, although peak travel times have several buses. Best bet is to travel via SITA, on Via Santa Caterina da Siena 15. It's about a block from the S.M.N. train station. Round-trip tickets are discounted slightly.

The SITA station has a sign outdoors directing you to where to buy tickets (the *biglietteria*) and an information booth outside of the ticket area. After you buy your tickets, you then must find out which lane your bus will be loading from; there is a large sign high up on the wall near the ticket office.

If you've rented a car (remember the 3-day, prepaid **Kemwel** deal at $107 mentioned in chapter 2?), you can drive to Siena and have a good bit of freedom in your day so that you might actually be able to get in two day trips in one day. That means that if you don't have to depend on local transportation and schedules, you may find yourself finished in Siena with enough time to go somewhere else—somewhere that would have taken a whole extra day of your life if you used public transportation.

Should you want to stay in Siena, there are many hotels: Go for either out-and-out elegance at the **Park Hotel Siena** (Via di Marciano 18, ☎ 0577/448-03), an old villa on the edge of town that has been converted to a deluxe hotel; or the **Jolly Hotel Excelsior** (Piazza La Lizza, ☎ 0577/28-84-88), right in the middle of town. The Excelsior is a stone's throw from where you will get off the bus, right next to the shopping, and close to all the winding roads you'll want to explore.

If you take the bus, it may make local stops as you approach Siena. Don't panic. Your stop is the end of the line, San

Domenico Church. When you get off the bus, note the public bathrooms (very clean, pay toilets) and the tourist information office where they sell you a map to the city. If you are standing with your back to the church facing the tourist information office, you'll see that there are two streets to your right. One bears off slightly, and the other turns more dramatically and goes down. The high road will take you directly to the Jolly Hotel, just a few steps away, and to the main commercial, real-people part of Siena. The low road will connect into the main streets of town and eventually take you to the Duomo.

If you have all day and want to see everything, take the high road. If you want to do this in a few hours and keep on moving, take the low road.

If you are doing this on a Monday morning, most of the stores in downtown Siena will be closed. However, if you take the low road, you'll see many touristy stores that are open, even on Monday. They knew you were coming! While some open at 9am, many more will open at 11am. In fact, the best time to be in Siena is on a Monday morning between 9 and 11am because you'll have it almost to yourself and you'll still get to go shopping.

The main shopping street is Via Banchi di Sopra, which leads right to the Campo and then goes up the hill as the Via di Citta. Take this to the Duomo (well marked) and then follow the signs back down and up the Via della Sapienza, which will bring you back to the bus stop at San Domenico.

Via della Sapienza has a good number of wine (this is Chianti country) and tourist shops, especially close to the bus stop, that remain open during lunchtime, too.

As you approach the Campo, you'll notice various alleys that lead into the square. Some have steps; others are ramps for horses. Each entryway seems to be named for a saint. Many of the alleyways that lead from the shopping street to the Campo are filled with booths or touristy stands. There are more free-standing booths on the Campo itself.

The Campo is surrounded by shops, many of which specialize in pottery, hand-painted in dusty shades and following centuries-old patterns. Some of them are even branches of other stores you will find up the hill, closer to the Duomo.

The best shops are clustered up the Via di Citta, close to the Duomo—you will automatically pass them as you walk around and up.

Don't miss the relatively new shop Antiche Dimore, Via di Citta 115, which sells homespun textiles.

Day Trip 3: Outlet Stores Near Florence

I can't remember when I've had more fun—my girlfriends Logan and Maria Teresa and I took a van with a chauffeur and did an outlet day from Florence. It was Maria Teresa who booked the van, she said she knew me well enough to know I would fill it with packages.

We did a hard day's work, and I wasn't crazy about the Ralph Lauren outlet or a few of the other outlets we went to, so the following list only highlights the great stuff that I loved and where I left the most money. They are in the order of how we drove to them, although it was the chauffeur who chose the order. Note that both Gucci and Prada have cute cafes for lunch; we ate at Prada.

GUCCI
Via Aretina 63 Regello, Localita Lecci, Montevarchi

I begin to stutter just remembering the findings: Gucci shoes for $40 (okay, they were on sale), a sports jacket for my son for $100, an enormous silk shawl for my step-daughter for $125, Logan's alligator wallet for $200.

The Gucci outlet is the closest to Florence; it is open on Sunday but closed on Tuesday; we asked a taxi driver about how much he would charge to drive us from Florence, to wait for an hour, and drive back, and the price he quoted was about $60. Start saving.

If you are driving, call ☎ 055/865-77-75 for exact directions. They do accept credit cards, and they have sales during which everything is half off the lowest price.

The outlet is very chic and modern, stark and well designed, up to the standards of any Gucci store. Ignore the busloads of tourists who are pushing about you. There are many salons—one for shoes, one for men's clothing, one for ready-to-wear, etc. The staff is lovely, and they take credit cards. After you have paid, there is a do-it-yourself detaxe desk.

I Pellettieri d'Italia
Localita Levanella, Montevarchi

I have listed the official name of this factory, although everyone just calls this "The Prada Outlet." Yes dear, you heard right. Montevarchi is an industrial area outside of Arezzo. How far is Arezzo, you are asking now? Well, about an hour or so by train from Rome and Florence—it's mid-distance between the two, actually, and right on the main train line.

It's about a half-hour drive from the Gucci outlet.

This situation is a little more formal, and you may feel like you are going to prison. You go behind wire and are given an ID number. The store is large and beautifully arranged and organized. There are other brands here besides Prada and MiuMiu (I found Helmut Lang), and there are shoes as well as sunglasses, clothes, handbags, totes, etc.

It's hit or miss, but worth the adventure if you are nearby. They now accept credit cards. They are open from 9am to 12:30pm and 3 to 7pm; ☎ 055/919-95-95 or 978-94-81. Open Saturday but closed on Sunday.

Malo (MAC)
Via di Limite 164, Campi Bosenzio

As soon as I gave away all my cashmeres because they gave me hot flashes, I discovered the Malo outlet where I almost wept with contempt for the insults of middle age. I was forced to buy cashmeres for others, but did get some suede shoes for myself.

Be still my heart—you could faint from the glory of all the colors, let alone the stunningly low prices. Two-ply cashmere

Logan's Outlets

BIG BERTHA CASHMERE
Via Dell'Industria 19, Perugia

Only Logan could come up with a resource with a name like this—it's a catalog company for cashmeres, and better yet, it does *not* close at lunchtime. There's a large selection in terms of sizes and colors.

Now then, a personal word. Ian and I tried to find this outlet while we were on the road between Perugia and Assisi. We were also looking for a nearby hotel for Ian to photograph for *Bride's Magazine*. I won't bore you with the details (I begin to cry), but we didn't find it. We also didn't try very hard, because it took 2 hours to find the hotel, and we were losing our sense of humor. I can tell you the location is closer to Perugia than Assisi. Local phone ☎ **075/599-75-72.**

TANO CRISCIO
Via Garibaldi 9, Casteggio, Pavia

DESMO
Via Matteotti 22b Donato, Fronzano, Reggello, outside Florence

Call ☎ **055/865-23-11** for specific directions; you will need to hit the *autostrada* going toward Reggello. No credit cards, but savings of about 30% on Desmo brand handbags.

ELLESSE
Via Filippo Turati 22, Ellera Umbria Ponte San Giovanni

I always thought this was a French line, but it appears to be made locally. Tons of tennis togs and other sportswear. The exit from the autostrada is Corciano; the factory is 500 meters (1,500 ft.) from the highway and is clearly marked. Local phone ☎ **075/503-91.**

sweaters were in the $100 price range; 4-ply were $150. I don't know if I was there for a sale, or if this is the regular drill, but you take half of the price on the tag. Ask!

Note, this outlet is the closest to Florence, but has moved to this address rather recently so there may be a conflict with other guidebooks. The sign outside not only says MAC but uses the same type face as MAC cosmetics, so it's confusing. Cope. If you are driving and want precise directions, call ☎ 055/894-53-06.

Many Americans are not familiar with the Malo brand because they only have a few stores in the U.S. This is one of the top Italian brands of cashmere, and we are talking about sweaters that would retail from $300 to $600 for a small pittance. I could barely breathe I was having so much fun.

By the way, Malo does make a few other things besides sweaters. Years ago my late husband bought the world's most chic bathing suit at a Malo store. They had hats and handbags when I was there, fabulous little suede slip-on shoes and some fashions à la Donna Karan in cotton and silk. I was there in winter so I would guess seasonal stuff turns up toward summer.

Chapter Seven

....

VENICE

WELCOME TO VENICE

There possibly isn't a more Magic Kingdom in the world: To me, Venice is the inspiration for Disney and for every other dream there is. It's historical, it's beautiful, and it's also romantic, but there's plenty of energy and shopping smarts. Venice has also changed a good bit lately—the town may be sinking, but new stores are still able to open their doors. So welcome to Venice, the shopping kingdom with a touch of the medieval and a soupçon of the modern.

I happen to prefer Venice off-season, but any time you can get here—even as a cruise passenger for a 1-day visit—is time enough to fill your soul and your senses.

In season, Venice is people, people everywhere; you have to be a little bit clever to actually enjoy shopping, or even to want to set foot in a crowded shop. Not to worry: Buy yourself a straw boater—yes, from that tourist trap (TT) right over there—buy a bag of pigeon food, and hit the back alleys where you have to get lost to get found.

Venice and shopping are made for each other; you're going to have the time of your life. In winter, the city can be a little bit chilly or damp, but the town is yours, and you will more than fill your senses . . . and your shopping bags.

- You can buy what they sell at Bergdorf-Goodman for a fraction of the U.S. price.
- You can walk into an ordinary shop in Murano and pay $45 for what would cost 10 times that in an ordinary shop in New York.
- You can load up on tourist junk, take it away from Venice, and turn it into great gifts for your loved ones—it won't even look like tourist junk.

When you start to collect intricate glass goblets on fluted feet of angel wings and find them for far less than in the U.S., you will thank your lucky bubble wrap.

When you can sit on top of the world at the **Terrazza Danieli** or the roof garden (or the canal-side terrace) of the **Bauer** and have coffee or a toasted cheese sandwich and enjoy the view of a lifetime, you, too, will share my enthusiasm for the glories of Venice.

Venetian Shopping History

Venice is about soothing all your senses; feeding all your being. Founded in the 5th century by survivors fleeing from Lombard invaders after the fall of the Roman Empire, Venice provided a cultural and political link between Eastern and Western civilizations for many centuries. By the 13th century, it was a leading and wealthy port of trade. People have been shopping here ever since.

The absence of cars allows leisurely browsing of the shops, churches, piazzas, and palaces. Every area contains boutiques stocked with the lace, fine glass, paper goods, and leather items for which Venice has become famous. The best thing about shopping in Venice is that you are forced to walk just about everywhere—even if you are just a museum person, you still pass by the shops and can look in the windows.

Conversely, even the most dedicated shopper is going to get an extra surge of excitement just from walking by the churches and museums. In Venice, culture and clutter, of the retailing sort, are all tied into one very attractive bundle.

Most shopkeepers speak English and are quite accustomed to tourists. All shops are anxious for business. Adjustments in price will reflect just how anxious for business shopkeepers are—in season (March to October), when tourists are plentiful, prices are higher, and bargaining is unheard of. In winter (except during Carnevale in February), things are so much sweeter—and cheaper.

GETTING TO VENICE

By Plane

Although the Venice airport is a tad inconvenient, it's not that difficult to use and is worth doing if you can afford water taxi connections. The airport makes European flight connections a breeze. Last trip, I went to Venice through Paris on **Air France,** a cinch. A round-trip ticket, with a Saturday night stay, was $200. If you are flying transatlantically on **Delta** or Air France, the price is even lower if you write it as a through-ticket.

Note that if you take a water taxi to/from Marco Polo International Airport and Venice proper, it will cost about $80.

By Train

To ride the regular express trains, I usually purchase an **Italian Rail Pass** (see chapter 2) or a **Eurailpass** or simply buy a ticket from Milan and hop onboard the fast train to Venice. Sometimes I do second class, but if I'm worried about a seat at what might be a peak travel time, I buy a first-class seat and a seat reservation so that I have a specific seat assigned to me. My most recent trip in a first-class seat cost $30 one-way and took a mere 3 hours. The concierge at the Hotel Principe de Savoia got the ticket, so it couldn't have been easier for me. Also note that many of the main hotels in Milan are 5 minutes from the Central Train Station.

Do learn how to read an Italian rail schedule, and allow yourself plenty of time for the asking of many, many questions.

I found an intercity train (fast train) on my timetable that appeared perfect—it was outbound from Venice and was stopping in Milan but was marked for Geneva. There was no way I could have known that was my train merely from reading the board in the station. If I'd taken the train marked Milano, I would have wasted 2 hours.

By Ship

I don't need to tell you that Venice has been a favored cruise destination for, uh, centuries. Some of the most famous shipyards in the world are outside Venice, and many of today's modern ocean liners are built right there. The number of passengers in recent cruise history who have come to Venice by ship has increased enormously in the last 10 years: In the new century, some 1 million people a year are expected just as cruisers. Ships disembark at VTP (Venezia Terminal Passeggeri), which is being renovated to handle the mob scene. The terminal has access for both ferries and cruise ships, and each area is color coordinated so that passengers can easily find the right check-in zones. For details, you can always call ☎ 041/533-48-60.

ARRIVING IN VENICE

You certainly don't want to drive to Venice, but if you do, and have a rental car, you will have to leave it in one of the major parking lots on the mainland in Mestre and come back later; you pay by the 24-hour period. So you'll probably be arriving by bus, train, or plane. No matter how you arrive, you will eventually need to arrange some sort of water transport (see below) to take you—and your luggage—to your hotel.

The key to smooth sailing, in all senses of the word, is to pack light and know that you can check baggage at the stations—even overnight or over many nights. In these days of international terrorism, it's not easy to find somewhere to leave unaccompanied baggage. Thankfully, the Venice train

Wedding Bells in Venice

Sure Venice is the most romantic place on earth; you may want to celebrate this fact not by buying glass or gilt but with a lasting memory—a wedding or reaffirmation ceremony, complete with gondola and wedding photos! **Samanatha Durell,** an American in Venice, can arrange it all. Fax her from the U.S. in Venice at 011-39-41/523-23-79, or use just the 041 city code if you are faxing from within Italy.

station will take your bags for several days, leaving you free to navigate the water bus in comfort.

But wait: The price to check baggage at the station is per bag, per 12-hour period, and it can get costly. It turned out that it was easier for me to just grab a water taxi (80,000L!) than check the bags for 50,000L and nights of worry (although Venice is virtually crime free).

Some hotels will arrange to meet you and will handle luggage for you; the **Gritti Palace** even has its own boat to take you back and forth from the airport. Put your Vuitton right here, Madame. Fax or e-mail your hotel in advance of your trip to arrange to be met. You'll pay for the service, but it may make your trip a lot more pleasant.

There used to be porters who met the water bus at the train station and then again at San Marco and would help you get to your hotel, but sometimes these guys are nowhere to be seen. This then is another reason to travel in winter; there were tons of them on my last December trip.

I personally choose to splurge on a water taxi when I arrive—it's about $50 and one of the nicest gifts I have ever given myself. A water taxi (*taxi acquei*) is a private boat hired to take you wherever you want to go; they are especially useful if you are coming from the airport and going directly to your hotel with a ton of luggage. There is a fixed tariff for water taxis that is adjusted every year or so. Know the rates (also listed in the booklet *A Guest in Venice,* which you can pick

Fávaro Veneto

14

Marco Polo Airport

Torcello

Burano

E13

11

Murano

Sant'Erasmo

Railway Station

San Michele

Ponte della Libertà

CANNAREGIO

SANTA CROCE · SAN POLO · SAN MARCO · **VENICE**

CASTELLO

DORSODURO

Airport on the Lido

LA GIUDECCA

Casino

Litorale di Lido

Airport ✈
Ferry Route — — —

Lido di Venezia

up at your hotel) so that you don't get taken. Last trip the fee was 90,000L, or just under $50.

The more reasonable approach to local transportation is the water bus (*vaporetto*). The water buses go around town in two different directions: one via the Grand Canal, the other via the Adriatic to San Marco. There are additional routes to various islands and specialty destinations. If you get on (or off) the water bus at the train station, you are at Ferrovia; the bus station is Piazzale Roma. The lines (and routes) are clearly marked; some lines offer express service with fewer stops. You can get a schedule at the Centro Informazioni ACTV at Piazzale Roma.

Buy the ticket before you board, if possible; it costs slightly more if purchased onboard. You can also buy tickets at any shop displaying a sign that says "ACTV." Prices have more than doubled in the last 2 years.

The water bus may be a little confusing at first, since there are different little floating stations for the different lines—read the destinations listed. Buy your ticket accordingly and give it to the ticket taker when he comes around to ask for it. Sometimes he doesn't ask.

Getting Around

Walk. Get lost. Enjoy it. Take the vaporetto (*vaporetti* is plural). And yes, take a ride in a gondola at least once in your life.

About Addresses

No city in Italy has a more screwy system for writing addresses; they are virtually impossible to read or to use because there is one address for mail and another for the actual building. My advice? Forget addresses. Walk; enjoy.

If you must get to a specific resource and haven't found it in your general lost-and-found, search-and-shop technique, ask your hotel's concierge to mark it for you on a map. Also take business cards that have maps on them so that you can get back to a specific source.

SLEEPING IN VENICE

My best trick? Don't sleep in Venice. Come in for a day trip. Padua is only 40km (25 miles) from Venice, an easy commute. Venice is just a 3-hour train ride from Milan. For something like Carnevale, where you want to be part of the action and then get out as fast as you can before you have a screaming breakdown (some 250,000 people jam San Marco each day on the Carnevale weekends!), this is an ideal ploy.

But since you've probably come to stay for a night or two or three, then just about any hotel will do. Some happen to be a little more magical than others. In Venice, you really pay for

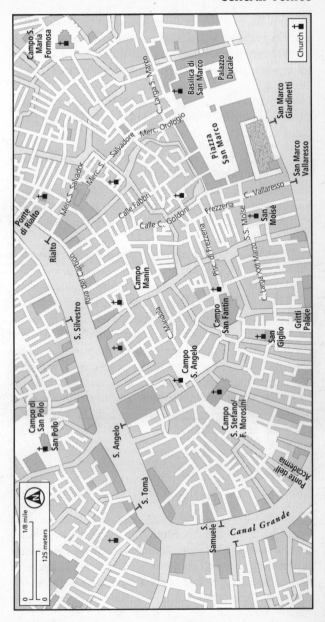

Central Venice

Church

Campo S. Maria Formosa

Basilica di San Marco

Palazzo Ducale

C. Larga S. Marco

Merc. Orologio

Piazza San Marco

San Marco Giardinetti

San Marco Vallaresso

Merc. S. Salvadore

Merc. S. Salvador

C. Vallaresso

Calle Fabbri

Frezzeria

San Moisè

Ponte di Rialto

Calle C. Goldoni

Pisc. di Frezzeria

S.S. Moisè

Rialto

C. Larga XXII Marzo

Campo Manin

S. Silvestro

Riva del Carbon

C. Mandola

Campo San Fantin

Gritti Palace

San Giglio

Campo di San Polo

Campo S. Angelo

San Polo

Campo S. Stefano/ F. Morosini

S. Angelo

Ponte dell' Accademia

S. Tomà

S. Samuele

Canal Grande

1/8 mile

125 meters

location. Since I tend to be there for only a short period of time and every moment is precious to me, I splurge on the hotel. As a repeat customer, I also know my way around from only a handful of hotels; not getting lost is money in the bank of time.

HOTEL BAUER
Campo San Moisè, San Marco 1459 (ACTV: San Marco or San Moisè)

Few moments in my life will I cherish with as much passion as when my private water taxi pulls up to the side of the hotel and I enter through the "water door." The Bauer is my palace, and I am the princess when my boat comes in. I especially like the approach from the water because the front door on the street is very 1950s, but the rear is very 1450s.

Rooms have recently been renovated in this hotel—my last room had 20-foot ceilings and a gilt wooden bed, and white embroidered damask was hung on the walls and bed. Naturally, there was a view of the Grand Canal. Add to that the fabulous bathroom amenities, the best shopping location in town (across the walkway from Versace, next door to the new Ferragamo, and two steps from American Express—how convenient), and Leading Hotels of the World charm, and, well, you can't beat it. As an added plus, I had breakfast on the seventh floor with all of Venice spread around me.

For reservations from the U.S., call ☎ **800/223-6800.** Local phone ☎ 041/52-07-022; fax 041/52-75-57; online: www.lhw.com/bauer.

HOTEL DANIELI
Riva degli Schiavoni, Castello 4196 (ACTV: San Zaccaria)

The Danieli also has a good shopping location; it's on the other side of San Marco from the Bauer. It, too, is a renovated palace, done more in the Byzantine fashion. Located on the far edge of San Marco, it even has its own gondola stop: San Zaccaria. Best yet, there is a rooftop restaurant and terrace with a view that cannot adequately be described. Have tea or drinks here, or just stop by to use the bathroom. Walk into the lobby, take the back elevator marked for the Terrace (Terrazza), and go up. Bathrooms are to your right. Then step onto the terrace and experience heaven on earth. Who could ask for anything more?

For U.S. reservations, call ☎ **800/221-2340**. Local phone ☎ 041/52-26-480; fax 041/52-00-208; online: www. ittsheraton.com.

HOTEL MONACO & GRAND CANAL
Calle Vallaresso, San Marco 1325 (ACTV: San Zaccaria)

I found this hotel around the corner from the Danieli, which means it has a great location; yup, this, too, is a shopping street. The hotel is not quite as grand as others, but it's not quite as expensive either. Nice views; dine from the rooftop à la Danieli.

Reservations from the U.S. are made through Prima Hotels (☎ **800/447-7462**). Local phone ☎ 041/52-00-211; fax 041/52-00-501. E-mail: mailbox@hotelmonaco.it.

IL PALAZZO
San Marco 1459 (ACTV: San Marco)

Okay, here's the true insider's secret: The hotel Il Palazzo is a recent invention cut out of the Bauer, above. It's the boutique hotel part, where the big names and celebs stay. All information above pertains.

4-Star Finds

HOTEL BISANZIO
Calle della Pietà, Castello 3651 (ACTV: San Zaccaria)

I was just walking along past the Danieli on the way to my girlfriend's restaurant (Al Covo) and on the sidewalk was a sign for this hotel, so I followed it, and lo, a find. It's set back from Riva degli Schiavoni, but it's brilliantly located and charming and real and funky and affordable. It's a Best Western Hotel with only 40 rooms.

For reservations from the U.S., call ☎ **800/528-1234.**
Local phone ☎ 041/42-03-100; fax 041/52-04-114; online:
www.bisanzio.com.

HOTEL FLORA
San Marco 2283A (ACTV: San Marco)

The hidden hotel of infinite charm in the heart of the shopping district that will steal your heart: Travel writer Patricia
Schultz took me here, as I had not discovered this hidden
secret. The hotel is reached through a tiny alley that leads to
its courtyard. It's in the middle of the finest shopping area and
not far from my beloved Bauer Hotel. The hotel is small and
charming with a hint of funky elegance. You do best to book
by calling or faxing and developing a personal relationship with
the hotel itself—it is family-owned. It's air-conditioned; breakfast is included in the room rate, as are taxes. A single room
with bath costs about $180; a twin room with bath is $200.
This hotel is technically rated with 3 stars, not 4 . . . but I give
it 4.

Local phone ☎ **041/52-05-844;** fax 041/52-28-217.

HOTEL SATURNIA
San Marco 2398 (ACTV: San Marco)

This hotel is not far from the Bauer. It's almost across the road
from the Flora but is far more visible. It's also a midpoint hotel
between the two extremes: The Flora is less expensive and less
formal. Rates at this hotel vary with the season—the least expensive price for a double room is about $250 and the high is about
$400, still making it a bargain by local standards. This hotel
can also be booked in the U.S. through SRS Worldhotels.
Breakfast buffet and taxes are included; there are demi-
pensione and full pensione prices depending on your needs.
Local phone ☎ **041/52-08-377;** fax 041/52-07-131; online:
www.hotelsaturnia.it.

Snack & Shop

AL COVO
Campiello della Pescaria, Castello

Okay, so this isn't on your ordinary list of legends and land-marks, but it's part of mine because Diane is from Texas and comes to me through my official foodie friends. Her husband is the chef, and he is increasingly getting famous and recognized by American authorities, so book now. The restaurant is on the far side of the Danieli, far enough away from the tourists to be pure and family-oriented. The food is fabulous (try Diane's walnut cake), and you will get the special treatment you crave from a great team. If you think I'm the only one on to this place, forget it. It came into my family of journalists because Marcella Hazan brought Faith Heller Willinger here, and Faith brought Patricia Schultz, and she told me, and . . . For reservations, call ☎ 041/52-23-812. Note that Al Covo now sells its own products as well.

CAFFÉ FLORIAN
Piazza San Marco, San Marco

So you sit there at sunset on the Piazza San Marco at a little table, drinking a strawberry version of the Bellini because it's straw-berry season and Florian won't use canned peaches like they do at Harry's (tsk, tsk). There's a tiny band shell, and they play schmaltzy music and all you want to do is sing and dance and laugh and cry. And that's before you see the bill. Just once before you die. No wonder Napoléon said that San Marco was Europe's most elegant drawing room. Ah, yes, they sell the china, the dishes, and their own house brand of coffee and tea and even spumante. A fabulous gift to bring home for someone who knows Venice.

HARRY'S BAR
Calle Vallaresso, San Marco 1323

There is a Harry's Bar, there is even a Harry (call him Arrigo), and no, Harry's Bar is not in the Gritti Palace, as many think.

It is where Hemingway and the gang liked to hang out and is located halfway between San Marco and the Gritti. This is the home of the famous Bellini. I have sipped Bellinis at Harry's— it was swell, and, yes, I saw everyone I knew. I have wondered just why Harry's is so famous and later discovered that the thing to do is not sip Bellinis (this is for tourists) but to dine upstairs with a chef whom many consider one of the best in the world. Me? I sit downstairs and nibble on the *croque monsieur,* which is fried to a crisp and makes a super lunch or snack. I also like their *latte macchiato* . . . milk stained with coffee.

Hostaria al Rusteghi
San Bartolomio 5529

This is an itty-bitty teeny-weeny deli/sandwich shop that you won't find if you aren't looking for it or are headed to the public toilets near the Coin department store. I always stop here to pick up little sandwiches for the train ride back to Milan. They are open from 9:30am to 3pm, Monday through Saturday. Each little sandwich costs 2,000L, a little more than $1.

Terrazza Danieli
Hotel Danieli, Riva degli Schiavoni, San Marco 4196

The rooftop of the Hotel Danieli has a wonderful restaurant called the Terrace (Terrazza). The view is spectacular, and the food ain't bad. Ian and I always try to book a lunch here while in Venice, but I have also been known to make this my first stop after I arrive via train from Milan in the morning. A mere cup of coffee overlooking the Adriatic is enough to make your heart sing. You can afford coffee here, so don't miss it!

THE SHOPPING SCENE

Hmmmm, let's see: Is this the place in the book where I tell you that things are changing fast and that Disney opened up a shop about three years ago? (There goes the neighborhood!)

Or do I ignore Disney (as you should) and figure it's for locals, it's to promote Paris Disneyland, and after all, Venice is the original Disneyland? Do I say forget all about those 101 Dalmatians and their friends and note that many stores have moved; many have joined the scene (big Ferragamo next to the Bauer, remember?), and some of the best stores have expanded either in square footage or with additional branches—*si, si,* there are now two branches of Venice Stadium.

Please understand the most basic law of shopping in Venice: Because of transportation, everything is essentially imported to Venice. That means higher prices than anywhere else in Italy. It means you'll pay top dollar for a Coca-Cola, a roll of film, or a pair of Italian designer shoes. Or a Disney T-shirt. Also, this isn't really a city for designer shopping, although you can buy most everything here.

Your best buys will always be locally made souvenir items, which are quite moderately priced. Also note that the tourist junk here is far more attractive than in any other major Italian city. There's also more than the usual number of hidden resources, since this is the kind of town where the best stuff is definitely hidden.

As for the souvenirs, I truly believe that at the beginning of each season the retailers in Venice have a meeting and peg the prices to exactly at what the lire-to-$10 ratio is trading in any given year. Thus everything is suddenly priced in the 15,000L to 16,500L price bracket, or $10; or whatever the current $10 equivalent is.

My Kingdom for a Goblet

I've gotten more and more into the traditional Venetian wine goblets with fishy or curvy stems laden with elaborate curlicues and doodads—which leave you breathless at the thought of the workmanship. These glasses sell for $250 and upward in New York. Way upward. In Venice they start at around $100, and very big, very fancy ones can be had for about $200, although, if you insist, you can find some splendid examples in the $500 to $600 price range. The problem, of course, is the shipping or the packing (if you are going to hand-carry your items). If you do have your glass shipped, make sure your shipper guarantees the items so that they will be replaced if they arrive broken.

In terms of sheer money saving, yes, you will save money if you buy in Venice, but, no, you won't save a lot, once you add on the cost of shipping and insurance.

The Best Buys in Venice

I have been known to go nuts for glass, handbags, paper goods, and local crafts—all can be best buys in Venice. More important, even if you've seen these items for less money elsewhere, they offer good value as items bought in Venice to be remembered as such and cherished. You don't want to buy your Carnevale mask in Rome just because you might get it cheaper, do you? Marbleized paper items are less in Florence, but only slightly less.

The very best buy in town? You can buy a bag of pigeon food in San Marco for 1,500L (less than $1) and feed the birds and have a ball. An excellent investment and a supreme bargain.

Glass   Murano is the glass capital of Italy, and Venice is the front door to the glass candy store. Even when it's expensive, glass usually costs less here than if bought in the U.S. Also in the glass category are mirrors and chandeliers.

Masks   Carnevale has its own rituals—mask-wearing among them. The city now sells scads of masks in every format, from cheap plastic ones to incredibly crafted ones made of leathers or feathers.

Silks   When you see the incredibly pleated teeny-tiny Fortuny silk baggies for jewelry or potpourri for $30 at Stadium (Venetia Stvdivm, see below), you'll know why Marco Polo came home.

The Worst Buys in Venice

If you can help it, don't buy:

- Clothing. Not a good buy in Venice, unless you need it or hit a sale or bargain.
- Designer items. Hermès is more expensive in Venice than in Milan.
- Film. Film is expensive everywhere in Europe; it costs about $12 a roll in Venice.
- Fake designer handbags. Give me a break.

The San Marco Rule of Shopping

If you are looking for the best prices on the average tourist items—from souvenirs to snacks—my rule is simple: Avoid San Marco.

San Marco is the center of the tourist universe and therefore the center of the highest prices. The farther you go from San Marco, the more the prices drop. Shop on the island where the train station is and you find the best prices in town. If you insist on TTs, hit the ones way past San Marco and the Hotel Danieli and on the way to the public gardens. You'll save as much as $1 per item. You'll also avoid the most severe crowds.

The Gondoliers

I don't care how touristy you think it is—riding in a gondola is part of the Venetian experience and something you must do at least once. While you can be hustled by a gondolier, there are fixed prices for their services that vary from season to season. Even if you have to save up for the experience, this is one treat that you shouldn't miss. *Tip:* Take your gondola ride at high tide—at low tide you'll have a view of the scummy exposed sides of the canals.

When there aren't as many rich tourists around, prices drop. The winter price can be 100,000L; the spring price for the same service is 120,000L, but you can try to bargain.

Night service, any time of the year, is 150,000L beginning at 8pm. These are the prices for 50 minutes of sailing time with up to six persons in the boat. For each additional 25-minute period after your first 50 minutes, the flat rate is 60,000L. You are also expected to tip.

Okay, that was the official line as taught to me by the city. In person, I find that knowing these prices is helpful, as is carrying around a copy of the freebie booklet *Un Ospite di Venezia* that is given away at your hotel and has a section on gondola prices. You bargain fiercely or find someone you like and forget the money. Gondoliers do 45 minutes, not 50; they want far more than the guidelines say they should get; they are especially not friendly when there are lots of tourists around. Their idea of a great fare is a chump who says "yes" to the quoted price and then lays a tip on top.

The gondolier will sing to you—it's part of the deal—but if you ask him to stop the boat en route so that you can get out for a look-see while he waits, or to provide extra services (other than posing in your family snapshot), he will expect more money.

All things are negotiable, but try to have a handle on costs before you get in—nothing spoils the magic more than a fight about money after the fact.

I've seen as many as six people squished into a gondola, so the cost can be amortized into a reasonable expense. You have not seen Venice until you've seen it from a gondola—it is worth the money. If you want an update or inside fact, call the hotline: ☎ 041/528-50-75.

Shopping Hours

High season is March to October, and shops are open from 9am until 12:30 or 1pm and then reopen from about 3 or 3:30pm to 7:30pm. If lunchtime closings bore you, remember that the shops on the nearby island of Murano do not close for lunch!

Off-season, most Venice shops are closed on Monday until 3pm. During Carnevale weekend, many things are open no matter what day or what time of the day. For Sunday shopping tips, see below.

Sunday Shopping

Venice, because of its high tourist population, is one of the few cities in Italy that does not close up on Sunday. *Si, si,* **Emporio Armani**, **Trussardi**, and **Versace** and the like are open on Sunday afternoon. Just about everyone is open on Sunday!

In season, a great number of shops (mostly TTs, of course) are also open on Sunday afternoon. Even out of season, there are enough shops open so that you may have a satisfactory shopping day.

Also remember those Carnevale weekends when retail is roaring all day on Sunday. Pre-Carnevale is celebrated in Venice on the two weekends preceding the actual event. There's tons o' shopping.

Sunday is also a good day to visit the islands; shops are open on both Murano and Burano. Check with your concierge for exact opening and closing times, but plan a day trip to Murano as early as you like—the fires are crackling at 9am, and shops are open nonstop until 4 or 5pm. On Burano, Sunday hours tend to be 10am to 1:30pm.

Street Vendors

One of the glories of Venice is the street action—not just the throngs of tourists but the zillions of street vendors who make it possible for you to do very thorough shopping in Venice without ever setting foot inside a store.

The street vendors stay open until the light begins to fade, which in the height of summer can be quite late. There are illegal salespeople hawking wares from blankets all over town—they usually operate during lunch hours and after hours as there is less chance they will be arrested then. Louis Vuitton anyone? Cartier perhaps? "This is real Chanel, lady."

Like other retailers, street vendors and cart dealers rig their prices to the needs of the crowd. Therefore, the farther you walk from San Marco, the better the prices at kiosks and carts.

Fairs & Mercatini

San Moisè is the location of many outdoor fairs, from antiques markets to the regular Christmas market. Vendors set up booths and sell from 9am to 8pm. What fun!

Buying Venetian Glass

I confess that up until the minute I walked into Bergdorf Goodman one fateful day, I thought that only old ladies liked Venetian glass. Then I took one look at a bowl filled with hand-blown Murano glass in the form of colorful hard candies and flipped out. Such style, such finesse, such color. If this is the passion of little old ladies, sign me up. I've had a sweet tooth ever since. Bergdorf's gets about $12 per glass candy. In Venice you'll pay from 3,000L to 5,000L, or about $3 per unit.

Once you get hooked on glass candies, a whole new world of glass design opens up. Fazzoletto (handkerchief vases) will surely be next. While you may not flip out for pink glass goblets with hand-painted roses and baroque gold doodads, you will gasp when you take in the designs made from the early 1920s right through the 1950s—all highly collectible works of art when they are signed by a big-name glasshouse. Even post-1950s glass is collectible: What you buy today (if you buy wisely) will be happily inherited by your children.

The colored strings of glass swirled into clear, white, or colored glass are called threads; the value of a piece—aside from the signature—is based on the composition of form, color, and threads or patterns; the way the piece reflects light should also be taken into account, although this is easy to look for in a vase and impossible to consider in a piece of candy. Smoked glass is hot now, as is glass matted with ash, and deco glass. Crizzled glass is crickly-crackled glass with a nice effect, but it won't last over the centuries and makes a bad investment.

The important names to remember are **Venini, Seguso, Brandolini, Poli, Barovier, Toso,** and **Pauly.** A vase from the 1940s went for $125,000 at auction at Christie's in Geneva in 1990; prices continue to rise. New pieces are not inexpensive as they are considered serious artwork.

Famous designers create styles for glasshouses, just as they do for furniture firms. The designer's name associated with a famous glasshouse can make a piece even more valuable. Do check for signatures, labels, or accompanying materials that uphold the provenance of your piece. If you are buying older pieces of glass—even from the 1950s or so—check the condition carefully.

If you are trading up and browsing for some of the important stuff, here's a quick-fix dictionary to make you sound like a maven:

Vetro battute Flat beaten glass with a scored surface.

Vetro sommerso Glass in bubbled, lumpy form is layered over the glass item—the rage in the mid-1930s.

Vetro pennelato No, it doesn't have pieces of penne pasta in it—this is painted glass with swirly streaks of dancing color that zip across the body of the item inside the glass.

Vetro pulegoso This is bubbled glass with the tiny bubbles inside the glass—it will never be confused with sommerso when you see the two in person.

Vetro inciso Flat beaten glass with scored lines all running in the same direction.

Vetro pezzato Patchwork made of various pieces of colored glass almost in mosaic form; introduced in the early 1950s.

Vetro a retorti Twisted glass with the threads swirled within the body of the work.

Murrina Slices of colored glass rods encircled with gold and sold as charms or pendants.

I must take some time here to warn you about the hawkers who offer you free trips to Murano and act as guides, etc. They are dangerous, emotionally and physically, and should be avoided. They not only get a percentage of what you buy but make their living by preying off tourists and telling half truths or lies that might convince you to buy something you weren't certain about.

If you want the free boat ride, ask your hotel concierge to book it. If you can afford to get there on your own, do so, and buy only from the houses of good repute. If you ship, be prepared to wait a very, very long time for your package to arrive.

Shipping

Anyone seriously considering glass, or mirrors, or chandeliers is also thinking about shipping. Almost all the stores, even the TTs, will volunteer to ship for you. I am not big on shipping, especially expensive items, but I have noticed that things shipped from Venice do tend to reach their destination—eventually. I have had several nervous letters from readers who have waited many months in a state of panic. My basic advice is simple: Don't fall in love with anything you cannot carry yourself. Always buy from a reputable dealer and pay with a credit card that has a protection plan on it.

Shopping Neighborhoods

Most of the shops are found in the historical and artistic center, between the **Rialto Bridge** (*Ponte di Rialto*) and **Piazza San Marco.** A new area of mostly designer shops has been evolving at **San Moisè.**

Looking at a map can be very confusing because of the cobweb of interconnecting streets, bridges, and canals. Finding an address can be equally difficult, as many streets and shops show no numbers, or the numbers are clear, but the street they are on is not clear.

Merceria One main street will carry you from Piazza San Marco to the Rialto Bridge: Merceria. It hosts hundreds of shops.

Many of the shopping streets branch off this one thorough-fare, or are very close. Merceria is not a water bus stop (San Marco is), but if you get yourself to Piazza San Marco and stand at the clock tower with your back to the water, Merceria will be the little street jutting off the arcade right in front of you. If you still can't find it, walk into any shop and ask. You need not speak Italian.

Piazza San Marco   The four rows of arcades that frame Piazza San Marco can be considered a neighborhood unto itself. Three of the arcades create a U shape around the square; the fourth is at a right angle to one of the ends of the U. There are easily a hundred shops here—a few of the shops are showrooms for glass firms and a few sell touristy knickknacks, but most are jewelry or glass shops (or cafes). Although many of these shops have been in business for years and some of them have extremely famous names, this is the high rent part of Venice and isn't very funky. I was quite shocked at the high turnover I noticed on my last visit: Many old reliable firms have packed up. One of the newer names to the area is **Michaela Frey,** a Viennese jeweler known for her enamel works who does a fab-ulous Saint Marks Square bangle bracelet for those who can handle a pricey souvenir.

Behind San Marco   Now, here's the tricky part. "Behind San Marco" is my name for the area that includes **San Moisè** and **San Giglio** (this way to the Hotel Bauer) and is best represented by the big-time shopping drag called **Via XXII Marzo.** This street comes off of Piazza San Marco from behind and forms an L with the square and Merceria. The farther you get from San Marco, the less commercial.

Frezzeria   This is the main shopping street also behind San Marco, but it goes off to your right if your back is to San Marco and you're facing the road to the Hotel Bauer and American Express. It's a small alley of a street that twists and turns more than most, and it's packed with small shops, many of which are artisan or crafts shops. There are also some designer stores woven into the texture of the landscape.

Giglio   This is a secret part of town tucked back and away from the tourist areas. It's also the home of the **Gritti Palace**. Unless a shop is actually on the piazza, it probably will have a San Moisè address, so you may get confused. Not to worry. Aside from the antiques shops, there's a good paper store and a little market for food for the train or a picnic. It's very civilized and quite divine back here.

Rialto Bridge   They might just as well have named it the "Retailo" Bridge—not only are there pushcarts and vendors in the walkway before the bridge, but there are also shops going all the way up and down the bridge itself. The stores are not like the crumbling, charming, old shops that line the Ponte Vecchio in Florence; they are teeny-bopper shops, leather goods stores, and even sporting goods stores. Despite the huge number of street vendors from Piazza San Marco to Campo San Zaccaria, street vendors here sell things I've never seen before. Most of it is extremely touristy junk.

Over the Bridge   Once across the Rialto, you'll hit a two-pronged trading area. In the arcades behind the street vendors to the left are established shops; in the streets and to your right are green grocers, food vendors, cheese stalls, and, in summer, little men selling little pieces of melon. You can have a walking feast for lunch in any season.

Once you make it past the immediate arcades, bear left and follow the shops and crowds toward **San Polo.** The shops here are a little more of the "real people" nature and a little less expensive. On the other hand, a fair number of them are smaller branches of the big designer shops found on the big island.

Piazzale Roma   This is by no means a hot retailing area, but it is where the bus station is and where you will get your vaporetto if you come in from the airport, or if you come by bus. (The train station is not here.) Where there are tourists, there are shops. In the case of Venice, or Venice in summer, where there are tourists, there are scads of street vendors selling everything from T-shirts like the one worn by your favorite gondolier to plates of the Doge's Palace.

Shopping Murano

Two different experiences are to be had here on the island of glassblowers—so watch out and don't blame me if you hate it. It can be very touristy or very special—it depends on how you organize your time, as well as what season you visit. Go by vaporetto in season, and it can be a zoo. Go by private boat, tour a glass factory, wander town, and then take the vaporetto back: It's easy, it's inexpensive, and it's fun. It can even be glorious depending on the weather, the crowds, and your appetite for colored glass.

On Sunday, most showrooms (and their adjoining shops) are open from 9am to 4pm. TTs open midday. Sunday on Murano can be heaven. Take no. 5 at San Zaccaria, in front of the Danieli. The visit to Murano can be combined with a trip to Burano (take no. 12), or you can turn around and come back home. It's a long day if you combine both islands.

Murano is also the perfect lunchtime adventure when stores in Venice might be closed. Do not bring small children or strollers with you.

If you want to take a private boat to the island, call one of the glass factories to come get you. Yes, you are obligated to tour the factory, but you aren't obligated to buy. Besides, the tour is fabulous. It's a perfect Sunday adventure; Sunday is a big day on Murano because they cannot close down the furnaces since the temperature must stay constant, but the workers don't work, so there are demonstrations and tours.

If you go by public transportation, you will arrive in the heart of Murano. When you get off the boat at Murano, you'll know it by the giant signs that say *fornace* (furnace). You have two choices, really: to work the area, or to realize quickly that this is one of the biggest tourist traps known to humankind. Walk briskly toward the museum and then head for the lighthouse.

By the way, you can also get a free ride to the island by private boat if you go with a hawker, but you *don't* want to do this! He gets 30% of what you spend in a secret kickback, and you get a lot of pressure to buy (see above). But if you can take the heat, you will be escorted to the fornace. And it may be hell, so beware!

Hawkers will automatically gravitate to you; you need not even look for them. It's better to ask your hotel concierge to contact someone from a proper factory for you.

Glass with Class

ARCHIMIDE SEGUSO
Fondamenta Serenella, Murano

One of the masters of the glass universe. They also have a show-room in Venice.

BAROVIER & TOSO
Fondamenta Vetrai 28, Murano

This is a very trendy showroom with the latest designs in hot colors and sophisticated styles. They will ship for you at moderate prices, but expect to pay several hundred dollars for a vase. This is serious art, folks, so if you're looking for cheap gifts to send home, forget it.

FOSCARINI
Fondamenta Serenella, Murano

This is a real showroom for important lighting fixtures that look like they were imported from outer space.

SENT
Fondamenta Serenella, Murano

This is a double showroom with jewelry and home furnishings. It's very modern and very chic.

VENINI
Fondamenta Serenella, Murano

The showroom on Murano is open to the trade only, and then only by appointment. Drat. There's a showroom at San Marco for mere mortals.

Other Glass Resources

For good, traditional showrooms that have it all, try either of the resources below. To find these shops, walk from the main drag toward the lighthouse, and you'll wander into a far less touristy world and a hidden street (Viale Garibaldi) of more glassblowers and shops. Once at the lighthouse, round the turn following the water (there's a sidewalk) to find several more glass showrooms. Both have boat service and will pick you up at your hotel in town and return you when you are ready to go back.

MURANO VENEZIA GLASS
Fondamenta dei Battuti 5, Murano

I asked the concierge at the Bauer Grünwald to pick a source for me, curious to see what he would suggest, and was pleased to find that this was his choice. They sent a boat for me and picked me up at my hotel, then returned me there when I was ready to go home. I even got a Coke along the way. A true delight!

The showroom is made up of a series of salons, organized by category of goods and by price. One room is devoted to chandeliers, other rooms to glassware. You'll also find beads and just about anything else you can imagine.

To get them to pick you up, call ☎ **041/73-92-22** at least 1 day in advance.

VETRERIA COLONNA FORNACE
Fondamenta Vetrai 10–11, Murano

This is another huge firm that will pick you up at your hotel and let you tour their scads of rooms of stuff. For pickup, call ☎ **041/73-93-89.** I don't mean to give this place short shrift, as I have enjoyed hours shopping here. Much like Murano Venezia Glass, above—the same but different. Do 'em both!

Shopping Burano

Although Murano and Burano sound like twin cities, they are not. But if you visit the two in the same afternoon (get the water bus from the lighthouse on Murano to Burano; it runs hourly, but go there for the exact schedule so that you can plan your time accordingly), you can sightsee and do some shopping at the same time. Many stores in Burano are open on Sunday afternoon, so you can combine the two islands in a fabulous Sunday outing.

As touristy and crass as Murano can be, Burano is totally different—I don't happen to like it as much, but I can see the natural, homespun attraction. Certainly the colors of the houses are divine. The shopping is awfully touristy. I get the feeling that Murano is in the glass business, and Burano is in the tourist business; there's something in the subtext of the air in Burano that lacks wonder. The lace is rarely handmade; there are few really good shops. But if you like to see, to stroll, and to avoid the throngs of pushing people in San Marco, this is a wonderful side trip. Don't think of it as a shopping adventure; rather, take your artistic eye and just enjoy.

You may want to poke into the fish market, **Fondamenta Pescheria,** held daily in the morning only—not that you're going to buy much, but it's fun and picturesque.

The lace-making school is the **Scuola di Merletti,** Piazza Galuppi (☎ **041/73-00-34**). The school is closed on Monday, open from 10am to 4pm on Sunday and from 9am to 6pm Tuesday through Saturday.

The boat to Burano from Murano is as big as the ferry that takes you to Nantucket, and you will have the same sense of adventure. Burano is the third stop, so don't have a breakdown wondering when and where to get off (the first stop is Mazzorbo; the second is Torcello). And yes, it's a bit of a schlep, so you'll be on the boat for a while.

When you arrive you'll see a narrow street lined with shops and think you are in heaven. That's because you haven't been in the shops yet. Pretty soon, you'll think you are in Hong Kong.

Here's the story of the woman in Venice who was buying a lace tablecloth. She had it spread out around her and draped all over—she was oooohing and aaaahing over it, but I knew it was from Hong Kong—like most of the lace in Venice—and I didn't know if I should tell her or not. Well, I didn't say a word because I didn't want to ruin her experience, but readers, you should know the facts.

If you don't like the lace shops, never mind; just take a good look at the colors of the stucco houses and storefronts—they are just fabulous. And the lace school is incredible.

Not all of the shops in the "heart of town" are open on Sunday, but the TTs are. Get the boat schedule before you wander so that you know how long you have—an hour on Burano is probably all you need. Note that when you return to Venice you will probably end up at a vaporetto stop other than San Marco and will have to buy a new ticket and transfer to get back to your hotel.

VENICE RESOURCES FROM A TO Z

Antiques

If you are the type (like me) who likes flea markets and junk and reasonable prices, Venice is not for you (unless you hit it for one of the triannual flea markets). There are also regular real-people flea markets, but they are on the "land" side.

The few antiques shops in Venice are charming and dear and sweet and—should I tell you, or can you guess?—outrageously expensive.

But wait, should you luck into the **Mercatino dell'Antiquariato,** held each April, September, and December, you'll have the giggle of your lifetime. This market is not large, but it's sweet and simple and the kind I like: heaps of stuff on tables laid out in a piazza, the very convenient Campo San Maurizio. The dates are established well in advance and set for each year so that you can call for the exact times (☎ 041/ 45-41-76). This is a 3-day event held on a Friday, Saturday, and Sunday; there is no admission charge.

Beads

LESLIE ANN GENNINGER DESIGN STUDIO
Calle del Traghetto, Dorsoduro 2793a

Talk about living out your best dreams: Leslie is American, lives in Venice, makes beads, and sells them from a fabulous little shop where you can buy ready-made jewelry or individual beads. The beads are made according to medieval (and secret) recipes but are inlaid with silver, which sparkles through.

Boutiques

ARBOR
Gran Viale Lido 10a, San Marco 4759

There are several branches of this boutique on the big island as well as at the Lido beach. Arbor carries the hot names, such as Byblos and Genny. The men's shop sells that stylish Italian look that thin men love to wear.

ELYSÉE
Frezzeria, San Marco 1693

ELYSÉE 2
Calle Goldoni, Castello 4485

This is not one but two very sleek boutiques carrying Mani, Maud Frizon, Mario Valentino, and the Giorgio Armani ready-to-wear collection for men and women. Armani is here exclusively. This also is a good place to check out the cheaper versions of Valentino—those licensed by GFT. Each shop has its own selection, including some shoes.

LA COUPOLE
Via XXII Marzo, San Marco 2366; Frezzeria, San Marco 1674

Once again, two boutiques carrying the same big names and many lines. A few of their makers include Byblos, Alaia, and the sort of local Malo cashmere; shoes from Moschino and earrings from Sharra Pagano of Milan. Both shops are small and elegant; prices are high.

Crafts

IL BALLO DEL DOGE
San Marco 1823

Cooperative of 14 artisans.

LA BOTTEGA DEI MASCARERI
Ponte di Rialto, San Polo 80

Located at the foot of the Rialto, this shop offers unusual papier-mâché masks that are a notch above the average fare. Elaborate masks begin at 100,000L, but simple ones begin at 25,000L.

LA VENEXIANA
Ponte Canonica, Castello 4322

You'll find masks and other carnival items here as well as some of the most incredible crafts work I have ever seen. Don't miss it.

MAX ART SHOP
Frezzeria, San Marco 1232

This store is right around the corner from the Hotel Bauer and the San Moisè designer shopping area at the start of Freezia; it will beckon to you from the velvet hung windows. Inside, choose from velvet pillows, clothes, Carnevale-inspired wonder, and Old-World charm.

Designer Boutiques

ARAMNI
Calle Goldin, San Marcoi 4412

BULGARI
Calle Larga XXII Marzo, San Marco 2282

CARTIER
30124 Venezia, San Marco 606

D&G DOLCE & GABANA
San Marco 1313

EMPORIO ARMANI
Calle dei Fabbri, San Marco 989

FENDI
Salizzada San Moisè, San Marco 1474

FOGAL
Calle Merceria dell'Orologio, San Marco 221

FRETTE
Calle Larga XXII Marzo, San Marco 2070A

GIANFRANCO FERRÉ
Calle Larga, San Marco 287

GIANNI VERSACE
Campo San Moísè, San Marco 1462

GUCCI
San Marco 1317

HERMÈS
Piazza San Marco, San Marco 125

ISTANTE
San Marco 2359

KENZO
Frezzeria Angolo Ramo Fuseri, San Marco 1814

LA PERLA
Campo San Salvador, San Marco 4828

LAURA BIAGIOTTI
Via XXII Marzo, San Marco 2400

LORO PIANA
Ascensione, San Marco 1290 & 1301

MALO
Calle della Ostreghe, San Marco 2359

MASKA
Via XXII Marzo, San Marco 2251

MAX & CO.
San Marco 5028

MAX MARA
Mercerie, San Marco 268

MONT BLANC
San Marco 4610

ROBERTO CAVALLI
San Marco 1316

SALVATORE FERRAGAMO
Campo San Moisè, San Marco

TRUSSARDI
Calle Spadaria, San Marco 695

VALENTINO
Salizzada San Moisè, San Marco 147

VERSUS
San Marco 1725

WOLFORD
Cannaregio 5666

Fabrics

GAGGIA
San Stefano, San Marco 3441

Traditional silks, velvets, pleats, block prints, and the to-die-for local look that is part costume and part local treasure. Fabrics by the meter, also clothes and styles for the home.

RUBELLI
Campo San Gallo, San Marco 3877

This Italian house is actually a source to the trade for reproductions of stunningly exquisite silken brocades and formal fabrics of museum quality. They have swatches, and they work with individuals, even if your last name is not Rothschild. Okay, the fabric costs 2 million lire per meter, but it's actually worth it.

VALLI
San Marco 783

Valli is a chain of fabric stores with locations in all major cities and factories in Como; their shop in Venice happens to be right along your path, so it's a good place to stop in. The specialty of the house is designer fabrics, straight from the factory as supplied to the design houses, so you can buy the fabric in the same season. It's not cheap, but you can save money. I spent $100 on some Gianni Versace silk and made a sarong skirt that I could never afford to buy from Versace ready-made.

VENETIA STVDIVM
Calle Larga XXII Marco, San Marco 2403; Mercerie, San Marco 723

Fortuny-style wrinkled fabric (mostly silks) in medieval colors that are pure artistry. There are long Isadora Duncan–like scarves and little drawstring purses that make the perfect evening bag. Prices begin around $200. Note that the store is in larger headquarters now. There are velvets as well as silks, and you should consider bringing your toothbrush so that you can just move in. Heaven on earth. Also check out their latest invention, "silk lighting." I bought silk tassels for about $50 each.

Foodstuffs

AL COVO
Campiello della Pecaria, Castello

On the back of your menu from Al Covo note that there is an order form for all the products. You take them away with you. These include olive oil, balsamic vinegar, pasta, and polenta. Ask Diane for details when you are there.

DROGHERIA MASCARI
San Polo 381

This is not a drugstore as you might guess from the name but the last remaining spice merchant in Venice. Located in a real people part of town, you get there by walking over the Rialto Bridge and going on to San Polo.

GIACOMO RIZZO
Salizzada San Giovanni Crisóstomo, 5778

Don't freak at the address; it's on the way to the Coin department store ... it's not out of your way at all, and please, don't miss this one. This is a designer pasta shop with prepackaged fresh gourmet pasta in weird and wonderful flavors such as chocolate and blueberry. There are also some specialty pastas in wonderful (or weird) shapes, from gondola to penis. (Who could make this up?) Pasta makes a great gift, at $6 per package. The company has national distribution throughout Italy, but this is the flagship store.

Glass

You'll recognize the difference between quality glass and touristy junk in a matter of seconds. Make a trip to the glass museum on Murano if your eye needs a little training.

F.G.B.
Santa Maria del Giglio, San Marco 2459

This is a tiny shop, off toward the Gritti; it specializes in blown glass bugs, which happen to be an art form. Many of the greats have begun with bugs and moved on. These may make you itch for a second, but will then fascinate you.

GALLERIA ALL ASCENSIONE
San Marco 72A

This very tiny shop is located in the arcade at the back side of Piazza San Marco (toward San Giglio). It features very fancy contemporary glass and collectibles. One of the very best stores in town.

L'ISOLA
San Zulian, San Marco 723; Campo San Moisé, San Marco 1468

There are a few branches of this contemporary gallery around town. It is the best source in Venice for the newer names in big glassworks. The San Marco address is across from the Bauer.

PAULY & COMPANY
Ponte Consorzi, San Marco 4392

They don't come much more famous than this house, which was established in 1866. Pauly & Company has worked for most of the royal houses of Europe. They will paint your custom-blown glass to match your china (but not while you wait). They ship.

SEGUSO
San Marco 143

You'll find bright colors and outstanding contemporary works here.

SALVIATI
Campo San Angelo, San Marco 3831

Among the most famous master glassmakers in Venice.

VENINI
Piazzetta dei Leoncini, San Marco 314

Credited with beginning the second renaissance of glassblowers in Venice (1920–60), Venini is among the best. Buy anything you can afford and hang on to it for dear life.

ZORA
San Marco 2407

This is the new guy in town. The shop is very close to Venetia Stvdivm, the best store for silks in town, so you will be here anyway. While the house makes glass, their specialty is glass picture frames, which are sophisticated and stunning and $400 each. There are also tassels, beaded flowers, and golden grape clusters. Even if you buy nothing, don't miss it.

Handbags & Leather Goods

FENDI
Salizzada San Moisè, San Marco 1474

If you have no other chance to shop for Fendi, this store is bigger than the one in Milan, modern, and right in the heart of your stroll across town. It's even near the American Express office, if you run out of cash. They do have sales; prices are about the same all over Italy, so your purchase will not cost less in another city. The store is located behind San Marco on the way to San Giglio, almost across the lane from the Hotel Bauer.

GUCCI
San Marco 258

Although I find this Gucci small and rather boring, without the flair of shops in other cities, it still offers the same gorgeous merchandise—sometimes on sale. You'll pass it on the way to the Rialto Bridge, so pop in if you have no other chance for Gucci.

VOGINI
Near Piazza San Marco, San Marco 1257A–1301

This was once my favorite leather goods store in Venice and one of a few faves in all of Italy. Now the basic glam is the fact that they sell the new line of Roberta di Camerino handbags, which are stunning and have a cult following thanks to marketing by Barney's in New York.

Home Style

ANTICHITA E OGGETTI D'ARTE
Frezzeria, San Marco 1691

Ignore the word *antique* here and concentrate on glam home style, cushions of gilded velvet and velvet devore and painted velvet and velvet dreams with fringe and beads. Fabrics from centuries past that will make you weep with their glory.

MARIO & PAOLA BEVILACQUA
Fondamenta Canonica, San Marco 337B; Campo Santa Maria del Giglio 2520

These are two different addresses; the San Marco one is the easiest for tourists. The shop is the size of a large closet and is filled with velvets, pillows, tapestries, and tassels. Even if you live in the Sunbelt, you will be tempted to do your home over in dark velvets.

RAIGATTIERI
San Marco 3562

Located near San Stefano, this shop specializes in faience. It's a two-part shop: One part offers country dishes, and the other more traditional ceramics. A faience plate will cost about $25, and they will pack it for travel.

Linen & Lace

FRETTE
Calle Larga XXII Marzo, San Marco

Here you'll find gorgeous linens from one of Italy's most famous makers for bed, bath, and lounging.

JESURUM
Mercerie dei Capitello, San Marco 4857

Yo—they moved. Jesurum has upheld and continued the tradition of Venetian lace making, which was all but lost in the early 1800s. Just before the art would have died out, two Venetians undertook to restore it. One of the two was Michelangelo Jesurum, who—along with restoring the industry and putting hundreds of lace makers to work—also started a school so that the art would not die.

When you enter the Jesurum lace factory and showrooms, be prepared to flip your wig. The old church has been left with all its beautiful inlaid arches and its vaulted ceiling. Beautiful lace and appliquéd table linens and placemats are displayed on tables throughout the room.

MARIA MAZZARON
Fondamenta dell'Osmarìn, Castello 4970

This is a private dealer who you must phone (☎ 041/522-13-92) to make an appointment to see her museum-quality treasures. Serious collectors only.

MARTINUZZI
Piazza San Marco, San Marco 67

This lace shop is almost as good as Jesurum, and it's located right on the piazza. This is the real thing: embroidered goods, appliquéd linens, very drop-dead fancy Italian bed gear. The atmosphere is more old-lady lace shop than church-goes-retail, but the goods are high quality.

Masks

If you saw the movie or play *Amadeus,* you are familiar with the type of mask worn at Carnevale time in Venice. Carnevale in Venice got so out of hand that it was outlawed in 1797. But it's back again, and with it a renewed interest in masks. One of the most popular styles is a mask covered with bookbinding paper that you can find at a *legatoria,* or paper goods store (see below). But there also are masks made of leather, papier-mâché, fabric, etc. If all this is more than you had in mind, not to worry—there are masks in plastic for $6 that will satisfy your need to participate. After 3 days in Venice, you'll swear you'll die if you see another mask, so make your selection carefully. Many of them seem like trite tourist items.

For a more special item, try any (or all!) of these famous mask makers:

ADRIANO MIANI
Calle Grimani, San Marco 289B

BRUNO RIZZATO
Ponte dei Barcoli 1831

F.G.B.
Santa Maria del Giglio, San Marco 2459

LABORATORIO ARTIGIANO MASCHIERE
Piazza San Marco, San Marco 282

LE MASCHIERE DI DARIO USTINO
Ponte dei Dai 171

MA BOUTIQUE
Calle Larga San Marco, San Marco 28

I found some excellent masks at **La Gondola** (Piazza San Marco 219)—many styles I hadn't seen elsewhere.

Since many of the crafts shops sell masks, also see the section on crafts, above.

Optical Goods

I bought pairs and pairs of eyeglasses on my last visit to Venice. Who would have thunk it?

DANILO CARRARO
Calle della Mandola, San Marco 3706

I wish I could take credit for this source, but Patricia Schultz brought me here after a friend of hers brought her. And so the chain is passed on . . . local makers of chic and fabulous frames that retail for about $65 per pair. All sorts of colors and many types of tortoise-y patterns. They also do a hot fashion color for a season and then never do it again. Best of all, they have a website, and you can shop electronically (www.otticacarraro.it).

FOTO MARTURANO
Ascensione, San Marco 1296

Right, I know this is a foto shop, but they also sell sunglasses, especially adorable (yet chic) kiddie frames. I bought Miss Julia, my niece, a pair of turquoise frames. They have two different qualities here: $25 for the good quality and $12 for the junky ones. But the junky ones are superb and perfect for a child who will outgrow them or break them (or lose them) anyway.

Paper Goods

Legatoria means bookbindery in Italian, and the famous designs are copies of bookbinding papers from hundreds of years ago. The best makers use the same old-fashioned methods that have been in the house for centuries. Many of the shops will make something to order for you, but ask up front if they will mail it for you; most won't. These papers have become so popular in the U.S. that the paper goods business now is divided between those who are staying old-fashioned and those who are counting the tourist bucks and loving it. When you walk into the various shops, you can feel the difference.

There are many $10 gift items in these stores. A calendar-diary of the fanciest sort costs $50.

Legatoria Piazzesi (Campiella della Feltrina, Santo Stéfano, San Marco) and **Il Papiro** (Calle del Piovan, San Marco 2764), the two most famous paper shops in Venice, are almost across the way from each other, right near Campo San Stéfano at Ponte San Maurizio. Piazzesi also sells old prints. Don't let the street address throw you; just keep walking and you'll see these two beauties. They are past the main tourist shopping but in a gorgeous part of town not far past the Gritti.

There's a relatively new chain of shops around town called **In Folio** that sells paper goods and books and gift items as well as sealing wax and wax seals. When I was a teenager, sealing wax was the rage in America; now it's got a nice medieval bend to it that tourists are scarfing up. There are five or six of these shops scattered around town: San Marco 55; San Marco 739; San Marco 2431; San Marco 4852; and Castello 4615.

Shoes

Check the "Handbags & Leather Goods" listing above for other sources.

BRUNO MAGLI
Calle XXII Marzo 2288, San Marco 1302; Calle Frezzeria, San Marco 1583

As you can tell from the addresses above, Magli has three different shops in Venice, although I swear I saw more. Not only is there a Magli every place you look, but they display different models, forcing you to visit each if only to drool.

CALLEGHER ROLLY SEGALIN
Calle dei Fuseri 4365

An old-fashioned shoemaker who creates everything by hand and made to measure. Unbelievable stuff . . . ranging from the type of creative and crazy things you might expect Elton John to wear (shoes shaped like gondolas) to very simple, elegant court shoes. He'll create or copy anything, although the price is about $500 a pair. Closed on Saturday.

SUPERGA
Calle dei Fabbri, San Marco 4673

This is one of the hottest casual shoe brands in Italy, with shoes for adults and for kids. Sizes, of course, are continental, so use the size chart in the back of this book, or ask them. I needed a lesson in kiddie sizes, which they happily gave me. (Kid's size 12 = 30; 13 = 31½; 1 = 33; 2 = 34.) Prices were steep for kiddie shoes, and I decided not to splurge, but you will go nuts for their bold designs, great colors, and futuristic contours . . . all with comfy crepe soles.

Weddings

I can't tell you how many people tell me they want to be married in Venice or ask me how to go about it. "Samantha" is my only answer. See the box on p. 148 for information on Samantha Durrell, who can arrange a wedding or reaffirmation ceremony in Venice, or call her directly at ☎ 041/ 523-23-79.

VENICE SHOPPER'S STROLL & TOUR

ALL-DAY TOUR: SAN MARCO TO SAN GIGLIO

1. Begin your day at the Piazza San Marco; hopefully it is January or February, and you can actually see the square and the architecture and even the pigeons—as opposed to the mobs of international tourists.
2. Walk completely around the piazza, under the covered portico. There are many old-fashioned glass showrooms here, a lace shop or two, several jewelry shops and TTs, as well as a few overpriced but still fun-to-splurge-on cafes. As you go around the square, get your bearings—look for

the back way out of the square, which you'll want later on. Don't miss **Michaela Frey** and her fabulous lion of Venice bangle bracelets.

3. Closer to the basilica, find the Merceria, which is a street leading away from the piazza in a relatively straight line toward the Rialto Bridge. Use this street as your guiding point to wind your way toward the Rialto Bridge. If done well, this area alone will take you more than half the day. Once you reach Riva del Carbòn, take a right, and you will be at the foot of the Rialto Bridge.

4. Cross the bridge, but don't shop yet! Enjoy all the fruits and vegetables at the market and the small shops tucked here and there. Visit **Coin Rialto** to see the architecture.

5. Walk back along Ruga Rialto and stop in any of the charming little boutiques that interest you.

6. Cross back over the bridge and buy what looks good. At least now you know what you couldn't get for less on the other side.

7. Wind your way back to the Piazza San Marco along the Merceria. Believe it or not, you will notice things coming back that you didn't see going.

8. Now that you have returned to the point of origin, head to your right from Merceria and move across San Marco to the "back" gate of the piazza and shop your way to San Giglio. This is a relatively straight line including a small ghetto of fancy-schmancy designer boutiques, an American Express office, Venetia Stvdvium for Fortuny-style silks, antiques shops, and Zora (next door to Venetia Stvdvium) for Venetian glass picture frames, which may make you weep from the power of their beauty . . . or the power of the price tags.

9. Finish up at the next plaza. Have a drink at the Gritti or enjoy a tiny market at San Moisè if you are lucky enough to find one.

Chapter Eight

....

MILAN

WELCOME TO MILAN
....

Milan: the world's most beautiful ugly city.

Sure, you may find it simply ugly as a first timer, but just wait. Milan grows on you. Milan worms its way into the soul of a shopper . . . and with a strong dollar-to-lire ratio, there's a lot of happiness in those worms.

Milan is not a one-night stand. Milan is not the kind of place you fall in love with at a glance. Milan is not pretty on the surface. But there's more style per mile than in just about any other city in the world . . . and the surrounding area is filled with factories and outlets and bargains galore. You can make day trips from Milan, you can rent cars from the Milan airport, you can do it all from northern Italy.

Milan's real strength is in the inspiration it provides, not only to the fashion world, but to visual and creative types of all sorts. Walk down the streets, press your nose to the windows, and you'll get *ideas*. There's no doubt that Milan is the real capital of Italian fashion. It's no secret that international *garmentos* comb the streets and markets to find the goods they will tote to Hong Kong to reproduce in inexpensive copies. A day on the prowl in Milan makes my heart beat faster; my pocketbook grow lighter; and, my shoulder grow weary—from carrying all those shopping bags.

What you see in Milan today will be in style in America in a year. What you adapt for your own lifestyle will compete with the cutting edge. Even if you can't afford to buy, you will feel invigorated by the city's creative energy just by walking its streets and window-shopping. Milan is not a great tourist town; it's a business city, and one of its businesses just happens to be fashion. So what's not to like? There's surely no business like shoe business. Or fur business. Or ready-to-wear.

When you learn how to ride the tram, you'll get a feeling of elation at having conquered a very special foreign city. When you sip cocktails in the garden at the Diana Majestic Hotel and look out at the wisteria, you'll know you have entered a world of special magic. When you get into the wholesale district and find cashmere twin-sets for under $250, you'll see beauty in the bargain.

Milan's Multiples

Don't overlook Milan as more than just a single city: It's a total destination. From Milan you can easily get in and out of Venice and into other northern Italian cities. Milan is less than an hour from Como and not far from Turin. From Milan, you can get to Switzerland—or anywhere! Milan is the hub of northern Italy and a great hub city for those who will rent a car to drive around for a weekend, a week, or a lifetime.

Arriving & Departing

Because Milan is this hub, there are plenty of ways to get in and out of town. But there are a few tricks to learn. There's also a bit of bad news, so watch this space carefully and be sure to ask a lot of questions.

The news is simple: In 1998, local authorities decided to switch all flights to Malpensa International Airport and to use the more user-friendly (and closer to town) Linate Airport for intra-Italian commuter flights. The hub has indeed been switched, despite a rough start. Meanwhile, several airlines have sued. Rulings keep changing with the courts and the times. This is, after all, Italy.

The division of labor did not work as planned, so one must watch flight designations carefully, as even intra-Italian flights may go to either Linate or Malpensa. When I fly to Milan from Paris I have my choice of airports depending on the airline and flight. It pays to investigate, especially if your time is limited or you are not on an expense account.

Remember: Linate is 15 minutes and $15 away from downtown and is the answer to all your questions. Malpensa is one hour away, and the taxi or limo ride costs about $100.

Note: Long-haul flights always have used Malpensa; this bit of news regarding the use of both Malpensa and Linate affects those who are traveling into Milan from another EU-city.

By Plane

Milan has two different international airports, as I just explained. In the old days you could save yourself a lot of time and money if you booked a flight that landed at Linate, which is much closer to downtown Milano than Malpensa. This may be less easy to do now.

Malpensa is changing rapidly; it has opened a new terminal and a new runway, and changes will continue in the next few years. Watch this space.

Right now, only three U.S. carriers can fly into Italy: **Delta, American,** and **United.** Code sharing has opened up possibilities for American travel; check out Delta's alliance with Swissair and Continental's codeshare with **Alitalia.**

If you arrive at Malpensa International Airport, you better have a rich sugar daddy, or be prepared to wait for the bus. The bus is easy to find and drops you right at the Centrale train station where you can hop on the metro or get a taxi to your hotel. Of course, you may want to spring for a car and driver, which will cost under $100 including the tip. (I use Europe Car Service, ☎ **02/942-51-00**; fax: 02/94-24-01-40; e-mail ecs@ecs-car.it; Malpensa transfer is about $75 plus tip.)

There is a new airport express train for those who can manage their luggage. Naturally, I've never taken it.

Just when you thought I couldn't dis Malpensa enough, may I offer up some happy news: Malpensa is out there in the wide open spaces in terms of getting out of town and hitting the road without going into Milan. It's also halfway to Como and the outlets, and yes, Switzerland.

For less than $10 you can take the bus from Malpensa into downtown Milan; the bus runs regularly on the half-hour. Buy your ticket at the marked booth and then line up outside. There are two bus stops outside, so be sure you don't take the employee bus to the parking lot. The bus will deposit you at the central train station in the heart of Milan.

Now then, this is a great service, and it's cheap, and it's fine and all that, but hey, you better be able to handle your luggage 'cause *mamma mia*, when they drop you at the train station, they drop you at the side of the building, and the taxi rank is in the *front*. There are no trolleys and no porters and no help whatsoever; go to the front for a trolley.

BY TRAIN

If you arrive by train, you will probably come in to the **Centrale Station** in the heart of downtown. Pay attention as you exit because parts of this station have been changed and (if this is a return trip) the layout may not be as you remember it. Most important, there are no longer any porters. Nor is there an elevator. Oy!

They've reworked the escalators at the front of the station so that a trolley can fit on them, sort of. I had some very frightening moments as I went down that very steep escalator, clinging for dear life to my trolley, hoping to balance it with enough counterweight so that we didn't go flying. There are pictograms on the trolleys and on the walls to show you how to get the trolley onto (and down) the escalator.

Arrivals and departures are now from the front of the Centrale Station. Centrale is connected to the metro if you can manage your luggage and prefer using public transportation rather than a taxi.

There are free trolleys, but they are usually at the entrances to the station: When you pop off the train, it's unlikely that you'll find a trolley when you need one. If you are traveling alone, good luck. You may want to pack your set of airline wheels with you, or invest in the kind of luggage that has rear wheels and a pull cord or handle.

DEPARTURE TIPS

To get the bus to either airport, take a taxi to the Centrale Station where the bus pick-up is. You do not want to enter the main part of the station to catch the bus. The ticket window is to the side, right where you caught the taxi when you arrived. Beware of gypsies and beggars who may annoy you while you wait for the next bus. Last time I took a taxi to Centrale—to catch a train to Venice actually—the driver asked me if I wanted the Pullman for the airport or a train, because he will drop you at two different places depending on which you want.

GETTING AROUND

Milan happens to be a good walking city—most of the shops, museums, and other attractions are in areas that you can easily navigate by foot once you get yourself to a specific neighborhood. This is why it pays to pick a hotel in the center of the action and near a metro stop.

If you need a taxi, they can be found in ranks, hailed in the street, or called. Note that when you call a taxi, the meter starts once the driver heads toward your pickup location.

Getting around town on public transportation is not hard. The metro is great, but does not get you everywhere you want to go. However, it gets you to and from your hotel and the best shopping districts. Note that most of the luxury hotels are within a block of a metro station.

Tram and bus systems are very good. Between these three modes of transport, you'll do just great. Buy tram or bus tickets at a tobacco stand (marked with a T sign out front) before you get on the vehicle. Enter from the rear, and place your ticket in the little box to get it stamped. Keep it; you can use it again within 75 minutes.

Metro tickets can be purchased in the station; you will need coins to operate the ticket machines, but there are change machines. Magazine vendors inside stations will not give you change unless you buy something.

Milan's *metropolitana* has three main lines, each color-coded. Tourists will probably find the red line most convenient, as it goes to some of the major shopping areas and also stops at the Duomo. Look for the giant red M that indicates a station. Many guidebooks have a metro map printed inside them—and so does the brochure *A Guest in Milan*, which most hotels give away for free. Local telephone books come in two parts, both of which should be in your hotel room (look in the closet). One part is a phone book as you know it, and the other is a map and city directory with pages of information on how to use the city and surrounding provinces, including a metro map and a bus-route map.

You can take a regular train to nearby communities, such as Como or Bergamo, or even to Venice, for a day trip. There's a large commuter population that goes to Turin, mostly for business, but you can go there to shop or to see the Shroud.

If you are using a train pass, do not blow a day of travel on a local commuter ticket. The same ticket can get you to Paris or to Como. Save the rail pass for the important stuff. A first-class, round-trip train ticket to Como costs about $15.

If you want to get to seriously out-of-the-way factory outlets, you'll have to rent a car or hire a car and driver. Hiring a car with driver is not outrageously expensive—about $200 a day (this includes the tip) for 150km, although there are half-day options. I use **Europe Car Service** and ask for Vincenzo, who speaks English. The rates were negotiated by my friend Claire on behalf of her firm, Aubin International, so ask for the Born to Shop/Aubin rate, ☎ **02/942-51-00;** fax 02/94-24-01-40. Yes I know there are more digits in one of the

Milan

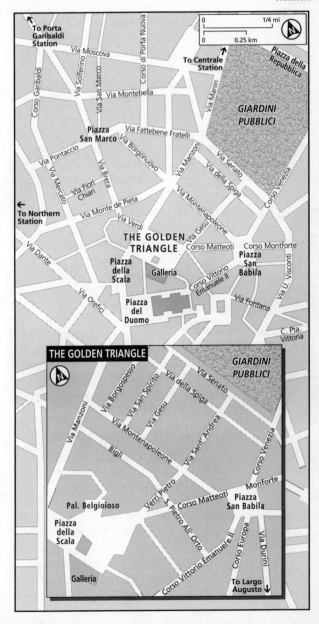

numbers, that's the way it is on the business card. Web address is www.ecs-car.com.

Note: On a rainy winter day in Milan, I booked the car service to drive me around. I was told there was a 4-hour booking fee at 210,000L, and then I was to tip. I used the car for only 2 hours as it was really hard to work. The driver wanted me to not only pay for all 4 hours but wanted a tip on top of that. I don't mind paying the 4 hours, which was the deal, but I figure two hours of free time is tip enough.

Another possibility is to hire a taxi driver. I did the Como outlets that way, and it was a positive experience. No, my driver did not speak much English, and I don't speak much Italian, but we had no problem. He drove me all over, waited for me while I shopped, and it cost about $25 for a half day. (I also think that knowing a taxi is waiting—with the meter running— keeps you quick on your toes. I might have spent 3 hours and $3,000 at **Ratti** if I had stayed longer.)

More Information

There is a local version of the Time Out guide, *Time Out Milano,* but it is in Italian. Buy it at any news kiosk in Milan. The national newspaper *Repubblica* has a Milan section toward the rear of the daily paper that has local listings, weekend happenings, and some flea markets or specialty shopping events.

SLEEPING IN LUXURY IN MILAN

FOUR SEASONS HOTEL
Via del Gesù 8

What would happen if the fashion angel came to Milan and decided to go into the hotel business? The Four Seasons, of course. You'll find this grand hotel discreetly located in the heart of the Montenapo shopping district. With up-to-date amenities and a posh atmosphere, it has a modern feel without seeming too rococo. For a shopper, it's simply the best location in town. As a result, it's become a fashion editor's hangout. There are two restaurants: Il Teatro, a Michelin 1-star and a more casual street-level cafe. It is the "in" place for visiting editors; a virtual zoo during Fashion Weeks . . . but a very chic zoo.

Note that the Four Seasons has not only extra lines for your computer but 110-volt electrical plugs; getting online has never been easier in my life as from this hotel.

For an extra advantage, hit up the concierge desk for their slick magazine on shopping in Milan. For reservations in the U.S., call ☎ **800/332-3442.** Local phone ☎ 02/770-88; fax 02/77-08-50-07.

GRAND HOTEL ET DE MILAN
Via Manzoni 29

This is a fancy-dancy hotel that's romantically small and dark. The wonderful decorating style takes you back in time and makes you wonder about the next century when the last century had some awfully perfect parts to it. Yet there's a subway stop right alongside the hotel, so you get luxury and real life wrapped up in one. Shuttle service to airports and to the train station. To reserve in the U.S., call **Leading Hotels of the World,** ☎ **800/223-6800;** local phone ☎ 02/72-31-41; local fax 02/86-46-08-61; www.lhw.com/ghmilan.

PALACE HOTEL
Piazza della Repubblica 20

PRINCIPE DI SAVOIA
Piazza della Repubblica 17

These two hotels stand together on the Piazza della Repubblica: They are both members of Westin's Luxury Collection. If you are a movie star, a big-name designer, or royalty, you stay at the Principe. (You do know that Demi Moore booked the presidential suite with its own private swimming pool!) If you are an executive on expense account, you stay at the Palace.

In each hotel, you get the elegance of a tip-top luxury hotel within walking distance of the main shopping district. The rooms are sumptuously decorated. Breakfast may or may not be included with your rate—ask. Don't wait around for a $35 surprise! That's $35 per day, not per week.

The metro stop, Repubblica, is on the corner. You can get just about everywhere via public transportation; you are also a stone's throw from the wholesale district, which leads to the train station and therefore also *from* the train station (which has a grocery store).

Note: The Principe has absorbed the Duca de Milano, a third luxury hotel that happens to be next door; they built a bridge and now call it The Towers. It's very swank; there's also a spa and health club. You can exit (or enter) the hotel from the original Duca doors.

Local phone: the Palace, ☎ 02/63-36; the Principe, ☎ 02/659-58-38; www.luxurycollection.com.

4-Star Finds

HOTEL MANIN
Via Manin 7

This is a tiny hotel decorated like an ocean liner from the 1930s. It's right near the gardens and the fashion district and is considered a find by fashion editors and those looking for a good location and an affordable price. Call ☎ 02/659-65-11.

JOLLY PRESIDENT
Largo Augusto 10

JOLLY TOURING
Via Tarchetti 2

You'll be jolly, too, when you learn about this hotel chain. There are two Jolly hotels in downtown Milan. The President is a business traveler's hotel, with small rooms of modern neo-Italian design. It's a great find because of its location. Largo Augusto is next door to Via Durini, designer shop row, and a block from the Duomo, which can be seen from your window.

The Jolly Touring is located near the Principe and the Palace and shares the same metro with them, but is a block closer to the shopping action. The rooms are much nicer than at the Jolly President. The hotel does cater to groups, but I was quite happy with my choice.

If you can handle a 4-star rather than a 5-star, this is a find. For reservations in the U.S., call ☎ **800/247-1277**. Local phone numbers are as follows: Jolly President ☎ 02/77-46, fax 02/78-34-49; Jolly Touring ☎ 02/63-35, fax 02/65-92-209; www.jollyhotels.it.

SNACK & SHOP

Café Corso Como
Corso Como 10

No that's not a typo, the name of the store is the address, and this is the rather new cafe in part of the store. It's very chic; a reservation in season is suggested, although when I got there in winter, I had no trouble getting a seat. There's a bar to eat at as well as tables; the look is Italian-Zen with a menu of pasta, salads, or sushi. Reservations: **02/65-48-31**; open from 11am until midnight.

Café di Gualtiero Marchesi
La Rinascente, Piazza Duomo

Shopper's alert: This is a must-do stop. It's on the top floor of La Rinascente and is fronted with glass.

It gets lots of light (even when it's raining) and magnificent, inspiring views of the Duomo. Although this is a popular place and most of the people here are tourists (expect to share a table if you are a single), it's so much fun that you must have lunch here once. I ate a sandwich of tomatoes and mozzarella, heated, with coffee, for about $10. There is table service; the waiter tallies your bill with a bar code and a computer wand. It's fabulous fun.

COVA
Via Montenapoleone 8

A lot like Sant' Ambroeus (see review later in this section), but more formal and touristy because it's on the list of so many out-of-towners. It's a local legend and an "in" place for tea, in between shopping breaks and sweets. Come at 5pm if you want to make the scene. Their chocolates are a status-symbol hostess gift in fall, their jellied fruit squares in summer. Note there's the old Russian system for paying if you buy food to go: Make your choice at the counter, pay at the front desk, and return to the counter to pick up your choice. *Note:* There's a rumor going around town that the real estate that Cova sits on is worth about $25 million, so if they've sold out by the time you get there, well, you can't blame them!

PECK
Via Spadari 9

This is possibly the most famous food store in Milan. Use it as your personal headquarters for picnic supplies. They also have a grill.

The main food shop is on a side street on the far side of the Duomo, away from the Montenapoleone area but still convenient enough to be worthwhile. I always buy a picnic to take back on the airplane. Somehow, few airlines are able to provide food like Peck's.

SANT' AMBROEUS
Corso Matteotti 7

I've fallen in love with this fancy space right off Montenapoleone. They have a bakery and candy shop for take-out orders, or you can stand at the bar or take a table. Sort of the Italian version of tea at the Ritz. They open at 8am if you prefer to breakfast here. I can eat their little *prosciutto crudo* sandwiches all day.

THE SHOPPING SCENE

Because Milan is the home of the fashion, fur, and furnishings businesses, you'll quickly find that it's a city that sells style and image. There aren't a lot of souvenirs. Near the Duomo, you can find the occasional piece, but the city lacks crass souvenirs and silly gift items. It's simply not a silly city. Milan is a city of big business: The souvenir stands are overflowing with an abundance of international magazines, not kitschy plastics. The big toy sold by street vendors? Plastic telephones for kids!

Although Milan was a medieval trading city, in its modern, post–World War II incarnation, Milan has sizzled and made its mark. The city hosts the international furniture salon every other year. There are fashion shows here twice a year, bringing a cadre of fashion reporters from all over the world to tell the fashion mavens just what Italy has to offer. Besides these, there are a zillion fairs and conventions and other business happenings, meaning Milan is always happening. Hmmmm, except in August.

Even if you aren't a fashion editor and don't plan your life around what comes trotting down the catwalk, you'll find that Milan's high-fashion stores offer a peek at what's to come. You'll also find that the markets and real-people shopping reflect the proximity of nearby factories . . . you'd be amazed at what can fall off a truck.

The best shopping in Milan is at these designer shops and showrooms, or at the discount houses, jobbers, and factory-outlet stores that sell designer clothing, overruns, and samples. If you really care about high fashion at an affordable price, you'll plan to spend January of each year prowling the sales in Milan—not London.

The Best Buys in Milan

Alternative Retail   Mavens will give me the evil eye for mentioning this, but Milan is a good place for a bargain. There are good flea markets and street markets, and the buys in Como cannot be underestimated.

I hit a home run a few years ago at **Il Salvagente,** the famous Milan discounter, where big-name clothes are marked down to reasonable prices during a January sale. My prize? A pink wool jacket from Mimmina—a big Italian name—for all of 268,000L. My girlfriend Mimi, an American fashion editor who covers the collections twice a year, regularly shops here and says that on her last trip, she "made out like a bandit." I got an e-mail from a radio show producer at NPR who said, "How did you find this place?" My last trip there? Nuthin'. Who said life was fair?

Meanwhile, I cannot rave enough about Como. It's more than just a resort town; it's heaven for bargain shoppers who want high-quality silks. I'm talking about the biggest and best French and Italian couture names, and more. Mantero? Did we say it's time to buy **Mantero,** oh yes, *si, si, si.* Remind me to tell you about the scarf that cost $500 in Munich that was $250 in Italy. Of course I bought two—you needed to ask?

Designer Home Design Again, maybe not a best buy in terms of price, but a best in terms of selection or unique opportunity. The hottest trend in Milan of late has been that all the big designers are doing home furnishings, from dishes and ashtrays to sheets, and then some. **Versace, Dolce & Gabbana, Missoni,** and **Ferragamo** are all into home design now. It's luxe, it's expensive, and it's gorgeous. Just press your nose to the **D&G Home** store, take one look at dark red silk brocade, leopard prints, and majolica and know that when it works, it works! But wait, I now also shop for home design in the outlet store that **Lisa Corti** has in her workrooms—fabulous stuff and half the price of Saks.

Designer Selections While designer merchandise is expensive, the selection and the possibility of a markdown or discovering a small, reasonably priced item is greater. **Etro** isn't a bargain resource and is available in other Italian cities, but it will please you to no end to buy here and to soak up the atmosphere of class, elegance, and northern Italian chic. The Etro outlet, right in town, will also please you to no end.

Fragrance, Makeup, & Bath Products   I am calling special attention to this category because the more I research it, the more I am convinced you can make it work for you. Under normal circumstances, designer lines—especially French and American—are outrageously expensive in Italy.

However, **La Rinascente** has a policy for non-Italian passport holders that allows you to show your passport at the point of purchase and receive an immediate 10% discount at the cash register! This is good for perfumes, makeup, and even Italian bath bubbles and spa items.

Meanwhile, in the last year, Milan has gone makeup crazy, meaning that no longer are French and U.S. brands the must-haves they once were—there are possibly six new brands of makeup, all jazzy and affordably priced. See p. 233 to learn about designer makeup (Armani, Versace) as well as Madina, Kiko and other new brands.

The Worst Buys in Milan

If you can help it, don't buy:

- Ceramics and faience. They're hard to find, and therefore expensive.
- Postcards. There's a bad selection.
- Important antiques. They're prohibitively expensive.
- Masks, marbleized paper goods, or traditional Italian souvenirs. These items are best bought where they're made.

Milan Style

In terms of clothing, Milanese style is much more conservative, chic, and sophisticated than the more flamboyant southern Italian style. In Milan, if you don't buy from a trendy designer, you'll actually load up on basics—good cashmere sweaters and shawls, knits, shoes, handbags, and furs. That's right: furs! Northern Italy is one of the few places in the world where it's not only politically correct to wear fur, but part of the fashion scene. In Milan, attitude is part of fashion so you can wear all black and be chic; it need not be expensive or laden with labels—you just need the look and a pair of great sunglasses.

Much of what is for sale in Milan is of the same design school as the English country look; this will interest Europeans far more than Americans who are looking for hot looks, not tweeds and V necks. Also note that a large influence in Italian fashion these days is the American mail-order catalog look—Levi's, J. Crew, L.L. Bean, etc. I didn't come to Italy to buy things like this; you probably didn't either, and will someone spare me from Gap wannabes? Still, there's plenty of trendy stuff for the Ferrari in your soul.

Milan is a great place for spotting color trends. Yes, *fashionistas* always dress in black because it's easy, but Italian fashion highlights a few new, key colors each season. Even if you just window-shop, you'll soon see that almost all clothing in any given season, no matter which designer is presenting it, falls into a few color families. Each season will have one or two hot colors that define the season; each season will also have a wide selection of items in black because black is the staple of every Italian (and French) wardrobe. The best thing about these colors is that other designers and even mass retailers in America will pick up these same shades, so that what you buy in Italy will carry smoothly into the fashion front for several years.

Another aspect of Milanese style comes in furnishings, home decor, tabletop, and interior design. No matter what size you are or what age you are, you will see things to light your fire in this city of desire.

Shopping Hours

The big news in Milan is that shopping hours are not as strict as elsewhere; nor are they as strict as they used to be. Furthermore, Milan now has stores that are open on Sunday!

Lunch Hours   Many of the big-name designer shops in Milan are open "nonstop," which means that they do not close for lunch. If you don't want to take a lunch break, shop the Montenapo area.

Dime stores like **Standa** and **Upim** have always been open nonstop; **La Rinascente**, Milan's most complete department store, has always been open during lunch as well. Of course, most of the Standa stores in Milan have become FNAC stores, but they are open, too.

Monday Hours   Most stores in Milan are closed on Monday through the lunch hour (they open around 3:30 or 4pm). Note that La Rinascente does not open until 1:45pm on Monday. Most of Italy is dead from a retail perspective on Monday morning. But wait!

- Food shops are open.
- Factory stores are frequently open on Monday morning. If you are heading out to a certain factory or two, call ahead. Make no assumptions.
- Como factories are open on Monday morning!

Sunday Shopping

Laws have changed, and all of Italy's big cities have Sunday shopping now; mostly big department stores are open. If you want to shop on a Sunday, try for a flea market. Or go to Venice, which is wide, wide, wide open on Sunday. Milan is far more dead on Sunday than other communities, but you can get lucky—at certain times of the year, things are popping on Sunday. During fashion weeks, stores in Montenapo district often open on Sunday; they also have specific Sundays when they open beginning in October going on until Christmas.

Some stores in the Navigli area are also open on Sunday.

The regular Sunday stores are **Corso Como 10** and **Virgin Megastore**. Sunday hours are most often noon to 5pm.

In season, Como (only 20 minutes away) is wide open on Sunday, although you may want to call ahead to verify that your favorite factory shops will be open on the Sunday that you want to shop them. Some people go to Ancora for Sunday shopping.

Exceptional Shopping Hours

Summer Hours   Summer hours begin in the middle of July for some retail businesses; August is a total loss from a shopping point of view because most stores are closed. Sophisticated people wouldn't be caught dead in Milan in August; shoppers beware.

When stores are open in August, they close at lunch on Saturday and do not reopen until 3:30 or 4pm on Monday.

Holiday Hours   The period between Christmas and New Year's Day can be tricky. Stores will close early a few days before a major holiday and use any excuse to stay closed during a holiday. Sales begin in the first week of January (usually after Epiphany), but store hours are erratic before then. There are weekend candy markets around the Duomo in the weeks before Lent.

Night Hours   Stores usually close between 7:30 and 8pm. Should you need an all-night pharmacy, there is one at Piazza Duomo and one at the Centrale train station.

Money Matters

There is an electronic currency exchange machine near the Duomo on the La Scala side but when I tried it, U.S. dollars were not being dispensed. Exchange machines cheat you anyway, so try to avoid them. Instead, use ATMs and your bankcard from home.

There's a BankAmericard ATM in the thick of the shopping district at **Banca Commercial Italian** (Via Manzoni 5), and there's a bank at the Centrale train station that is open Saturday and Sunday. There are also banks at both airports.

American Express's travel office is at the corner of the Via Brera and the Via Dell Orso: It's Via Brera 3. This is in the thick of the shopping district, so you need not go out of your way to get here.

Personal Needs

I needed shoe laces in Milan—sounds simple, huh? Forget it! Since **Upim** has gone upscale it's become harder and harder to find the basics of real life. **Upim** used to be a lot like Woolworth's. Now it's trying to be more like La Rinascente. It's unlikely you'll find everything you need in real life at an Italian department store, so try Upim as well as any number of pharmacies and grocery stores. P.S., the shoelaces? **Footlocker** on Victor Emmanuelle!

Look for a green neon cross if you want a pharmacy. There's a very good pharmacy in the Centrale train station, and they speak English. In fact, the train station has an excellent selection of shops selling basic items you may have left at home: try **Free,** an enormous grocery store that sells everything from food and souvenirs to health and beauty aids—even condoms.

Shopping Neighborhoods

Golden Triangle/Montenapo   All of the big designers have gorgeous and prestigious shops here. You can easily explore it in a day or two, or even an hour or two, depending on how much money or how much curiosity you have. Although the main shopping street is **Via Montenapoleone,** sometimes this area is referred to as Montenapo.

This is the chic part of town, where traditional European design flourishes along with Euro-Japanese styles and wild, hot Italian New Wave looks. It includes a couple of little streets that veer off the Via Montenapoleone in a beautiful little web of shopping heaven. This is where you'll find **Gucci, Ferré, Versace, Fendi, Ferragamo,** and **Krizia** boutiques as well as some very tony antiques shops.

There are furniture and fashion showrooms to the trade that are so fancy and secluded that you would never know they are there. There are also some reliable real-people shops, like **Brigatti,** a sporting goods emporium, that you'll enjoy.

The outermost borders of the neighborhood are **Via Manzoni** and **Corso Venezia,** two major commercial streets. Use

Down by the Station

My European friends virtually insisted that I include the wholesale district of Milan, that area between the Centrale train station and the Repubblica metro station. Many friends tell me that they take vacations to Milan just to shop for bargains in the nearby factories and in this area, which is filled with discounters and jobbers. Obviously it's hit-or-miss shopping, but if you've got time to spare, you might want to hightail it over here. Note that stores here are closed Saturday and Sunday, and some of them close during lunch hours. There is a booklet you can get about the showrooms in the area (see "Train Station/Ingrosso," in the "Shopping Neighborhoods" section).

The stores here like to call the area the San Gregario Quarter: These are mostly small stores that sell wholesale. However, they will sell to the public. New clothes arrive weekly, and what impressed me most was that the very latest styles were available.

The easiest way to "work" the area is just to go up and down the side streets off the **Via Pisani,** beginning with Via Boscovich and then moving on to Via San Gregario. But other streets have stores too, such as Via Napo Torrinai (look at **Anacleto, no. 5**). There are sources for men's, women's, and children's clothing, and some stores also sell shoes and boots. On Via Carlo Tenca, try **Fiume Giovanni** (no. 15) for menswear from top northern Italian factories.

them mostly for finding your way—although in the past year Corso Venezia has become a hot address for designer bridge lines. Your real shopping streets will be **Via della Spiga, Via Sant' Andrea,** and of course—**Via Montenapoleone.** But don't miss the back streets of this little enclave, streets like Via Gesù, Via Borgospesso, and also Via Manzoni (which is not a back street).

For anyone with limited time in Milan who wants to absorb a lot of the scene in just a few hours, this is the top-priority shopping district for looking around. You might not buy your souvenirs here, but you'll see the stuff that dreams are made of.

Duomo   The Duomo is the main landmark of Milan. It's an incredibly detailed and gorgeous cathedral; not a store. It is on the Piazza del Duomo and is happily surrounded by stores. You guessed it, there is even a **Virgin Megastore** to one side and the country's leading department store, **La Rinascente,** to another side.

Via Montenapoleone angles away from Corso Vittorio Emanuele II as you move away from the Duomo, so the Golden Triangle and Duomo neighborhoods sort of back up to each other. This connection makes it very easy to shop these two areas in the same afternoon. When you are finished with them, there are two other shopping neighborhoods, Brera and Jolly Augusto, that you can connect with on the other side of the Duomo.

You did come to Milan to shop, didn't you?

Corso Vittorio Emanuele II   This neighborhood is filled with big stores, little stores, and half a dozen galleries and mini-malls that house even more stores. The most maddening part about this area is that you can hardly find an address. Just wander in and out and around from the Duomo to **Piazza San Babila,** which is only 2 or 3 blocks. At San Babila, turn left and you'll end up at Via Montenapoleone for entry into the Golden Triangle. Or you can do this in the reverse, of course. But don't forget to check out this intersection. Because the San Babila area is very important, you'll find everything from the new Benetton superstore to Upim to plastics mongers and fashion mavens.

At the front end of the Duomo, off the piazza, is a shopping center of historical and architectural landmark proportions, the **Galleria.** This is one of the most famous landmarks in Milan, and some tout it as the first mall in Europe. Other galleries in Europe also make the same claim, but who cares? Take one look at the ceiling and you'll marvel. Then visit the **Prada** shop.

The Galleria has a vaulted ceiling and looks like a train station from another, grander, era. Inside there are restaurants and bistros where you can get coffee and sit and watch the parade of passersby. Several big-time shops are here besides **Prada**—don't miss **Rizzoli** for books in English. If you go out the back end, you will be at La Scala. Behind La Scala is the **Brera** area.

If you are at the piazza with the Duomo to your back and have not turned right to enter the Galleria, you can walk straight ahead toward the **Virgin Megastore** and yet more retail. The arcade across from the Duomo is filled with many old names of Milanese retailing and some newer shops, too, including a **Missoni** jeans store that sells their sports line. **Galtruco** is a very famous fabric firm where you can buy every imaginable type of yard goods, including the designer fabrics from local mills.

Brera   Brera is one of the most famous shopping districts of Milan because it has slightly less expensive rents. It's the part of town where young designers can break into retailing and high style, and it has both designer shops and up-and-coming trendsetters.

It's a fair (but not difficult) walk from the Duomo.

The main stretch of Brera is rather commercial, with shops oriented toward teens, and quite a few jeans stores as well as very obvious branches of the famous international retailers: **Laura Ashley, Shu Uemura,** and **Naj Oleari,** etc. Behind all this, there are narrow and bewitching back streets closed to vehicular traffic that call out to you to explore them. Many of them host the most expensive antiques dealers in the city; some of them are the ateliers of new, hot designers.

There are designer shops in here also, including **Il Bisonte** (Via Madonnina 10) and **Angela Caputi** (Via Madonnina 11). Don't miss **Etro,** Via Pontaccio 17, at the corner of Vicolo Fiori. And while you're in this neck of the woods, don't forget that **London's Lush**—that adorable deli of bath bombs, face masks, and homemade soaps and suds first created in England—has opened up here at via Fiori Chiari 6; the store is not identical to the English (or Canadian) versions and therein lies its charm.

The best way to see it is during the Brera antiques street fair (third Saturday of each month), when vendors put out tables in the narrow streets and a well-heeled crowd browses. But any day is a good day. Carry on from Brera to Solferino (the street just changes names) and then over one to Garibaldi.

Largo Augusto/Durini   Another option is to move from the other side of the Duomo to **Corso Vittorio Emanuele II,** and over to **Via Durini.** Via Durini is only a block long, but it's a good-sized block and it's crammed with fabulous stores. It veers off at an angle from San Babila and runs straight to Largo Augusto.

Via Durini has blossomed into an important Milanese fashion street: Mr. Armani offers three different **Emporio** shops; **Calvin Klein** has opened up shop, and there are designer showrooms, cute little clothing places, very chic fur salons, and furniture design showrooms.

Please note that you can catch a bus to **Il Salvagente,** the discounter (see p. 225), at Largo Augusto, or walk via the **Corso Porta Vittoria,** and be there in 10 minutes. I usually walk because I enjoy window-shopping along the way.

Train Station/Ingrosso   In the area between the Centrale train station and the Repubblica metro station, at the base of the luxury hotels run by Sheraton, a grid system of flat streets makes up the *garmento* wholesale (*ingrosso*) and discount district of Milan. There are scads of stores here: You can browse and just go in and out—about half of them are closed for lunch, and all of them are closed on Saturday and Sunday. The area is trying to fashion itself as a fashion destination, calling itself **"CMM"** (Centro Moda Milano); it now has a printed brochure of the showrooms and has special hours for holiday shopping and during Fashion Weeks. Get the brochure for free at any showroom or take a look at the website: www.centromodamilano.it; fax them at 02/93-57-22-18.

If your time is limited and you crave high style and multiple marvels, this is not your destination. If you like a bargain and don't mind hit-or-miss shopping, step this way. I had a ball here last time I visited because I got lucky—cashmere twin sets for $250 (total price), stores that take credit cards and smile, Tod's boots for $200 a pair, lots of brand names and lots of selection.

For Euro visitors who specifically come to Milan to beat the high prices in other parts of Europe, this is your cup of tea.

Buenos Aires   Don't cry for me Buenos Aires, I've got my credit cards. Corso Buenos Aires is one of Milan's most "real" shopping streets. It's also more reasonably priced than the high-rent streets. If you are a serious shopper, but value is important to you, this is your kind of neighborhood. This is a great place for teens to shop.

The street is almost a mile long and features more than 300 shops: It is one of the most concentrated shopping areas in continental Europe. The best stores are located around the Lima station of the metro.

There are tons of bars, cute restaurants, markets, and fabric shops. This is also the place for jeans stores, unisex fashion stores, moderately priced shoe stores, and knock-offs of the latest Milanese designer goods. Avoid shopping on Saturday because it's always mobbed. Remember, this is where the real people shop, so few people will speak English. The clientele is not always chic; the scenery is neither cute nor charming.

Many of the shops have no numbers; often the number by a store represents the block rather than the store address (so many shops may be called "3"), but it's all easy once you're there. Just wander and enjoy—you can't miss the good stuff. Oh, yes, Standa is gone (the flagship **Benetton** is there now) but **Upim** is there, with a supermarket in the basement. You can get there easily by taking the no. 65 streetcar from the Centrale train station and getting off at Corso Buenos Aires (about 3 stops). Or take the metro to Loreto and walk toward Venezia or vice versa.

Magenta   For the opposite type of experience, get to the corso Magenta, a rich residential thoroughfare where the best bakeries, cafes, and shopping brands are located to serve those who live in this area; it's the equal to Paris's 16th or 17th arrondisement. From October to May, do remember to wear your fur.

Navigli South of the Porta Ticinese is the canal area of Milan. The canals have been mostly built over, so don't spend too much time looking for a lot of water (wait for Venice): There's just the one canal. Yet the Navigli is becoming a funky shopping neighborhood. You can wander around here for an hour or two if you like colorful junk shops, secondhand shops, artist's studios, and the feeling of getting in on the ground floor of up-and-coming Italian style. Cash only; no one speaks English.

The two streets running along the canal are called **Alzaia Naviglio Grande** and **Ripa di Porta Ticinese.** You can walk down one, cross a bridge, and walk back on the other side. There are some cute restaurants, and you can make an afternoon out of it if this is your kind of thing.

There is an antiques market held on the last Sunday of each month on both sides of the Naviglio Grande. Tell your taxi driver either that you want *"mercatone dell antiquariato"* or the name of the street, Ripa Ticinese, which is one of two streets hosting the market along the canal.

Every Tuesday and Saturday there is a regular street market along the Viale Papiniano. This is a great place for designer clothing that fell off trucks and all sorts of fun fashions and accessories. Plan to be there early—9 to 10am is fine. In addition to two lanes of stalls selling clothing and dry goods, part of the market is fruit and food.

To save money, you can hop on the red line of the metro and get off at San Agostino and be right here.

Porta Vittoria The Corso di Porta Vittoria begins shortly after the Duomo and changes its name to **Corso 22 Marzo.** Just use your feet. I like this walk because it takes you by **Il Salvagente,** the discount designer store, and enables you to see something of middle-class Milan along the way.

The walk along Corso Porta Vittoria takes you through an upper-middle-class neighborhood where you'll find branches of many favorite stores, like **Max Mara** and **Bassetti**. This is where well-off locals shop, and it's very non-touristy, not unlike the Corso Vercelli. There is a nice branch of **Coin**.

After the street name changes to 22 Marzo, you'll turn left on Via Fratelli Bronzetti to get to **Il Salvagente**. Hail a taxi to take you back to your hotel if you have too much loot.

Aprile & Beyond   Not for the average tourist, Aprile stands for the plaza (piazza) of the same name: XXV Aprile. It is an up-and-coming neighborhood that attracts design mavens and fashion editors because of a handful of important shops in the area, including **High Tech** and **Corso Como 10**. The few retailers who have set up shop here are inventive, creative, and exciting, so take a look if you want to be in with the in-crowd. If you are more interested in sightseeing, and don't have much time in Milan, this area may not be for you.

Piazza XXV Aprile is between the Moscova and Garibaldi stops on the green line. After this plaza, Corso Garibaldi changes its name and becomes Corso Como.

MILAN RESOURCES FROM A TO Z

Antiques

Milan's antiques markets are great fun, but don't be afraid to get out of town to explore a few more. In Pavia and Brescia, there are antiques markets on the second Sunday of each month. On the third Sunday, in Carimate (Como), there's a flea market. Begamo Alta also celebrates on the third Sunday, in Piazza Angelini. Many villages have antiques markets on certain Sundays only in April and October: Ask your hotel concierge for details. For markets in Milan proper, see "Flea Markets," later in this chapter.

Antiques stores are mostly located in the Brera area, on or off Via Madonnina, with a few fancier ones in the Montenapo area. The Montenapo shops do not offer affordable items for mere mortals.

Serious dealers include: **Legatoria Conti Borboni** for antique books, at Corso Magenta 31; **Amabile** for carpets, on Via Brera 16; and **Mauro Brucoli** for furniture, on Via della Spiga 46. There's a tiny gallery of about eight or ten shops right near the Sheraton Luxury Hotels—the Palace Hotel and the Principe di Savoia—and the Jolly Touring. Take the Repubblica metro and walk or taxi to **La Piazzetta degli Antiquari** (at Via Turati 6).

Bath

Lush
Via Fiori Chiari 6

I am assuming that most readers already know the Lush chain, either from visits in the U.K. or Canada or from the press. If you have no idea what I am talking about, this is going to be a must-do experience. For those who already know and may even be bored with the gimmick, snap out of it— what's brilliant here is that the concept has been adapted to local specialties, so you find things like Lemoncello shampoo, not sold in stores outside of Italy (there's also a store in Bologna). While prices are not bargain basement, the novelty factor is high. This street is right off the via Brera; even men like it.

Mimosa
Via Solferino 12

This small shop sells bath products from several international brands; what you want are the local brands. I've fallen for a line of mud products called Guam made by Lacote, which, despite either of these names, is indeed an Italian firm. Many of the products are made with algae, and then there's mud with algae—my fave. There are products for body, face, and for bath. The shop's owner does speak English and will explain products and how to use them.

Books

There's a small international bookstore upstairs at the Armani Superstore (via Manzoni 31) and another, larger one upstairs at 10 Corso Como.

MONDADORI
Corso Vittorio Emanuele II

This is a big, modern bookstore with as much crammed downstairs as there is on the street level. They have an enormous selection in every category and a very good travel department. They offer some books in foreign languages, including English, and some gift items. There are now similar bookstores, sort of American-style super stores if you will, in the area and in other parts of Milan. It's a trend.

RIZZOLI
Galleria Vittorio Emanuele 79

Large bookstore with books in several languages; travel department toward the front of the store, although they may not have the latest editions of guides. Open evenings and on Sunday.

Boutiques

FONTANA
Via della Spiga 33

Modern Italian design of the most expensive and highest order. The interior is swank and very Milano, with lots of marble and sleek woods. The counters are suspended from thin wires and seem to hang in midair.

GIO MORETTI
Via della Spiga 4 & 6

There are three different Gio Moretti stores: one for men, one for women, and one for children (across the street). You'll see all the big names here: For women, stock up on Sonia Rykiel, Complice, and those designers who don't have their own free-standing shops.

MICHELE MABELLE/MILANO MONAMOUR
Via della Spiga 36

The name is enough to make you fall in love. Inside you'll find Norma Kamali, Kansai, and Thierry Mugler, plus wild sequiny T-shirts, a glitzy interior, and piped-in rock music.

RUFFO RESEARCH
Via Della Spiga 48

Two different stores, next door to each other, one for men and one for women. It's leather, it's trendy, it's fairly priced considering how cool it is and you will swoon at how leather can be made to wrap, droop, flow, swing, and dance around the body. The leather is so light and fine that it drapes like fabric. Much of the work is created by Greek designer Sophia Kokosalaki, but the force behind the scenes is the president of the firm, Giacomo Corsi, who insists on innovative style for both the men's and women's lines. Hides come from Tuscany and are worked on by the most famous Italian leather workers in order to get them light enough to meet the requirements of the design technology. The results are downright revolutionary.

Cashmere

LORO PIANO
Via Montenapoleone 27

A three-story temple to cashmere and luxe, selling not only men's and women's things but items for the home. There's also interactive displays like videos and tests you can perform to see how the fabrics hold up, proving this is an art and a science.

MALO
Via della Spiga 7

One of the most famous names in Italian quality cashmere, Malo has opened a shop that sells both men's and women's lines; in summer there are non-cashmere items, too. Not the factory outlet, which is located outside of Florence (see chapter 6).

MANRICO
Corso Magenta 11

The address says it all—this is a local source for those with money who are in the know. There's also a store in Aspen, so you get the idea.

Costume Jewelry

ANGELA PINTALDI
Via San Pietro All'Orto 9

This is very serious costume jewelry. Her work is similar to Bulgari, but funkier. For the last decade, Pintaldi has ruled as the "in" creator of creative and expressive jewels, frequently made with semiprecious stones. She also works with ivory and other materials, based on color and texture—pure magic meets pure art.

Department Stores

COIN
Piazza Giornate 5; Corso Vercelli 30–32; Piazzale Cantore; Piazzale Loreta

Pronounced "co-*een*," this store is not as convenient or as much fun as La Rinascente. But if you find yourself near one of the stores, by all means check it out. (There are four different locations.) I also find that Coin has more energy than La Rinascente and is more likely to have hot styles and designer copies. In fact, Coin specializes in designer-inspired looks at moderate prices; they have completely re-created themselves in the last 2 years and are far more upscale than ever before.

FIORUCCI
Corso Vittorio Emanuele II

This is a small department store for teenagers; most of the store is on the lower level. It specializes in trendy junk but happens to be great fun.

GIORGIO ARMANI SUPERSTORE
Via Manzoni 31

I don't know what to call this except a department store, although the word "showroom" comes to mind . . . as does "showcase" as does *"ohmigod."* I am horrified and delighted with the store and think all students of retail, marketing, and merchandising should rush here for a look-see. Everyone else, well, you are on your own.

The store is almost a city block long in size; it has three levels, some of which bleed through from one to the next to add height and drama. The giant video screen says it all—this is a store for people who don't know how to read (although there is a small bookstore upstairs). There's also a cafe, a branch of Nobu, a florist, and all the Armani lines, many of which have goods that are not sold elsewhere, such as the home furnishings line, which looks like something designed by Terrence Conran. I am partial to the jeans line because the logo is AG, which are my son's initials. To me the best part of the store is the large makeup bar, because the Armani makeup is great, and relatively hard to find even in Italy.

LA RINASCENTE
Piazza del Duomo

Being across the street from the Duomo and in the center of Milan makes this store seem more exciting than it is, although if I go in need of a design fix, I come away impressed.

There's a lot of merchandise in the store, and this is a good place to see a lot and absorb trends and makers quickly. The style of the store is in the American-Anglo model, so don't expect all goods to be Italian or to feel very Italian while shopping here.

Check out the handbag department for a good selection of low-to-moderately priced items. This is one of the few places in Italy where you can get a nice-looking $100 bag. Other good departments are children's and active sportswear. The ski clothes are sensational, but expensive. I also like the basement housewares space, especially the small gourmet food market.

The big fashion names are not well represented in women's fashion, but there are lots of "real-people" clothes at fair (for Italy) prices.

I bought a pair of wool gloves in January in a hard-to-find fashion color for $10, so I was pleased enough with the accessory department. There are lots of hair ornaments, but again, you pay for their novelty and fashion cachet.

The store does not close for lunch during the week, except on Monday, when the store opens late (1:45pm). The hours are extraordinary, especially for Italy: Monday to Saturday 9am to 9pm. The store does have some special Sunday openings now.

Here's the best part: There's a cafe (seventh floor) that overlooks the spires of the Duomo. Note that this is a full-service department store; along with the cafe there are hair-dresser and beauty facilities, free alterations except on sale goods, banking facilities with an ATM, customer service, etc.

OVIESSE
Corso Buenos Aires

Technically this might be a lifestyle store, not a department store; it is the antithesis of the Armani Superstore. This is a temple to cheap thrills; the most exciting copies of fashions for the least amount of money you have ever seen . . . it is the Italian version of H&M and then some. I went nuts here and dream of going to all their other stores. Skirts for $20. Knit polo shirts for $15. You get my drift. Sizes up to 52, although the sizes run a little small.

UPIM
Corso Buenos Aires; Piazza San Babila

Bury my heart at the Piazza San Babila, because I will never forgive the Upim powers for what they have done to this store. Who takes a great dime store and turns it into Penney's, I ask you?

They don't close for lunch; they may have inexpensive cashmere sweaters (if you come in the winter) and they are worth exploring, but, gosh, I liked the old Upim better. The Buenos Aires store is larger; it also has a grocery store in the basement. The lower level at San Babila has trendy fashion and men's fashion as well as lingerie; on the street level there's mostly women's fashion with some accessories and makeup, an arrangement is reversed on corso Buenos Aires.

Designer Boutiques

AMERICAN & CANADIAN BIG NAMES

Obviously you didn't go to Italy to buy American designs. Still, there is an American invasion beginning to take place in many different financial brackets. **Timberland** has three stores in town, **Footlocker** is everywhere (try Corso Vittorio Emanuele II for convenience's sake), and **Guess** has opened quite a temple to teens, their second store in Italy, at Piazza San Babila. (The other is in Florence.)

Calvin Klein is in a large, sparse, very minimalist fancy-dancy space on the fashionable Via Durini. There is also a CK Milan store; and, there are plans in the pipeline for a **CKCollection** store as well.

Among the foreign-based arrivals is the makeup guru from Canada, by way of Estée Lauder: **MAC** is now in a very spiffy shop in the Brera district, having already moved off Via Spiga.

Jean-Louis Ginibre's Secret List of Jazzy Record Dealers

Jean-Louis Ginibre, the editorial director of Hachette Filipacchi Magazines in New York, has passed on his favorite Milan sources for secondhand jazz LPs for collectors:

THE BLACK SAINT
Via V. Monti 41

IL DISCOMANE
Alzaia Naviglio Grande 38

METROPOLIS DISCHI
Via Padova 104

VINYL MAGIC
Via Tribaldi 29

Continental & U.S. Big Names

BCBG MAX AZIRA
Via Durini 23

BODY SHOP
Via Brera 30

CARTIER
Via Montenapoleone 16

CELINE
Via Montenapoleone 25

CHANEL
Via Sant' Andrea 10

ESCADA
Corso Matteotti 22

FOGAL
Via Montenapoleone 1

GAULTIER
Via della Spiga 20

GIEVES & HAWKES
Via Manzoni 12

HELMUT LANG
Via Sant' Andrea 14

HERMÈS
Via Sant' Andrea 21

KENZO
Via Sant' Andrea 11

LAURA ASHLEY
Via Brera 4

LOUIS VUITTON
Via Montenapoleone 14

MICHAELA FREY
Piazza Cordusio

SWATCH
Via Montenapoleone 12

TIFFANY & CO.
Via della Spiga 19A

UNGARO
Via Montenapoleone 27

WOLFORD
Via Manzoni 16b

YVES SAINT LAURENT (YSL RIVE GAUCHE)
Via Pietro Verri 8

ITALIAN BIG NAMES

ALBERTA FERRETTI
Via Montenapoleone 21a; Philosophy di Alberta Ferretti,
Via Montenapoleone 19

ANTONIO FUSCO
Via Sant' Andrea 11

BENETTON (SUPERSTORE)
Corso Vittorio Emanuele II

BLUMARINE (ANNA MOLINARI)
Via della Spiga 42

BOTTEGA VENETA
Via della Spiga 5

BYBLOS
Via della Spiga 42

CERRUTI 1881
Via della Spiga 21

D & G BASIC
Via Sant' Andrea 10

DOLCE & GABBANA
Via della Spiga 2; D&G, Corso Venezia 7

EMILIO PUCCI
Via Montenapoleone 14

ERMENEGILDO ZEGNA
Via Verri 3

ETRO
Via Montenapoleone 5

FENDI
Via Sant' Andrea 16

FERRAGAMO
Via Montenapoleone 3

FIORRUCI
Corso Vittorio Emanuele II (Galleria Passarella 1)

GENNY
Via della Spiga 4

GIANFRANCO FERRÉ
Via Sant' Andrea 15

GIANNI VERSACE
Via Montenapoleone 11; Atelier Versace, Via Gesù 12; Versus, Via San Pietro all'Orto 10; Versace Jeans Couture, Via Carducci 38

GIORGIO ARMANI
Via Sant' Andrea 9; Armani Superstore, via Manzoni 31

JIL SANDER
Via Verri 6

KRIZIA
Via della Spiga 23

LAURA BIAGIOTTI
Via Borgospesso 19

LES COPAINS
Via Montenapoleone 2

MARIELLA BURANI
Via Montenapoleone 3

MARINA RINALDI
Corso Vittorio Emanuele II at Galleria Passarella 2

MARIO VALENTINO
Via Montenapoleone 10

MASKA
Corso Vittorio Emanuele II

MAX & CO.
Via Victor Hugo 1

MAX MARA
Corso Genova 12

MILA SCHOEN
Via Montenapoleone 2

MISSONI
Via Sant' Andrea 2

MISSONI SPORT
Piazza del Duomo 21

MIUMIU
Corso Venezia 3

MOSCHINO
Via Sant' Andrea 12; Via Durini 14

NAJ OLEARI
Via Brera 58

NAZARENO GABRIELLI
Via Montenapoleone 23

PRADA
Via Sant' Andrea 21; Via della Spiga 1/5

ROBERTO CAVALLI
Via della Spiga 42

SAMSONITE
Corso Matteotti 12

STRENESSE
Via Manzoni ang. Via Pisoni

Discounters

Also see "Outlets (In Town)," later in this section.

ELDORADO
Via Montenapoleone 26

Considering the address and convenience, this store is a must-do: a discount store selling high-end fashion names right in the heart of the biggest fashion stores in town and not far from the metro station. Now then, I can't tell you I was knocked out by what I saw, but there were Lagerfeld shoes, MiuMiu clothes, and some Helmut Lang items. The names were in place; I just wasn't tempted, and the store wasn't nearly as much fun as Il Salvagente. Still, when in the neighborhood, take a quick look.

IL SALVAGENTE
Via Fratelli Bronzetti 16

American and European styles from big-name designers in suits and dresses; even in larger sizes, but you just have to hit it right. Men's clothing is on the second floor. This looks like a prison; you enter through a gate, walk down the drive and turn into the door where you will be asked to use a locker for your bags and maybe even your handbag. During sales it is mobbed. Il Salvagente is the most famous designer discounter in Italy. This is an operation that makes Loehmann's look classy, but if you are strong enough, my God, can you find stuff here. Attention savvy shoppers.

While the labels are still in the clothes, the merchandise is not well organized, so you must be feeling very strong to go through it all. There's so much here that you have a good chance of finding something worthwhile, but you could strike out.

Clothes are located in several parts of the store and upstairs as well; there are dressing rooms. Not everything is new. Some have been seen on runways or are over one season old; not everything is in perfect condition.

On various visits, however, I've seen Krizia, Gianni Versace, Valentino, Guy Laroche, Trussardi, made-in-Italy Lacroix handbags (for $100 each!), and more. On my most recent visit, I was truly dizzy from all the choices. I once happened on the January sale when prices at the cash register were 30% less than the lowest ticketed price.

Remember: The atmosphere is drab; the display is zero. This place is for the strong and the hungry. Hours: 10am to 12:30pm and 3 to 7pm; closed Monday morning and July 15 to August 30. On Wednesday and Saturday the store does not close for lunch and is open nonstop from 10am till 7pm.

SALVAGENTE BIMBI
Via Balzaretti 28

There is a separate shop for children's clothing called Salvagente Bimbi; the layout is similar to the mother shop, but the store is harder to find—take a taxi, of course. It is hard to find a taxi to get you home, so you may want to ask them to call you a cab. "Taxi" in Italian is *taxi.*

Note: I used a car and driver to get here, and my Milanese driver was lost. Still if you are looking for expensive kids clothing at affordable prices, this is the place.

SEVEN GROUP
Via San Gregorio 49

This was my favorite showroom when I hit the wholesale district near the train station last visit; it's a large, open space, not crammed and crowded like many jobbers. They are open to the public, they do take plastic, and they do give tax-back refunds! They don't speak a lot of English, but who cares? I bought my cashmere twin set here and was tempted by many of the fashions. The bad part is that prices are not clearly marked, and you feel like you're a big pain every time you ask a question. Still, the quality and styling were sublime.

STOCK HOUSE
Via Panizzi 6

This is inside, in the courtyard. This is the venue of an adorable man, Antonio Leuce, whom I met at a street market. He sells designer clothes—the very best names in Italy—from his shop in a van, and even takes U.S. dollars.

There are men's and women's clothing as well as women's fashion accessories; we are talking big names and big discounts. The clothes are at least a season old, and possibly older, but are at least 50% off retail. You can get here in a taxi or via bus 58 or 60; hours are Tuesday to Saturday 9:30am to 12:30pm and 3:30 to 7pm.

VESTISTOCK
Viale Romagna 19 & Via Boscovich 17

A chain of discount shops in various neighborhoods, including the very convenient Buenos Aires for Viale Romagna and the train station district for Via Boscovich. If you hit it lucky you can chose from labels such as Les Copains, Moschino, Versace, Montana, etc. There are men's, women's, and kids' clothes as well as accessories, so go and have a ball. Take bus 60, 90, or 91 for the Buenos Aires area shop, or call ☎ **02/749-05-02** for more specific directions.

If you prefer the store between the train station and many major hotels, it's open nonstop, 9:30am to 6:30pm, Monday to Friday. There were Tod's boots when I visited and plenty of men's clothing in large sizes.

Flea Markets

The following markets sell all manner of old and/or used things—what we Americans consider a flea market. The words the Italians use to describe such a market are *mercato di pulci*. Note that more and more flea markets are opening all over Italy, so ask your hotel concierge if there is a new market and check the pages of the monthly magazine *Dove* (pronounced do-*vay:* Italian for "where," not the flying bird) for fairs and flea markets in nearby communities.

BOLLATE ANTIQUE MARKET
Piazza Vittorio Veneto, Bollate

Take the train or a taxi to this suburb on the north side of Milan, where there is a Sunday *mercato dell'usato*, or antiques market. Unlike most Sunday markets, which are held once a month, this market is held weekly. Most of the dealers sell English antiques, if you can believe that; silver is especially hot, as are old prints. There's not much in the way of bed linens, but there are some old hats and a fair amount of furniture. About 300 dealers.

Consider renting a car for this day in the country, or hop the bus: take the no. 90 or 91 to the **Piazza della Liberta in Bollante.** Open from 8am to 6pm.

BRERA ANTIQUE MARKET (MERCATONE DELL' ANTIQUARIATO)
Via Brera

This flea market, held on the third Saturday of each month, is a local favorite. Because it takes place right in the heart of downtown Milan (in the shadow of La Scala, in fact), this is a drop-dead chic market to be seen prowling. About 50 antiques dealers set up stalls, and many artists and designers turn out. To find it, just head for Via Brera. Do wear your fur and walk your dog if at all possible.

NAVIGLI ANTIQUE MARKET
Grand Navigli

If flea markets are your thing, be in Milan on the last Sunday of the month. Then you can spend the mid-morning at this fabulous flea market, which stretches all the way from Porta Ticinese to Porta Genova and the Viale Papiniano. With approximately 400 dealers, some say it is the most stylish flea market in all of Europe.

While the market is open from 8am to 2pm, do remember this is Italy, not New York—things are most lively from 10am to noon. You'll find the usual antiques and wonderful junk, and the crowd is one of Milan's top see-and-be-seen. Take the no. 19 tram to Ripa di Porta Ticinese.

Food & Wine

ARMANDOLA
Via della Spiga 50

This is a teeny-weeny, tiny, itty-bitty deli with fresh foods, dried mushrooms, tuna in jars, and all sorts of fancy, expensive and yummy things. In the Tuna Quests, I paid $15 for a jar of tuna fish—the recipient said it was worth the price. Sometimes I buy a ready-made picnic here; you can't beat the location for convenience.

ENTECA COTTI
Via Solferino 42

Considered one of the best wine stores in Milano. They also have serious olive oil, as is the custom at a good enteca.

FREE
Centrale train station

Don't snicker, I do a lot of my gourmet food shopping here because it's convenient. Buy magic coffee here as well as Italian specialty food items for gifts and home use.

PECK
Via Spadari 9

You can eat in their restaurant or just do take-out from the deli, the most famous in town. Near the Duomo.

Home Style/Showrooms

ALCHIMA
Via Torino 68

One of the longest-running shows in modern Italian design, Alchima started it all and continues to be top-notch for seeing and believing. The very latest is always on display. Whether you buy or not, you must stop in.

ARFLEX
Via Borgognona 2

One of the big names in design, Arflex's showroom is filled with all manner of wild, creative home furnishings. A lipstick-red leather sofa, anyone?

CASSINA
Via Durini 16

One of the long-standing big names in post–World War II design, Cassina makes mostly office furniture, but all of their pieces are quite avant-garde. Colors are bright, deep, and vibrant, and the design lines are beyond clean. I popped into this showroom recently to look at the leather chairs designed by Mario Bellini—which are the prototype for the plastic Bellini chairs that my friend Alan makes with Bellini (at a Target store near you). Even though I was just snooping, the people in the showroom could not have been more gracious.

LISA CORTI
Via Conchetta 6

I don't even know how to describe this space or shopping situation—it is a showroom, but it's also different. First off, you should know or understand who Lisa Corti is—an artist and magician with color and textiles, whose work is sold at Saks and is best seen in the pages of the Saks home-furnishings catalogs, which always have at least one full page in color with stacks of her things.

Corti is best known for her home design for table and bed and sofa, but also makes clothes for women and children and other accessories, and at one time, dishes or ceramics. She is an artist and does it all; her work is her signature. Even her postcards are glorious (and free). Perhaps a look-see on the website might help: www.lisacorti.com.

The showroom is in the middle of nowhere; if you take a taxi have the driver wait for you. There is a front door on the street, but I didn't find it and went in through the courtyard. I also called (☎ 02/58-10-00-31) from my mobile phone, as I thought I was lost.

The showroom inside is the real showroom and work-room; the shopping op is sort of like being in the factory out-let. The prices are not low, but are just a fraction of the U.S. price. I paid about $150 for a quilt that I had paid $250 for in the south of Italy, and that costs $350 at Saks. They do detaxe, and someone there does speak English. You might want to call ahead before you make the trek; store hours are 10m to 1pm and 3 to 7pm.

POLTRONA FRAU
Via Manzoni 20

No, this establishment was not named after a German house-wife; Poltrona Frau is one of the most famous names in Ital-ian design. This is the place to buy leather-upholstered furniture that costs a fortune, but will be considered a collectible for the next century.

Linens & Lace

BASSETTI
Corso Vercelli 25; Corso Garibaldi 20; Corso Vittorio Emanuele II 15

A famous name in linens for years, Bassetti makes the kind of linens that fall between ready-to-wear and couture—they're more affordable than the big-time expensive stuff and far nicer than anything you'd find at the low end. Although they do sell colors, their hot look is paisley fabrics in the Etro vein. There are branch stores in every major Italian city.

JESURUM
Via Verri 4

A branch of the Venetian linen house, famous for old lace bro-cades, really swanky stuff—with prices to match.

FRETTE
Via Montenapoleone 21

This line has gone so far upscale that they now call it "home couture" with items such as pajamas and robes and leisure clothing as well as sheets and bedding for sale. Naturally there is a business in custom-created bed linen as well.

PRATESI
Via Montenapoleone 27

The biggest and best shop right now is the flagship space in Milan, where prices are 25% to 40% less than in the U.S., and there's merchandise galore.

Climb the stairs to the large showroom for the best selection of sheets, tablecloths, and other linens. Don't neglect the mezzanine level for children's sheets and other items appropriate for setting up a nursery.

Pratesi's annual sale is in January, and it's well worth planning a trip around. Here's an example: I priced a king-size sheet set in the Milan store at 775,000L. The sale price for the same set in January was 30% less, or 542,000L ($340). And, as an American, you'll receive an additional 19% off if you file for a refund on the IVA. This same linen set retails for just over $1,000 in the U.S.!

T&J VESTOR
Via Manzoni 38

For the most part, I don't suggest you buy sheets or towels in Europe, because these products are often better and cheaper in the U.S. However, when you get to T&J Vestor, it's another story. This is the house that acts as distributor for Missoni bed linens, and these Missoni sheets (and towels) are something to behold. They are expensive (around $100), but they are unique, and if money is no object when you worship at the altar of style, this is your kind of store. There are branches in almost all big Italian cities.

Makeup

Don't look now, but there is a color war in Italy, centered in Milan where everyone is suddenly doing makeup. This was probably instigated by the success of the Versace makeup, which was actually launched a few months after the Versace murder and was obviously created before he died. With the success of makeup artist lines in the U.S., several Italian names have jumped into the fray. Most of the names are not familiar to Americans; some of them have pedigrees, however. And then there's Armani.

DIEGO DELLA PALMA
Via Madonnina 13

This is embarrassing, but here goes: I am forever getting Diego della Palma, a well-known local makeup artist and Diego della Viale, the creator of Tod's shoes mixed up. That said, Palma is an artist with connections to the Italian couture houses; he has a small shop that also sells his line, where you can make an appointment for lessons and a makeover. The address is adjacent the Brera district on a great shopping street.

GIORGIO ARMANI
Via Manzoni 31

As we go to press, the Armani makeup does not have very much distribution in Italy or elsewhere in the world. This could be because the line is so new, and the intent is to keep it very exclusive. Regardless, you can see it all and play with it all at the Armani flagship; the line is also sold in Milan's La Rinascente. I have tested many of the products and adore the pearlized liquid foundation that really does add light to the face.

KIKO
Corso Buenos Aires 43

By the time I got to Kiko, a cute little shop in the best part of the trendy shopping (near metro stop Lima) on Buenos Aires,

I could no longer tell one brand from the next. I can't quite tell how this line differs from Madina, although it is not as sophisticated in the packaging and marketing. Still, the line is well priced and is getting raves from local fashion editors.

MAC
Via Fiori Chiari 12

MAC, the professional color line from Canada, now owned by Estée Lauder, which has gone global, has a freestanding store in Milan, newly relocated to the Brera area. Aside from the products, you can get a makeup lesson or just play with the colors. The professional line is sold; all charitable promotions, such as products whose profits go to good causes, are continued in international stores.

MADINA
Corso Venezia 23

With stores in Milan, Tokyo, and New York, Madina is the color story the press is in love with: Madina—sort of the Italian version of France's Terry de Gunzberg—used to do makeup for the opera at La Scala. She is married to the man who owns the most famous luxury cosmetics factory in Europe. The stores are small, but the packaging is very, very slick. Imprinted on the tablets of color are slogans in English—"color is seduction"; "color is power," etc. Terry also does something like this, by the way.

There are hundreds of shades; the strength of the line is said to be in the intensity of the colors and their staying power. I tested several items, and while I like them, I don't find them any more extraordinary than other brands. Prices are moderate to low—a paintbox of 12 shades of cream eye shadow for $15 is a steal, and a great gift for anyone. There's also a wide selection of brushes and several styles of makeup bags. There is another store in Milan, via Meravigli 17, which is on the corner of corso Magenta an upscale residential area with nice shopping.

NAJ OLEARI
Via Brera 28

Because this fabric designer is known for her bright colors, it makes sense that the firm would branch into color cosmetics, which are even sold in most big department stores as well as the flagship boutique. The line is so successful that now spa and treatment products have been added. Don't ask me, I don't make the news; I only report it.

PERLIER/KELEMATA
(ARMONIA NATURALI)
Corso Buenos Aires 25

You may remember Perlier as a French bath line; it was bought by the Italian Klemata family who now has a chain of very spiffy bath and makeup stores all over Italy. There is probably a store coming to a mall near you in no time. This year they joined the color wars and added a color makeup line under the Perlier branding; it is sold only in their stores, which are named "Armonia Naturali." There are four other shops dotted around Milan.

SHU UEMURA
Via Brera 2

Uemura is the king of color, and the man who started it all over 20 years ago in Japan, where he brought professional makeup to the public. His products have a cult following, and he is clearly in a league above all others; so are his prices.

VERSACE
Via Montenapoleone 11

The Versace makeup lives and is now sometimes found in duty-free shops. The colors are a tad over the top, but the packaging is fabulous, and a lipstick still makes a nice gift. The line is sold in the U.S. at a few department stores and in Versace boutiques.

Markets

To a local, there's a big difference between a market and a flea market. A market sells fruits and vegetables and dry goods, and a flea market sells old junk. See p. 227 on Flea Markets.

SAN AGOSTINO MARKET
Viale Papiniano

First, I must admit that no other guidebook calls this the San Agostino Market. I call it that because San Agostino is the name of the closest metro stop, and it helps me remember where this market is located on the Viale Papiniano.

This is a T-shaped market. The cross of the T is the fruit, food, and vegetable market; the long stroke is the dry-goods market. The dry-goods portion goes on for 2 blocks, so don't quit after the first block. Everything in the world is sold here, including a few designer items that seem to have fallen off the backs of trucks (but are carefully mixed in with less valuable items). For example, one dealer in the dry-goods market seems to specialize in bath articles, but also has a small selection of Missoni bathrobes.

You'll find everything from the latest teen fashions to tapes and CDs, kitchen supplies, car supplies, pet supplies, aprons, and housedresses. There are also socks, towels, batteries, luggage, underwear, sewing thread, running shoes, designer shoes, lace curtains, and fabrics by the bolt. The market is open on Tuesday and Saturday.

Menswear

A note about menswear: *Born to Shop* French Correspondent Richard Duvauchelle shops discount in America and retail in Milan to beat prices in his native France. He says regular retail in Milan is less than in most European capitals but that prices in America are better, especially if you hit a big department store sale or use American off-price stores. However, Richard is 6'3" and has an American-type body rather than a

European one; he can easily find a fit in Milan, right off the rack. For those too lazy to use the size chart in the back of this book to translate a U.S. size to an Italian one, add 10 to your European size: A size 42R is a size 52R.

ADER
Via Settembrini 33

M. Duvauchelle found this store in Milan. He says it's for guys who don't want to go to the big names and fancy, expensive shops, but who just want good quality clothes and sports jackets at fair prices. Prices here, he reports, are excellent for Europe, bargains when compared to those in France, but not as good as at American clearance sales or off-price shops. He bought sports jackets off the rack in the $250 to $300 price range. The store was open on Saturday, whereas discounters in Milan are not.

BOGGI
Piazza San Babila 3

Boggi specializes in the English look, the preppy look; whatever you call it, you'll find cable-knit sweaters and plaid hunting trousers. There are several shops; the main store is near Via Montenapoleone. It's not cheap here, but the quality is very high.

CASHMERE COTTON AND SILK
Via Madonnina 19

This is one of those fancy stores on the little side streets of Brera that is worth looking at, if only for its charm. Walk down a rather long corridor until you get into the store, which is modern with an old-fashioned feel. Inside, you'll find Milanese yuppies scurrying around, choosing among the shirts, sweaters, and suits made only of the three fibers in the store's name. Prices are very, very high, but the shopping experience makes you feel like royalty.

EDDY MONETTI
Piazza San Babila 4

One of the leading sources for Anglo style in Milan, Monetti deals with rich gentlemen who want to look even richer. They hand-stitch suits and shirts but also sell off the rack. The Monetti customer likes special service and hates to shop; he wants to come here and be pampered and know that he'll walk out looking like a million dollars, not lire.

ERMENEGILDO ZEGNA
Via Pietro Verri 3

For centuries, the family has excelled in the quality wool business. Until recently, the ready-to-wear was a small sideline, but now the world's richest men can buy the best suits that Italy ready-makes in a smattering of freestanding boutiques. There's one in Paris, one in Florence, and this shop in Milan, which is the closest to the mill in Biella, and serves as the family flagship store. The shop is large and modern and sells classic tailoring to discriminating men. Although the house is famous for its wools, you can get other items, including cotton or silk dress shirts.

TINCATI
Piazza Oberdan 2; Via Verri 1

An old-fashioned men's store, or haberdashery (as they used to be called), with fine woods on the walls and an upper mezzanine filled with stock. Very good Old-World reputation. Not for hotshots who want the Euro-Japanese look. Its shirts are famous because they come with a tab that passes between the legs (trust me on this) and an extra collar and two cuffs.

Outlets (In Town)

ETRO
Via Spartaco 3

This began life as an employee store in the firm's offices, but it's open to the public and is the kind of secret that every smart shopper in Milano knows about. They do close for lunch from 1:45 until 2:45pm. Saturday hours are 10am to 1:45pm. Closed Sunday. They take plastic. Now then, did I have fun? I get sweaty just remembering.

The tiny shop has two levels; the clothes are downstairs. There are bins of things; I got men's pocket squares for $25 each; silk suspenders for $15. There is fabric by the meter and everything else.

FRETTE HOTEL LINEN OUTLET
Via Visconti di Modrone 15

In bed linen, Frette has two different consumer lines: an everyday, rather average line that I don't find particularly special, and an upscale line meant to compete with Pratesi. There is a third line, from the hotel division, which makes sheets for many of the world's 5-star palace hotels (like the Ritz in Paris and the Four Seasons in New York). This division has an outlet store right in the heart of town; don't miss it if you enjoy the outlet rummage.

The outlet store is actually the employees' store right in the office building. You enter the building and then hang a left into the shop, where things are in boxes, on shelves, and on a few racks. As at all outlets, it's hit or miss. No one speaks English; no credit cards. Much of what you see has been made for the hotel business. Prices are excellent compared with the quality of the goods. Besides bed linen, there are bathrobes, etc.

The outlet shop is not far from the Jolly President Hotel and is worth the adventure even though you may come up empty-handed.

There is another Frette outlet in the suburbs (Via Vittorio Veneto 45, Concerezzo; ☎ 02/606-93-90) that has everything and is not confined to the hotel line, as is this resource. For more on out of town outlets, see "Beyond Milan," at the end of this chapter.

LISA CORTI
See "Home Style/Showrooms" earlier in this chapter.

MAGLI
Via Manzoni 14

Warning: Bruno Magli is a Bologna-made shoe source that does not really believe in outlets; this store is in retail space and doesn't feel all that permanent. But it's right in the heart of the shopping district, so what the heck? If they are closed when you get there, please let me know.

Orphan shoes and leather goods go here to be sold off; the shoes and bags weren't too impressive, but the leather jackets at $200 each were to kill for. Maybe I'm just annoyed that they didn't have shoes for big feet. Who knows, you could get lucky.

Paper Goods

FABRIANO
Via Verri 3

The new kid in town—and all the big Italian cities—Fabriano is a modern graphics gallery of paper goods with adorable and very chic squiggles: a pair of shoes, or a hat, pasta, espresso in a cup. Among the best gifts: the tiny folding notebooks that fit into a pocket or handbag and cost about 12,000L.

PINEIDER
Corso Europe 13

Italy's most famous name in paper goods and old-fashioned, heavy-duty, richer-than-thou stationery is Pineider, with stores in every major city. The Milan shop is right near Piazza San Babila.

Perfume

For the most part, perfume is expensive in Italy, and you must be smart to catch a bargain, so buy at the airport duty-free or in La Rinascente, where you get a 10% discount at the checkout counter if you show your passport. There are several branches of the enormous German chain **Douglas** dotted around the main shopping districts: You may want to ask about their Douglas Card, which can be used in any of their stores worldwide and will bring you extra perks. If you are a fan of the scent **Acqua Di Parma,** note they have their first freestanding store, Via Gesù 3. If money is no object, pop into **Profumo,** Via Brera 6, where American and English imports are sold at higher prices than you are used to.

Secondhand Fashion

I spent a day touring many of Milan's tony secondhand shops because this form of alternate retail is so important in Paris and New York. I wish I could say this was great, that I bought stuff, or I think you'll want to do it, too. I am listing the best shops, but with the understanding that this kind of shopping is very hit or miss, you are on your own.

L' Armadio di Laura
Via Voghera 25

This is by far the largest and the best, but it is a bit out of the way, although the woman there when I was shopping (who speaks English perfectly) said that most people come on the metro. The area is industrial; the building is frightening on first approach—only because everything is unfamiliar. You press the button on the console, enter the gate, cross the courtyard and enter through a door slightly to your right, at maybe one o'clock on the clock system of direction-giving.

The store smells like used clothes; it's the same musty smell all of these stores have, but it's not a dirty clothes smell. Designer clothes are packed into racks; there are some shoes and handbags and accessories. There are some sizes larger than 46. (Thank God!) Hours are Tuesday through Saturday 10am to 6pm; in summer the store is also open on Monday.

Mercatini Michela
Croso Venezia 8 at San Babila

I like this store because it's easy to get to and has very expensive clothes. I've never bought anything, but it's easy to pop up (the store is upstairs in an office building) and check. Sometimes you can find Pucci. They do a big business in wedding gowns.

Shoes & Leather Goods

Shoe shops obviously abound with shoes in just about all price ranges. The greatest problem with cheap shoes is that they wear out more quickly than well-made shoes. You can stick to brand-name shoes in Milan, or explore some of the low-cost no-names—it's all here. No-name shoes start at about $30 a pair. Better no-name shoes cost $50 a pair. Just wander the middle-class neighborhoods where real people shop.

In expensive shoes, there are two completely different schools of thought: English-style, conservative, country classics that you wear for 20 years, and high-fashion fluff bundles that will last only a season or two but will signal the world that you are a major player.

Please note that I have listed several of the big-name leather goods firms under "Italian Big Names," above, because they are more or less icons in the business and most of them also have clothing lines. The following names are not as famous in the U.S., but they deserve attention while you are studying the scene in Milan.

FRATELLI FIGINI
Via Spadari 3

This is a source for locals but is known throughout the world for simple, well-made, excellent shoes for men and women. Prices are slightly less than those of some of the more famous names. If you care for the quality of the shoe, not the fame of the brand, this is an excellent resource.

HOGAN
Via della Spiga 22

The casual shoe division of Tod's, Hogan is a cult shoe little known in the U.S., with weekend shoes and boots for men and women. Hey, if it's good enough for Princess Caroline of Hanover (also Monaco, you know, Grace's girl) you might want to check it out.

REDWALL
Corso Matteotti 7

Redwall is the manufacturer of various designer accessory lines, which they are allowed to sell in their own retail stores, which happen to be opening up all over the world. One of their biggest names is Moschino, but there are other names, from the internationally famous to the not-famous-at-all.

SUPERGA
Via San Pietro all'Orto 11

Don't let the address throw you. This is in the Montenapo area and is worth seeing and doing, believe me. First of all, to spare you the stuttering and suffering I went through, I will give you a pronunciation lesson. Despite the fact that you immediately see the word "super" in the name, forget it. Instead, say *sueperga, grazie:* now you've got it.

Superga has stores in all major Italian cities; the flagship in Milan is relatively new, very hot, and really worth looking at. I first found the line because I saw shoes I wanted for my 6-year-old niece, but they were above my budget. Still, they have great designs for kids and adults in casual shoes, sneakers, and sports shoes. The line is expanding like mad, with stores to be launched all over the world. You heard it here first.

If you knew the line before, when it was just a sneaker source, check it out again because they have all sorts of platforms, glossy patent-leather running shoes, and *fashionista* must-haves.

TANINO CRISCI
Via Montenapoleone 3

This maker of classic styles for men and women does not have the problem of the shoes wearing out—in fact, the main reason locals buy this brand is that the shoes actually look better as they age. Prices are very high, but the goods are worth the investment. Prices are lower in Italy.

VALEXTRA
Piazza San Babila 1

Known throughout Italy for their colored leather goods, this store will sell you a handbag to go with your Joseph's coat of many colors. This is a status brand with inventive designs that aren't over the top.

VICINI
Via della Spiga 1

Relatively new to retail, Vicini used to make shoes for other designer firms before opening their own stores, which are just beginning to go global. (Been to Cyprus lately? Saint Petersburg maybe?) The store is small, the shoes are stunning and very expensive. Vicini is sold in the U.S. at Neiman's and Bergdorf's.

Sporting Goods

BRIGATTI
Corso Venezia 15

Located on the edge of the Golden Triangle, Brigatti is a giant of a store, with floor-to-ceiling wood paneling, wide stairways, and stock-filled cabinets that are higher than three men. They carry all major brands, plus a wide selection of no-names. Tons of Fila. You really do not need another sportswear listing in Milan: This is where you find the colored gear you've seen on TV during Olympic telecasts.

DANZA
Corso Europa at Via Cavallotti

For exercise and dance buffs, this store (there are several branches around town) offers exciting looks (and colors) that you won't find back home. Prices can be stiff, but you'll be the only one in your aerobics class in the outfit. Buy dance and exercise togs for men, women, and even children. This large store is conveniently at the end of Via Durini.

PETER SPORT
Piazza Liberty 8

Around the corner from the Duomo, Peter Sport is my backup or control store for sporting goods and active sportswear. I prefer to load up at Brigatti, but I always check here to make sure I'm not missing out on anything. Peter Sport has three levels, a creaky elevator, and more stuff than you could ever dream of wearing, even if you are a professional athlete.

Tabletop & Gifts

HABITAT
Corso Vercelli 10; Piazza Diaz (across from the Duomo); Corso XXII Marzo 25 (near Il Salvagente)

Habitat is what the locals consider a moderately priced store. (We remind you that nothing in Italy is moderately priced.) Still, you may find some gift items here, or at least be able to pick up on the latest Italian design trends. Worth a visit for those who are into design.

HIGH TECH
Piazza XXV Aprile 12

By Milan standards, High Tech is an enormous place. The second floor of this two-story selling space is completely devoted to home furnishings, all with the look we've come to associate with the city of Milan. Begun by Aldo Cibic, formerly of Memphis Milano fame.

IMMAGINAZIONE
Via Brera 16

As always, the Via Brera is a great place for finding new, hot looks. This shop is no exception—it's crammed full of weird but wonderful stuff, including tableware, gift items, and cuff links.

LISA CORTI
See "Home Style/Showrooms," earlier in this chapter.

LORENZI
Via Montenapoleone 9

After you finish with plastics, head to Milan's head cutlery store, where you can also buy pipes and other gifts and gadgets for men.

MOLIGNONI & C.
Corso Porta Vittoria 47

If you bemoan the fact that Milan is so sophisticated it's hard to find any country wares, you'll be delighted to find this pottery shop, which sells various *faenza* (faience) patterns in everything from plates and platters to jars, lamps, and small gifts. The selection is large, and the location good—only the hours are a little unusual. This store opens at 9am (few do) and closes at 1pm for lunch, then doesn't reopen until 4pm, a little later than most shops. If you are in need of Italian ceramics and faience, you'll be hard-pressed to find another convenient source in Milan.

MORONIGOMMA
Via Braccio da Montone (at Via Giusti)

This store has plastics from all over the world, so don't buy any of the expensive American products. Instead, get a load of the Italian designer vinyl, the car products, and the household items.

With its affordable prices, this may be the only store in Milan where you can go wild and not be sorry the next day. It's conveniently located at the start of Via Montenapoleone, on the far side of the Piazza San Babila; there are many other wonderful design hangouts in the area.

RICHARD GINORI
Corso Giacomo Matteotti 1; Via Dante 9/11; Via Panfilo Castaldi 42

The Richard Ginori store in Milan is large and fancy, with parquet floors and the atmosphere of a fancy china shop. Ginori has a wide selection, not only of its own designs, but of every major maker—Lalique, Baccarat, Aynsley, etc. Prices are outrageously high; you may do much better at a U.S. discount source or catalog.

However, Ginori wants to please. They offer free delivery to local hotels and help with applying for an IVA tax refund.

SHED
Viale Umbria 42

This former cheese factory has furniture designs from French big names as well as Italian and Japanese movers and shakers. A must-do for those with an eye for design—even if you don't buy a thing. Furthermore, the location is within walking distance of my trusty clothing discounter Il Salvagente.

TAD
Via di Croce Rossa 1

Despite an unfamiliar-sounding address, this is in the heart of the Montenapo area and right near the metro station. (How else would I find it?) Tad is a store filled with ideas, so even if you don't buy anything, stop by and stare. Multilevel shop with candles, gifts, some home furnishings, etc.

Teens

Teens need no specific addresses; just plop them onto Corso Buenos Aires. Or, try these specialty label stops.

DIESEL STORE
Galleria San Carlo at San Babila

All the Diesel products (way beyond jeans) as well as a Style Lab; teen heaven.

ENERGIE
Via Torino 19

The superstore for the Miss Sixty brand of hot fashion and jeans.

ONYX
Corso Vittorio Emanuele 11 and 24

Cheap thrills and an amazing scene filled with technology and great clothes at great prices, sort of the local version of H&M.

MILAN ON A SCHEDULE

TOUR 1: MILANO PRONTO

No time to go shopping? You're traveling with a man who paces in front of stores and makes you nuts? You're between business meetings and only have an hour to yourself? For your Milan visit, may I suggest this spree:

1. Begin at the Galleria and walk briskly through it, pausing to look at the ceiling, to stare at the original Prada, and maybe to dash into Rizzoli for guidebooks in English . . . and maybe a hat for him at Borsolino . . . and something wonderful for you at Prada—the fur-lined sleeping bag, perhaps. Cut through the mall, heading to your right to La Scala, and hit the Via Verdi at a brisk pace: Now you are headed toward the Brera district.

2. After the Via Verdi changes names to become the Via Brera, begin window-shopping until you get to Via Fiori Chiari, which comes up on your left. You are now in the most charming neighborhood in Milan; it's so beautiful that you don't even

need to go into the antiques shops. But you may. Just don't ignore the old buildings, the narrow doorways, the painted shutters, the flowers . . . then you get to Lush (no. 7): It's British, not Italian but with an Italian accent, and so much fun you must indulge.

3. Stroll a few short blocks until you get to an alley on your right. Turn into it, then look left in the middle of the block and enter Etro, one of the seats of Italian luxury goods. The store's front is on the Via Pontaccio, which runs parallel to Fiori Chiari, but the doors to get into this three-part store are on this side alley. They have a newer store on Via Montenapoleone, but the fragrance store is here, and this part is small, charming, and fabulous to sniff around.

4. When you leave Etro, backtrack and cross the Via Fiori Chiari and head on to Via Madonnina, continuing to window-shop. Merge onto Via Mercato, then veer toward the Duomo to the famous gourmet food store Peck (Via Spadari 9). Didn't Mother tell you the way to a man's heart was through his stomach? Buy something fattening and eat it while you walk, or buy a total picnic and take it to the Castle. Peck has several shops in the area, including a sit-down restaurant, Peck Rosticceria (Via Cantu 3), and a wine shop, Bottega del Vino (Victor Hugo 4). There are other food shops in this warren of streets, including a little supermarket.

Wander from here to the Duomo, about a block away, and light a candle that you got to go shopping at all. Didn't buy much? Well, maybe next time. If you didn't eat lunch at Peck or want to continue the tour, you can grab a bite at the cafe at La Rinascente and then shop this department store. You can then amble along the Corso Vittorio Emanuele II and grab hold of the tony Montenapo area (see next section).

TOUR 2: BIG NAMES TO BARGAINS: ALL-DAY TOUR

This tour is best done as a walking trip, so wear comfortable shoes and carry your high heels in your tote bag, because you'll want them for trying on clothes when you get to the bargains. Of course, you may end up buying a new pair of shoes before you get to the bargains, but better safe than sorry. I bought three pair last time I wandered around this part of town.

With a whole day at your disposal, you can see the best of two worlds: Milan's Golden Triangle of designer shops and Milan's best discounters, where you buy the clothes you saw in the Golden Triangle at better prices.

1. Begin your day in the high-fashion district of Via Montenapoleone, lovingly called Montenapo, the main drag of the Golden Triangle where most of the major designers have boutiques that are downright amazing.

    Start with Montenapo itself, then hit the side streets. The streets to prowl are: Via Sant' Andrea, Via Gesù, Via Santo Spirito, Via Borgospesso, and Via della Spiga. About half of the stores on these streets are internationally known, designer-related shops; the others are small, but chic, local treasures devoted to jewelry, antiques, children's clothes, or leather goods.

    Concentrate on Italian names because the French ones are way too expensive. If you need a break, stop for coffee at the Four Seasons Hotel, which is in a convent on Via Gesù and has a small indoor cafe overlooking the garden.

2. When finished with the Montenapoleone area, walk toward San Babila and the resale shop Michela (Corso Venezia 8 at San Babila). Perhaps your bargain shopping will start here. If you don't get lucky, not to worry.

3. Now head toward the Duomo on Corso Vittorio Emanuele II from San Babila. Be sure to stop at La Rinascente (located right at Piazza del Duomo). There are some snack shops on the corso for a quick bite: Paper Moon is not far away if you want the truly chic shopper's lunch, or you can stay at La Rinascente and go upstairs to its cafe and have a sandwich and a view of the Duomo and a small bite of heaven.

4. Refreshed from lunch and maybe a nap, you're now ready to explore the bargains part of this tour. If you are doing this as one big walk—it's possible, but grueling—make sure you've already been to La Rinascente before you reach Via Durini, because you will be walking in the other direction as you head for the bargains at Il Salvagente. Or, grab a cab and ask for Via Fratelli Bronzetti 16.

5. Pass between the iron gates (yes, you are in the right spot), and go into the courtyard and through the doorway to your left. Shop till you drop—and then some. Call for a taxi to drive you back to your hotel; you should be too loaded down to walk. Way to go! Congrats!

MILANO MAGIC TOUR

As I've said, I've come to love Milan in a new way, and I know it's because of my adoration for the combination of the street market I call San Agostino (see "Markets," earlier in this chapter) and the bargains to be had in Como, which I do together in a Monday-Tuesday, one-two shopping punch.

When scheduling a trip, I arrange to be in Milan on a Sunday (my travel day) so that Monday I can wake up ready to go to Como. Milan has little retail on Monday, and can be depressing, as can all of Italy on a Monday. The trip to Como is possibly the best Monday morning activity you will find anywhere in Italy.

BEYOND MILAN

. . . .

Lake Como Area

GETTING THERE

If you have a train pass, count out your usage, because it's a waste of money to use one of your travel days for the trip to Como. I bought myself a round-trip, first-class ticket for about

$15. I bought it at the ticket counter in Milan's Centrale station; the transaction was in Italian, so I didn't get too much of what was happening.

The ticket was marked "via Monza," and I panicked that I would have to make a connection in Monza—I did not.

The ride was a simple 20 minutes on a commuter train—nothing to it. On my last trip, I booked a car and driver from Europe Car Service (see p. 189) for a half-day and 150km (93 miles). The cost was about $200, which I thought was more than fair.

Arriving in Como

The train station (**Como San Giovanni**) is nice: There's a tourist office window to answer questions, a map of the area posted in the hallway, and many free brochures. There's also a news agent and a bar.

Out front, you'll find a line of taxis and vans with, finally, some English-speaking help. I hired a taxi for the morning to take me around and wait for me. I was told that the flat fare from the train station to the **Ratti** outlet was a mere 10,000L! You can also get a taxi to drop you at Ratti for 10,000L and come pick you up at the agreed-upon time or when you call. Get your driver's radio number (or Ratti will get you a taxi).

The town proper is located below the train station, within walking distance. However, if you've come on a Monday, most of the town will be closed in the morning, so you might as well head first to your hotel (if you are staying for a while) or the silk outlets.

Sleeping in the Como Area

Grand Hotel Villa Serbelloni
Lake Como, Bellagio

I call this the poor man's Villa d'Este, but it's almost as grand and posh and fancy and swell. Rooms can be booked with half board or full board; rates differ with the seasons. This hotel is open year-round. Bellagio is on a higher point of land at the middle of the lake, about 30km (19 miles) from Como, and, therefore, farther north from Milano.

Like the Villa d'Este, this hotel is a palace, with gorgeous rooms, a fine kitchen, and a health and beauty center. The Serbelloni family once lived here (but, of course); it became a hotel in 1872. You can book apartments by the week (the week always begins on a Saturday) or on a daily basis in winter.

Considering all this grandeur, the hotel is approximately $250 for a double in low season and $300 in high season. To make reservations from the U.S., call ☎ **800/233-6620**. Local phone ☎ 031/95-02-16; fax 031/95-15-29.

Villa d'Este
Via Regina 40, Lake Como, Cernobbio

Look at any list of the ten most famous hotels in the world, and you will undoubtedly see this one. The grand hotel was created from a 16th-century palace in 1873 and has stayed grand ever since. There are several places to eat here, if you just want to gander a look while you are in the area. Or maybe you just want to sink into the new spa.

The hotel is 5 minutes from the Como train station and minutes from the Swiss border; it's about 40 minutes from Milan. Please note that this is a seasonal business—the hotel is open from March through November. Doubles begin around $400.

In the U.S., book through **Leading Hotels of the World** (☎ **800/223-6800**). Local phone ☎ 031/34-81; fax 031/34-88-44.

The Shopping Scene

The town of Como was the center of the medieval silk industry. (Como no longer has its own worms.) It's at the southern end of Lake Como, about 50km north of Milan, and offers all the charm you want in a teeny, old-fashioned village on the edge of a lake surrounded by forest and Switzerland.

The town caters to the wealthy landowners who live in the villas surrounding the lake as well as to the merely rich and/or fashionable who stop by for the weekend (as Gianni Versace used to do). There are also loads of day-trippers and visitors, many of whom are visiting from Switzerland.

Best buys in the village shops are in clothes, silk scarves, and leather goods. While you'll find lots of antiques, most of them are fakes or reproductions. If you love it, and the price is right, who cares? Remember that U.S. Customs wants an item to be 100 years old or older for you to bring it back into the country duty-free.

If you love fabrics, you owe yourself a visit to **Seterie Moretti** (Via Garibaldi 69), located right on Como's main square, on the corner of Via Galio and Via Garibaldi. The shop was closed on Monday morning when I got there! They do open on Monday afternoon, however.

Seterie Moretti distributes signed fabrics to retail sources such as Galtrucco in Milan and Liberty in London. They retain the screens and rerun them without the designer name and with a slight variation in design. As a result, you get fabrics that look familiar, but are slightly different. There are five rooms of fabrics at Moretti. They speak English and accept credit cards.

Another silk maker is **Mantero,** with a showroom at Via Volta 68. The business was run by eight brothers about a hundred years ago—the firm actually produces wool, cotton, and silk. The silk comes from China (as does much Italian silk) but is screened in Italy; it's the ability of the craftspeople who work the screens that makes Italian silk so famous these days. Get a look at Mantero's silk scarves—you will go wild. I have recently begun buying them, about $250 each (regular retail, not at the outlet) for the huge shawl size. Rumor has it this firm makes the silk screens for Hermès.

Not only are there house designs (nice botanical prints), but also goods that have been licensed by designers such as Chanel, Ferré, and Saint Laurent. Not bad, eh? I bought Richard a Ferré tie for $45 that was so sophisticated I could have wept: whites and beiges and grays with seashells in a row. There was a scarf, the type I like, for about $200 but it wasn't the one I wanted so I gave it up. Later I found what I wanted for only $50 more in a regular retail store. Undoubtedly, this outlet has the most sophisticated merchandise, but the discounts are not huge, so don't panic if they don't have what you want.

These two stores are in the "downtown" Como area and are within walking distance.

The downtown also has cute stores, although no big designer names. I was fond of the local branch of **Standa**.

The star of the area, however, is **Ratti** (Via Cernobbio, ☎ 031/23-32-62). The shop is at the base of the estate of an old villa that is not visible from the road. However, it is on the main road right off the lake, so it's not far at all.

Your taxi driver knows his way here blindfolded. If you are driving yourself, ask for directions—but this is a no-brainer (thank heavens).

You will have no trouble getting in, although because no one here speaks English, having an Italian-speaking driver will make you feel less tense and could be a great morale-builder.

The Ratti outlet store has two rooms jam-packed with the goodies you want to buy—from men's ties and women's silk scarves, to pillows, handbags, blouses, and even bolts of fabric. When I went, there were tons of Etro bathrobes, bolts of Versace fabrics, and enough ties to make you swoon. Now then, about prices: They are cheap, but not dirt-cheap. I paid $40 for designer ties. I'm talking big-name designer ties, but, nonetheless, Filene's Basement frequently has the same names for $30. I estimate that if you are a keen shopper, you could happily spend a couple of hours here. But you can also do it in 10 minutes. It depends on the stock and your style.

MORE OUTLETS NEAR COMO

EMPORIO DELLA SETTA
Via Canturina 190, Como

The Emporium of Silk sounds pretty good, huh? Many big designer names are represented in this clearinghouse for silk from the local mills. Discounts in the 40% range. There are seasonal sales in January and July to add to your savings. Local phone ☎ 031/59-14-20.

Mantero
Via Volta 68, Como

Note that this factory is closed Saturday and Sunday. Regular hours are 9:30am to 12:30pm and 2 to 6pm. They do take credit cards, showing just how sophisticated they are. Besides their own distinct line of silks and scarves and ties, there are big-name designer goods as well. You will die and go to heaven; this is the thrill of a lifetime. Local phone ☎ 031/27-98-61.

Seterie Martinetti
Via Torriani 41, Como

By now you surely know that *seterie* means silk maker in Italian. This is rumored to be one of the best silk resources in the area, although there are so many good ones that it is hard to qualify them all. You'll find the usual scarves, ties, robes, and yummy items from the usual cast of international big-name designers. Closed on Monday morning. Local phone ☎ 031/26-90-53.

Past Como

Not far from Como, you find yourself in Switzerland, headed toward Lugarno. But don't panic, you're also on the way to **FoxTown,** which is a 5-minute drive into Switzerland across the Italian border. So what? FoxTown is an outlet village with 140 stores, a casino (for husbands, no doubt), and a cafe. There's quite a large number of big-name designer outlets here, including **Gucci, Prada, Nike, Diesel, and Versace.**

For specific directions, call ☎ 410/848-828-888. They are open 7 days a week, 11am to 7pm nonstop. If you are driving, you want the Mendriso exit, which is 7km (4.3 miles) from the Swiss-Italian border; www.foxtown.ch.

Remember Armani

For those with cars and a spirit of adventure, head over to the new Armani outlet at the Intai factory, near Bregnano (which is between Milan and Como). Take the Autostrada/A9 to the Como exit and head for Bregnano; look for the factory at the crossroad of SS35. For more specific directions, call ☎ **031/88-73-73**. The shop is closed on Monday; otherwise, the hours are 10am to 1pm and 2 to 7pm. They accept credit cards.

Parabiago

Parabiago is an industrial suburb of Milan, where many of the shoe factories and leather-accessories people have offices. Many consider it within the metro-Milano area, not a day trip, however no public transportation goes here, and when I asked my driving service about getting there, they made it clear they considered it out of town. If you take a car, a taxi, or drive yourself, do remember that even factory stores are closed at lunch.

CLAUDIO MORLACCHI
Via Castelnuovo 24, Parabiago

While you're in Parabiago, stop by Claudio Morlacchi—the factory looks like a house, but don't be alarmed. Push the large wooden door and enter into a light, airy courtyard. To the right is a room with a small but wonderful display of all the shoes the Morlacchi people make. Among Morlacchi's clients are Lanvin and Guy Laroche.

FRATELLI ROSSETTI FACTORY
Via Cantù 24, Parabiago

There is a Fratelli Rossetti boutique in Milan (Via Montenapoleone 1), but why shop there when you can go to the factory in Parabiago? The Rossetti factory has no ads and no markings; it kind of looks like a prison from the outside. The shop is in a separate building from the factory and houses a large selection of men's and women's shoes and boots in a big open room with blue rubber flooring. The shoes are displayed on L-shaped tables. The help does not speak English, but is very friendly. Men's shoes in traditional styles cost $65 a pair; more elaborate slip-ons cost $125; boots range from $100; high-heel pumps begin at $80.

Biella

Biella is a mill town in northern Italy, famous because it is the headquarters of the **Zegna** woolen mills. It's also known for the **Fila** outlet store. Paola, from the Delta flight, gave me this info.

There are other nearby outlets.

ERMENEGILDO ZEGNA
Via Roma 99, Centro Zegna, Trivero

This is the one you've been looking for. This is the really big time of the big time. Of course, price tags—even at discount— can also be big time, but there is no finer or more famous name in Italian wool and cashmere. Trivero is near Biella. They take credit cards, and they are used to tourists and visitors; follow signs to **Centro Zegna**. Local phone ☎ 015/75-65-41.

FILA
Via Cesare Battisti 28, Biella

Here's an exception to factory stores being open on Monday morning—this factory store does open on Monday, but only at 3pm. They close at noon, not 1pm, for lunch daily and reopens at 3pm. Needless to say, Fila is an enormously famous name internationally for sportswear. They are most famous in the U.S. for their tennis gear, but they make clothing and gear for all sports; their ski stuff is sublime. There are bargains for all members of the family, and the store is conveniently located near the cute part of the old city. Local phone ☎ 015/34-141.

FRATELLI PIACENZA LANIFICIO
In Biella

Another cashmere mill. Wools as well; also mohair, which is big this year. There are bargains, but you are still looking at price tags over 1 million lire for a cashmere coat. Rumor has it that Escada gets their goods here. Local phone ☎ 015/614-61. Call for an appointment and directions.

MAGLIFICIO DELLA ARTEMA
Strada Trossi 31, Verrone-Biella

Located right outside Biella, this is yet another cashmere resource from the famous mills; watch for Artema signs. They sell the Zegna line as well as other Italian labels, including some designer names from the big-name circuit—rotating according to availability, of course. They sell everything from underwear to outerwear. Open Tuesday to Saturday, from 9am to noon and 3 to 7pm; closed all day on Monday. Local phone ☎ 015/255-83-82.

Vercelli (Beyond Biella)

Vercelli is actually a province; it includes the city of Biella. It also includes a zillion mills, more known for their wool and cashmere than for silk, but some silken luxuries can be found. Vercelli is about a 2-hour drive (one-way) from Milan, so I didn't go. Let me know how it is if you get there. I did have the concierge call from Milan; he also said that the Loro Piano cashmere factory is nearby.

LANAFICIO LUIGUI COLOMBO
Borgosesia, Vercelli

Chris Columbo discovered America; Carolyn Blain discovered this mill from her friend Yuki. They sell cashmere. That's all I know. Local phone ☎ 0161/45-80-03.

SAMBONET
Via XXVI Aprile 62/64, Vercelli

When I told Logan the saga of my enthusiasm for the cashmere mill and my reluctance to go on a blind trek, she threw
in another nearby resource. From the sublime to the ridiculous, guys, this one sells pots and pans—big-name pots and
pans and stainless and flatware and silverplate, including seconds from Krupp and the Cordon Bleu lines. Local phone
☎ **0161/59-71.**

Toward Turin & Genoa

SERRAVALLE

MacArthur Glen has opened an Italian outlet mall midway
between Milan, Torino, and Genoa. You take the highway A7
to the Serravalle Scrivia exit. The mall is done in the American cutie-pie mall style; it is open seven days a week, nonstop
from 10am until 7pm. There are currently 60 big name outlets; no bus service as we go to press, but MacArthur Glen has
traditionally gotten very organized *after* their mall openings,
so there may be more services as things get going.

Toward Bologna

The people who own the Chelsea outlet malls in the U.S. and
several European outlet malls in partnerships are breaking
ground on an outlet mall outside of Milan on the way to
Bologna. It should open in 2002.

Chapter Nine

······················

NAPLES & THE AMALFI COAST

WELCOME TO NAPLES

···

It's a new world, Golda, and my beloved Faith Willinger says they have cleaned up Naples enormously. She says I should shut up and stop whining about a few taxi cheats, she says then was then and now is now. So I won't tell you my unhappy stories about Naples from visits past. Hmmmm, maybe I will, but later on. Meanwhile, we all have Faith. Keep with Faith, baby.

With Faith writing about Naples for *Travel & Leisure*, and every French travel magazine I read profiling the city as the best of the hidden weekend destinations, I just had to give it another try. After all, any place with palm trees and Ferragamo in the same spot can't be too dangerous to anything besides my credit rating.

So welcome to Naples, where the shopkeepers in some of the stores told me to take off my watches (yes, I do wear two), lest I attract a thief. Welcome to Naples, where the clerks at Ferragamo were not only rude, but refused to redo my tax refund papers when I decided to buy *more*.

Welcome to Naples where I had the best pizza of my life, where I fell madly in love with the scarves at Rubinacci, and where you are less than an hour away from Capri.

Welcome to Naples, Faith's favorite version of Miami Beach, and my idea of what Rome should have been.

NAPLES STATE OF MIND

Many visitors associate Naples as a suburb of Rome, or think the two are related because they are only 2 hours apart on the train. Wrong. Naples is its own kingdom; it has its own dialect, culture, and tradition, and I don't need to tell you, has made its own contributions to the world, from pizza to Sophia Loren.

Naples fits together psychologically with the rest of southern Italy, Sicily, and the islands, but it is so different from Rome that it seems like another country.

GETTING THERE

If you come for the weekend, you may want to fly into Rome and rent a car for the 2-hour drive to Naples; this gives you a car for driving along the Amalfi coast as well. You can also take the train from Rome. The Naples train station is clean, modern, and not frightening.

If you prefer to fly directly into Naples, there are some non-stop flights—especially from large Euro-hub cities. The 2-hour flight from Paris to Naples, round-trip, costs about $300 when bought 7 days in advance with a Saturday night stay.

The Naples airport is small, easy to manage, and a true pleasure. It's about a 20-minute drive into Naples; a 1-hour 10-minute drive to Positano. And don't make a face like that, yes they fly real jets into this airport—there is nothing to be afraid of.

If you arrive by cruise ship, the port (the Maritime Center) is next to the heart of town and well situated for your explorations and adventures. Note that the ferries and hydrofoils to the islands (Capri, Ischia, etc.) use different piers in other parts of town, one alongside the Maritime Center and the other around the bay, about 2 miles away.

Arriving in Naples

While it was a pure pleasure to arrive in the Naples airport, the taxi ride to the hotel left a little to be desired. Actually, the ride itself was fine, and the route most charming. The meter read 27,500L on arrival at the Hotel Vesuvio (about $14). *Then,* the driver said the total cost was 60,000L—this including the surcharge for the luggage and the airport tax.

Need I tell you that there is a surcharge for luggage (all of 1,000L per bag), but none for the airport, and we were cheated? I bet you had already guessed it.

Departing Naples

If you leave from the Naples airport, luggage carts are free, and there is a small mall upstairs for last-minute shopping. There is a duty-free store at the gate-departure area that you know is a joke because there are no non-EU international flights from this airport so duty must legally be charged. Still, if you haven't had time to shop for gifts, there is a good selection.

THE LAY OF THE LAND
....

Naples is an enormous city. On a day trip, you will probably only want to visit the nice shopping areas and the nice hotels, and have a look at the museums, the palm trees, my castle, and the sea. Watch your handbag.

On a weekend, you will feel more like you have seen some of the sights and gotten a grip on where everything is. If you want to visit the islands and perhaps the Amalfi Coast, Naples is easily a 5- to 7-day destination.

If you think of the Castelo and the Hotel Vesuvio as the heart of the world, then the various areas to visit can be read as you tell time: The castle is at 6 o'clock, the Maritime Center is at five o'clock, the Via Constantinople and the National

Museum are at 1 o'clock, the historic old town and street of angels are at 2 o'clock, etc.

Warning

Please be sure to study a map of Naples before you go off on your own. The reason I knew I was being cheated by one of my taxi drivers was that he kept heading in the wrong direction, and I *knew* it was the wrong direction.

Location, Location, Location

Don't forget that part of the charm of Naples is the location—you can get to Pompeii, Sorrento, the entire Amalfi Coast, and Capri very easily. More below.

Information, Please

Check out *Qui Napoli* ("Where Naples") for listings, directions, tourist information, and dates of the monthly flea market at Via Caracciolo. Note that English language guidebooks are scarce in Naples, so you should come prepared or know how to read Italian. *Time Out Naples* is perhaps the best guidebook in English for a thorough view of the city (but it's unlikely that you can find it in a Naples bookstore).

GETTING AROUND

There are taxis at the gates of the Maritime Center; do be clear with taxis about where you are going and vigilant about the use of the meter, as they may attempt to cheat you. One of my favorite scams is that they drive you to the wrong place and then tell you they didn't understand your accent, but meanwhile the meter is running. This happened to me when I asked to be taken to my ship at the Maritime Center and was instead taken in the other direction to the train station. Although I was

Naples

National Museum
Parco di Capodimonte
Via del Capodimonte
OTTOCALLI
CAPODIMONTE
Albergo dei Poveri
ARENACCIA
Orto Botanico
Via Arenaccia
Via Santa Teresa Corso A. di Savoia
Via Vicenzo Troli
Via Miracoli
Via San Michele
Via Ferone
Via Foria
Airport
Capodimonte
Via Salvator Rosa
Via Materdei
Via Stella
PIAZZA CAVOUR M
Via Carbonara
Via S. Antonio Abate
Corso Garibaldi
VASTO
Via Casanova
Corso Novara
Stazione Centrale
Piazza Cavour
Via E. Pessina
Via Sapienza Pisanelli
Il Duomo
Via Tribunali
Piazza Garibaldi
CENTRALE M
Via Vicaria Vecchia
SANTA CHIARA
Piazza Bellini
Piazza S. Domenico
San Gregorio
Corso Umberto I
Corso Garibaldi
Stazione Circumvesuviana
Piazza Dante
Via Biagio dei Librai
Via Duomo
Piazza del Mercato
Via B. Croce
Università
Via Marinella
MONTESANTO
FUNICULAR M
Stazione Cumana
Via Monteoliveto
Via A. Diaz
Corso Umberto I
Via Nuova Marina
Corso Vittorio Emanuele
Via Medina
Via A. Depretis
Via Cristoforo Colombo
Bacino del Piliero
Via Toledo
FUNICULAR
Piazza Municipio
Stazione Marittima
Via S. Carlo
Molo Beverello
Bacino Angiono
Piazza Plebiscito
Via Chiaia
Piazza d. Martiri
Via Morelli
Via S. Luca
Via N. Sauro
To Chiaia & Mergellina
Via Partenope
Golfo di Napoli
Castel dell'Ovo

0   1/4 mi
0   0.25 km

Church
Information ⓘ
Lighthouse
Metro Ⓜ

screaming *"aqua!"* *"mare!"* and *"barco!"* and tapping my driver on the shoulder and pointing in the right direction—he paid no heed.

When we got in our taxi at the hydrofoil station in Naples, on return from Capri, we quickly noticed that the meter wasn't on and began to fuss. The driver said there was a flat fee of 15,000L. Because we had paid 7,000L in a legit cab to get to the hydrofoil, we refused to pay any more.

Outraged, we told our next driver as we got in the cab that we would only pay what was on the meter. Of course, he said. Then he drove us into a traffic jam; then we had to stop for gas (with the meter running, of course); then we had to go around the circle until he found the best place to let us out— it was the most expensive taxi of the trip.

Note that the Maritime Center is a tad to the side of town, and you will not be walking anywhere from there. With the need to start your explorations some place, you may want to direct the taxi to a hotel (see "Sleeping in Naples," later in this chapter) or ask to be dropped right in front of Ferragamo (Piazza dei Martiri 56–60), which will plunk you down in the heart of the luxury shopping.

All hotels can get you a taxi; there are taxi ranks, usually at big squares, where you can usually find a cab when you are out and about. If the driver is honest and goes by the meter, round up the tab as a tip.

To call a radio taxi, dial ☎ 3296. Remember that traffic is fierce during rush hour and can run up the tab on the taximeter.

There is a metro, with two different lines. There are several train stations; one, Centrale, has trains that will take you to Pompeii and as far as Sorrento.

You may also want to book a car and driver for the day; your hotel can do this for you. If you rent a car to drive yourself (concierge can do this for you or you can get one on arrival at the airport), don't try to drive in town. And remember, when driving the Amalfi Drive: no Lemoncello for you!

SLEEPING IN NAPLES

....

EXCELSIOR HOTEL
Via Partenope 48

Location, location, location—although this hotel is almost next door to the Vesuvio, it has a corner location, which means it has three-dimensional views. You owe it to yourself to venture to the roof garden for lunch at La Terrazza and a stare out at the deep blue. Cruise passengers enjoy lunch here—you can even see your ship.

The hotel is more ornate than Vesuvio. Each room is different and is furnished with antiques. The hotel has been refurbished, so if you haven't been here for a few years, fret not.

The hotel is a member of the Luxury Collection and is part of the Starwood family. Local phone ☎ **081/764-01-11**; fax 081/764-97-43; www.elcelsior.it.

GRAND ALBERGO VESUVIO
Via Partenope 45

Although the hotel is more modern than you might be expecting, that means everything works. This is, after all, the Leading Hotel of the city, located right on the Bay of Naples with a view directly to heaven. That is my castle right over there, and nothing thrills me more than this view. Oh yeah, on a clear day you can see Vesuvius.

I also like to hang out in the lobby because this is *the* hotel in town and the one that attracts royalty, presidents, rock stars, opera stars, and where Enrico Caruso himself made history.

There's a new fitness center/spa, you can eat on the rooftop, and you are walking distance from much of the fancy shopping. Do you need more?

Okay, then here's more. One night we were so exhausted that we could not even make it upstairs to the famed culinary restaurant Caruso on the hotel's roof, so we sent out for a pizza. When it arrived, the hotel sent it to room service, which placed each of our pizzas under a silver dome, sent up a table with roses and silver and fine linens, and let us feast.

There are shopping packages as well as a Shopping Fidelity program in which you get a numbered personal card that entitles you to discounts, gifts, or privileges at the city's best shops.

U.S. reservations through Leading Hotels of the World. Local phone ☎ **081/764-00-44**; fax 081/764-44-83; www.lhw.com/vesuvio.

MAJESTIC HOTEL
Large Vasto a Chiaia 68

This is a 4-star hotel, not as grand (or as expensive) as the others but in a great location near the Villa Communale (flea market here once a month) and the upscale shopping neighborhood. The hotel is more like a modern 4-star deluxe; suites include Jacuzzi baths. There are fax and PC outlets in every room. You can also rent videotapes to play in your room. A double room is about $170 with breakfast and taxes included. Local phone ☎ **081/41-65-00**; fax 081/41-01-45; www.majestic.it/impguest.html.

SHOP & SNACK
••

CANTA NAPOLI
Via Chiatamone 36

This is one of my favorite pizza places and casual dining spots; it's great if you have kids with you, too. The walls are painted with the local scenery, the waiters are dressed in costumes, and the pizza is incredible. Located directly behind the hotels Vesuvio, Santa Lucia, and Excelsior. They even have a website you can check out: **www.connect.it/cantanapoli/**.

LA TERRAZZA
Hotel Excelsior, Via Partenope 48

This restaurant serves both lunch and dinner, but I prefer it for lunch because you can see more, although it is indeed romantic at night. Because of the location of the Excelsior hotel, you get a three-sided view of Naples and the Bay of Naples that is breathtaking. The food is good, too. They are open every day, even Sunday. Reservations: ☎ 081/764-01-11; fax 081/764-97-43.

THE SHOPPING SCENE

Shopping in Naples is very different from shopping in other Italian cities. You must remember that you are in the south now (y'all), and the good stuff is hidden, especially from tourists. Therefore the shopping is on various levels, and the truly best stuff is available only to insiders.

I can't say that anyone chooses to come to Naples for the designer shops, but you'll find plenty of places to drop a few dollars, have an ice cream, enjoy the day or the weekend or even the week, and make pleasant memories. Most important, you can buy **Perugina** chocolates and begin to get used to how much coral and fake coral and/or cameos can be yours.

Walking up and down and around the fancy shopping district in Naples is actually a treat. There are gorgeous antiques stores and great places for an afternoon *gelato*. It's a nice, half-day shopping excursion, after which you can eat, quit, or move to secret sources or even museums (all with good gift shops). Note that it takes more than a weekend to have a bespoke suit made.

Shopping Hours

The stores are normally open from 9 or 9:30am to 1:30pm and 4 or 4:30pm to 8pm. Nothing is open on Sunday. On Monday, remember that you are in Italy. That means that nothing is open in the morning, and some things will open around 4 or 4:30pm.

On Saturday in summer, stores will close for the day at 1:30pm, but in winter they do re-open in the afternoon. If you need a pharmacy on a Sunday or on off-hours, there is a listing in the newspaper with the open stores, or your hotel concierge can guide you to an open pharmacy.

Even street markets get going late here, 9am in fine weather. Don't get to a flea market before 9:30am.

Neighborhoods

Maritime Station & Hotel Heaven   Cruise passengers disembark at the clean, modern, safe Maritime Station, right in Naples near the Castel dell'Ovo, a 2,000-year-old fortress which is a monument; a nice touch, adding a little romance to a commercial seaport. There are several shops in the terminal; my favorite is **Taylor,** a tailor shop that obviously lost something in the translation. There are tourist traps (TTs), a newsstand, and some pay phones—it's a good place to buy a postcard or make a phone call. Outside on the quayside, a few vendors sell their wonderful, touristy souvenirs, including Hermès-style scarves for $10. There's also a bank and a currency exchange office.

The port of Naples is just completing a 3-year renovation meant to transform the entire area. Much of the $100 million budget went to commercial services, which will not affect cruise passengers, but there should be some refinements for cruisers, including a more modern cruise terminal, and a nice new statue out front.

While the Maritime Station is not far from the heart of Naples, it's not really within walking distance to anything. There are taxis out front. Naples is a full-time commercial port, so the Maritime Center is not in the middle of nowhere—as in many Italian coastal towns—and for a $5 or $10 taxi ride (going by the meter), you can be taken about any place you want to go.

My personal trick is to take a taxi to a fancy hotel where I will change money (if I have no lire or euros), make phone calls, send faxes or use the business center for e-mail, use the bathroom, and get free tourist literature and maps. The hotels are just down the road from the pier and the Castel dell'Ovo, so I call it Hotel Heaven. You just ask if you can use the services and then pay the rate, which is usually minimal.

I head for either the **Grand Albergio Vesuvio,** Via Partenope 45, or the **Hotel Excelsior,** Via Partenope 48. Obviously, these two are next door to each other—if you are a hotel freak like I am, you may want to look them both over. If you want the Leading Hotel of the World's member, Vesuvio is for you. Excelsior is fancier in many ways and is the Luxury Collection hotel from Starwood. Both hotels have great concierges who will help you with whatever you need. You can walk to all the shopping from these hotels, so that's why it's safe to leave your car here and go on foot. See "Sleeping in Naples," above.

Hotel Heaven (the neighborhood) stretches past these hotels to a series of casual bars, ristorantes, and pizza places—all adorable. Just keep walking, and you'll have your pick.

Castel dell'Ovo   Located directly across the street from the Hotel Vesuvio, the Castel is on a small island, which also houses several adorable alleys for exploring (no shops, sorry) and many restaurants, bars, pizza places, and seafood eateries. It's adorable and great fun.

Luxury Shopping   The main upscale shopping district is a few blocks from the strip of luxury hotels on the waterfront. Just walk along the water (with the castle to your rear) until you come to a clump of palm trees that represent the Piazza Vittorio, turn right, and head "up."

Now it gets slightly tricky as this is a district, and you don't want to miss all the parts—you can, and will, miss part of it if you don't look at a map.

The Via Calabritto is one of the main tony shopping streets (Prada at no. 9) with many of the big-name designers (but not all!). It stretches from the Piazza Vittorio to the Piazza dei Martiri and the large **Ferragamo** shop. **Versace** is down the street from Ferragamo. You get the drift. There's a chunk of big names in a nugget right here.

There are a few side streets off the Piazza dei Martiri that will make you feel like you're in Italy; there are some antiques shops located down the Via Domenico Morelli.

The area is not without charm. Equally charming is the fact that you then easily segue to the Via dei Mille and Via Gaetano Filangieri, which have the rest of the luxury shops—**Bulgari, Zegna, Hermès, Frette,** etc.

Via Chiaia This is a real-people shopping street that's between the luxury shopping district and Via Roma. Use it to cross over from one neighborhood to the other or to get to Via dei Mille—it's all an easy walk. Shopping-wise, there's very little to distract you. Italy-wise, it's great fun.

Via Roma The Via Roma is the commercial heart of town; it is called Via Toledo lower down and becomes Via Roma near Piazza Dante. This street stretches for 2 miles from the Piazza del Plebiscito, right near the Maritime Station, through the center of town, passing the Piazza Carita on its way to the Piazza Dante and then ending near the National Museum.

Centro Antico The core of the old town (*centro antico*) includes the famous Via San Gregorio Armend—this is the street of angels, where all the miniatures and *presepios* (crèches) are made. But don't look for Via San Gregorio Armend on your map, as it's a small area around the church of the same name. Instead you want to find the rectangular area between the Piazza del Gesu and Piazza Dante, reaching over to the Duomo as its other border. The main streets for shopping, gawking, sightseeing, and absorbing the soul of Naples are Via Croce and Via Tribunali. Via Croce will change its name a few times, so fret not. The area is part of a living history, outdoor-museum program that labels the buildings and tells you the path to walk (and shop).

Port Alba Adjacent to the old town, you find the Port Alba, a medieval doorway that leads to a million bookstores. Just beyond this is the Via Constantinopli, filled with antiques shops. Once a month there is an outdoor flea market on the weekend (except in August); see the next section, "Antiques & Flea Markets."

Antiques & Flea Markets

FIERA ANTIQUAIRA NAPOLETANA
Via Caracciolo

This one is a little tricky, as there is often confusion about the dates; we were sent on the wrong weekend by knowledgeable people, and the listing in *Dove* magazine was equally unclear. Luckily you can call the market offices directly and get the dates for the year (☎ **081/62-19-51**).

A weekend event, the fair is considered the best in southern Italy; it runs from 8am to 2pm.

MOSTRA MERCATO CONSTANTINOPOLI
Via Constantinopli

A weekend fair never held on the same weekend as the other fair (Via Caracciolo, see below), this is a more casual event in the street of antiques shops with dealers set up on sidewalk and under tents. Don't bother going if the weather is bad. For dates call ☎ **0347/486-37-15** or e-mail antiquario@ tightrope.it.

Local Heroes

MARINELLA'S
Riviera di Chiaia 287

This itty-bitty tie shop is one of the most famous addresses in Naples. Come holiday season there are lines stretching down the street, no ties in stock, and shoppers are issued chits, which they gift wrap to present. The store creates custom ties, as long, short, wide, or thin as you want or need.

MARIANO RUBINACCI
Via dei Mille 1

If you shop Capri, you may know this name—Mariano's sister has a small shop in Capri that sells cottons and cashmeres.

But the shop in Naples is large, sells designer clothes, and offers a sort-of-Ralph Lauren–local-preppy look, complete with a series of silk scarves that would make Mr. Dumas-Hermès weep with envy. The scarves depict various scenes in Neapolitan history or geography or iconography and are sold in some hotel and museum gift shops as well. Prices vary depending on the difficulty of the silk screen and range from $140 to $200. The best luxury souvenir in town.

MAXI HO
Via Nisco 20 & 23; Riviera di Chiaia; Piazza dei Martiri; Via dei Mille 32; Via Cimarosa 85; Via Luca Giordino 28

Despite its silly sounding name, this is one of the best stores in Naples. The various addresses are mostly in the luxury district and are not branches of the same store, but extensions of the store selling different looks. Each store sells a different group of designer brands geared for a certain look or age group.

Note: To get to the Via Cimarosa and Giordino shops you must take the funicular from Piazza Amedeo to Piazza Fuga—a fun adventure.

UPIM
Via Nisco 11

Upim is a chain of dime stores, famous throughout Italy. There is a branch right in the heart of the fine shopping, a two-level store with tons of clothes, home fashions, and even underwear. I buy a lot of La Perla copies at Upim and love them; **www.upim.it.**

Shoppers Beware

Whether you are on your own or on a ship tour, you may be taken to "factories" to go shopping—be careful, they may or may not offer the real thing, or real deals. They certainly offer kickbacks to your guide.

POMPEII

. . . .

I never got to Pompeii—I fell in love with the hypermarket Citta Mercato. My friend Carla tells me that locals prefer the Carrefor, but that is a French chain located closer to the airport. In Pompeii, there's also a McDonald's nearby. Besides, the shopping in Pompeii is, uh, dying out . . . .

If you are out and about and near Pompeii, you will want to visit Torre del Greco, about 10km (6 miles) west (on N18), which is the cameo city. The most famous place here is **Basilio Liverino** (☎ 081/881-12-25), which sells directly to fine jewelers (Bulgari is a client) but will sell directly to you if you are a serious shopper and book an appointment ahead of time. The more touristy resource is **Giovanni Apa,** at 1 Via de Nicola (☎ 081/881-11-55), but you can ask for Bruno Gia who speaks English.

CAPRI

. . . .

Welcome to Capri

I'm told that many *garmentos* in the bathing suit and lingerie business go to Capri for a few days each season to see what everyone is wearing (or not wearing, as the case may be), and that many American styles originate from here. Indeed, Capri got its reputation as one of the original havens for the rich and the famous.

In Capri, I'm always too busy with the jewelry stores, the sandals, the latest incarnations of Tod's shoes and handbags, the cottons and the cashmeres, and even the lemons to get to the beach or to notice who's not wearing what.

Capri is a shopping port . . . Capri is a shopping day trip . . . Capri is a spree.

So welcome to a town that has streets that are more like alleys, where you stroll in total contentment, remembering Jackie

Kennedy . . . and places to get lost and found. Welcome to one of the major TTs in the world (Blue Grotto); welcome to the kind of place where you can buy lemon booze, ride in a convertible '57 Chevy stretch (with fins), buy plastic pens with your name on them in Italian, or sink deeply into **Gucci, Prada, Fendi, Hermès,** and all the better names of international and Italian fashion.

Getting There

You may arrive by cruise ship (and tender ashore) or by hydrofoil from Naples, Amalfi, Sorrento, or another port or resort town. Regardless of how you actually arrive, you'll land near the funicular that takes you up to Capri proper. Sunglasses, please. If you have luggage, there are porters at the pier. They happen to be very honest, so don't fret.

Although I usually get to Capri via cruise ship, on my last visit I took the hydrofoil from Naples. The trip lasts about 45 minutes, costs $10 each way, and is most pleasant if you are on a larger vessel with space around you. There's a ferry or hydrofoil almost every hour; they all arrive at the same place in Capri but do depart from different stations in Naples depending on which line you book.

SECRET SOURCE

If you want a private boat to take you to Capri, contact **Gianni Chervatin,** former GM of the Grand Hotel Quisiana in Capri, who arranges jet set details for the rich and famous (☎ 081/ 837-68-95). There is a public hydrofoil every half-hour in season.

The Lay of the Land

The island of Capri is rather big and has much more to it than just the resort town of Capri. From a serious shopping perspective, you can skip Anacapri.

In fact, I think you'll be surprised at the sprawl of downtown Capri. Best yet, a lot of it is hidden in back alleys, so take some time to look at a map. If you follow the main tourist trail, you'll miss the best stuff.

Getting Around

You can get up to the town of Capri very easily by funicular; it's 3,600L round-trip out of season. It's possible that the price goes up in season. When you alight from the funicular, you are standing in the Piazza Umberto. The main square of the town, which is mostly a cafe and a church, is a few feet away. The town of Capri itself is rather compact—you can walk everywhere.

If you want to explore Anacapri, the town bus station is about 100m (300 ft.) past the funicular station in downtown Capri. Be advised that it is a narrow road with a lot of hairpin turns.

The Shopping Scene

It's not Rome, but as cruise ports go, Capri ain't bad. There are a lot of stores and a sprinkling of designer shops—small branches of **Prada, Gucci, Fendi, Ferragamo, Malo, Albertti Ferretti, Exte, Tod's, Ferragamo, Hermès,** etc. I've heard a rumor that Cartier will close, but they were there when I visited recently.

As a beach town, Capri has become famous for its sandals, and there are scads of no-name shops selling the latest looks, as well as copies of the latest looks.

There are several *profumeri* (perfume shops). Each one carries several brands on an exclusive basis, but no single shop carries every brand. If you inquire about a brand a store doesn't carry, the clerk is likely to try to trade you over to the brand they sell, rather than tell you to walk down the street or around the corner. There is also lemon perfume.

The emphasis in Capri is on high-quality goods and cheap sandals; the resort fashions are very body-revealing, in the southern Italian style. Note that the style of goods and the shopping experience is so totally different from Positano that there is virtually no overlap.

SHOPPING HOURS

Stores open around 9 to 9:30am and close at 1pm, although more and more are staying open during lunch. Those that close will reopen around 3:30pm and stay open until 7pm. Big names tend to be open nonstop.

The TTs down by the port usually stay open during lunch and are often open until 8pm in the summer.

Stores are open on Sunday.

Note that the season begins March 15 and ends October 15; most stores are closed out of season. It's not unusual for the same owners to have a similar shop in Cortina or another Italian ski resort for the winter season.

The Best Buys in Capri

Cottons & Cashmeres   Despite the heat, cashmere is one of the leading lights of Capri. There are several specialty shops that sell premium cashmeres—some of them also sell cottons.

Jewelry   Until I visited Capri and saw its magnificent jewelry, I'd never been one for important (or even real) jewelry. Now, I've been converted. There's a good bit of latitude on price. If you have a few thousand dollars, you may be very happy.

Lemons   We're still in southern Italy, so there's lemon vodka galore. I also buy fresh lemons in the market down near the port.

Shoes   Capri has all sorts of shoe stores, from the fancy **Ferragamo** shop and little hole-in-the-wall stores that sell $30 pairs of sandals to stores that sell **Tod's** and other designer brands. I bought a pair of Tod's for $150 that retailed at the time for $225 in New York, so even with resort prices, you can still save. Tod's cost more than that now, but there's still some savings.

Shopping Neighborhoods

Marina Grande   This is where your ship's tender or your ferry or hydrofoil comes to port; on the pier, there's a Customs office and a pushcart vendor selling fresh fruit in newspaper cones and ices. You'll also find several TTs teeming with Blue Grotto souvenirs, a liquor store, a mini-mart, and the funicular, which takes you up to Capri proper.

CAPRI

I divide downtown Capri into several neighborhoods, just to make sure you know what's available:

Main Street Capri   Capri has two main streets, Via Vittorio Emanuele and Via Camarelle. The former dead-ends to the latter when you hit the **Hotel Quisisana.** If you are facing the hotel from Via Vittorio Emanuele, bear left to explore Via Camarelle.

The island's toniest shops can be found here, selling everything from antiques and jewelry to expensive resortwear and affordable sandals.

Back Street Downtown   Hidden from view, but running parallel to Vittorio Emanuele, is a pedestrian alley—Via Fuorlovado—that is crammed with real-people shops. Don't miss the chance to prowl this street; it's far more charming than the main tourist thoroughfare.

Via Roma   The Via Roma in Capri is what the British call a high street; it's where the bus station is located and where you'll find the main thrust of the town's real-people shopping.

ANACAPRI

This is a city (higher in the hills) that can be reached by a snake-like road that will thrill or terrify you. There's a beautiful church and a few sights and views; the shopping is limited to a few TTs and one huge department store that carries everything: **Mariorita,** on the central square.

Big Names

BENETTON
Via Vittorio Emanuele 43

CARTIER
Via Vittorio Emanuele 47

FERRAGAMO
Via Vittorio Emanuele 21

GUCCI
Via Camarelle 35

HERMÈS
Via Camarelle 43

LOUIS VUITTON
Via Camarelle 9

MALO
Via Vittorio Emanuele 11

Finds

ALBERTO & LINA
Via Vittorio Emanuele 18

This is one of the leading jewelers in town, part of a family that owns several jewelry shops. In case you haven't already guessed, Italian women define themselves and their success in life vis-à-vis their jewelry, which they buy in places like this and wear all of the time. Yes, even to the beach and right into the sea. That's how we all know it's real gold.

CARTHUSIA PROFUMI
Via Camarelle 10

I am more amused by this store than serious about it, but I have met people who make this a ritual stop when they are in town. Before she had her own perfume line, Liz Taylor was supposed to have been a regular customer. Photo op with the tiles on the front of the store. This is a perfumer who makes a local scent that you can only get here; it's very lemony. Cute gifts.

LA COMPANNINA PIU
Via Fuorlovado 39i

This is a very fancy gourmet food store, not at all funky. They sell all sorts of imported foods, so watch out for the English brands—but much to see, touch, and taste.

MARCELLO RUBINACCI
Via Camarelle 9

This is my favorite shop in Capri—I come here first to stare at the colors, touch the cashmeres, sigh about the quality of quality, and then buy a few T-shirts. Since the T-shirts are about $50 each, this is my idea of extravagance. Hand-wash your cottons from this store; we had big-time shrinkage when we used the washer/dryer. This brand has expanded and has stores in Naples, Rome, etc.

SORRENTO

Most of you will probably arrive by car, train, or tour bus from Naples or Pompeii. A few lucky ones will arrive by cruise ship. However you come, you should stay long enough to see my favorite Lemoncello factory and to explore a good branch of **Standa,** the Italian dime store/grocery store, which, if you're on a cruise, may be your only opportunity to do a little real-people shopping and pick up a few affordable treasures. Dime stores are not plentiful in swanky resorts, believe me. Note that most of the Standas in Italy have been closed or turned into branches of FNAC, the French store for compact discs, books, etc. As we go to press, Standa is still open and is as described above.

Of course, Sorrento is more than a chance for a dime store. When you see the little square and the carriages that are pulled by donkeys in fancy dress hats, and the narrow alleys crammed with crates heaped with fruits and vegetables, when you see the faience spilling from the stores, when you stand at the overlook and peer down into the Bay of Naples, hmmmm, this is what we saved all that money for. This is what southern Italy is all about.

Sorrento is also the gateway to Positano and the rest of the Amalfi Coast. You can rent a car in Sorrento and drive yourself there. (If you're on a cruise, your ship will even arrange your car rental.) If you're feeling more adventurous, take a bus from the station in Sorrento. Even if Gore Vidal hasn't invited you to the villa for lunch, you're going to want to spend as much time as possible in these gorgeous, adorable, and ever-so-chic hill towns.

Getting There

You can take the train or a bus from Naples, drive, hire a car and driver, or take the ferry from Capri, a mere 8km (5 miles) away, or the hydrofoil from Naples.

If you are driving, forget all this hillside nonsense; you'll arrive right at town level and can ignore the port itself. If you're staying only a matter of hours and you like my hotel trick (see p. 270), then head right to **Grand Hotel Ambasciatori** (Via Califano 18), which has parking on premises. Parking in town is difficult.

The Lay of the Land

Like many Italian resort cities, Sorrento is built on a hill above the harbor. You will come to port at Porto Marina Piccola, and then catch a shuttle bus up into the heart of town, Piazza Tasso. You can walk, but it's pretty far, very steep, and the road is curvy and dangerous.

PHONE HOME

The public telephone office is right on the main square, between Piazza Tasso and Piazza Lauro on the Corso Italia. They sell phone cards there, or you can use a credit card. To dial the U.S., dial 001, then the area code, then the number.

Getting Around

If you arrive by car, park near the Via Fuonmura, in the heart of town, then walk. Or try my hotel trick, as noted on p. 270. Cruise passengers can take the ship's shuttle bus. If you miss it, or need instant gratification, a taxi to and from town and the marina costs about 10,000L. Like the taxi drivers in Naples, they'll try to run up the meter. Or, for 3,000L each way, you can take a public bus.

Taxis in town congregate at the **Piazza Tasso,** lining up on the Via Fuonmura.

The Shopping Scene

Sorrento has a lot of charm to it, visually, emotionally, and even from a shopping perspective. There's no serious shopping, but there are several opportunities here that you won't find elsewhere.

While Sorrento has only one or two designer shops (there's an **Emporio Armani**), it does have a branch of **Standa,** one of the best dime stores in Italy, so you can have some serious fun here. Along with a main shopping street, there's a pedestrian back street that's shady and picturesque.

And there are lemons to buy. And where there are lemons, there's Lemoncello. Don't drink Lemoncello and drive, especially when we're talking about the Amalfi Drive!

SHOPPING HOURS

Stores open around 8:30 to 9am and close about 2pm for lunch. They reopen around 4pm. When there are ships in port, hours can be a little more flexible. The major TT department store in town, **A. Gargiulo & Jannuzzi,** Via Fuonmura, is open (nonstop, mind you) from 8am to 10pm in season.

Banks are open Monday to Friday 9am to 1:30pm and 3 to 4pm. This town is closed on Sunday.

Shopping Neighborhoods

Piazza Tasso   This is the proverbial town square: It's in the middle of everything, and many streets branch off in different directions, with each street offering different shopping opportunities. The donkey carts that you can rent for a trot about town are also here.

Corso Italia   This is the main real-people shopping street. It goes across the city and has two different personalities. The portion leading away from town and toward the Amalfi Highway has two designer shops (**Emporio Armani** and **Furla**), plus a branch of **Standa,** the dime store.

The portion that stretches to your right, if your back is to the sea and the donkeys are in front of you, is the main shopping street, with branches of **Lacoste** (very expensive!), the leather goods and shoe store **Pollini,** and a few cafes.

Via Fuoro   This is everyone's favorite street because it's a pedestrian alley; no cars, just tourists. There are drug stores, grocery stores, ceramics shops—in sum, everything that's authentically Italian.

Via de Maio   This is the road that leads to the main square from the marina; the 2 blocks before you get to the square are filled with stores—some of which are quite nice. There are also two excellent pharmacies here.

Via Fuonmura   Leading away from town, this street just has a few stores on it and a hotel or two, but it's home to **A. Gargiulo & Jannuzzi,** the largest shop in town, which is frequented by cruise passengers. It is crowded, overpriced, touristy, and everything you think, but it also provides many services and is in cahoots with all the major cruise lines. And, it has good stuff—you just have to ask to see it.

Finds

A. GARGIULO & JANNUZZI
Via Fuonmura

This is the largest department store in Sorrento, and it was designed for tourists. In business since 1853, it's open from 8am to 10pm nonstop. It's air-conditioned and accustomed to foreign visitors. (They speak English perfectly.) This is not a TT, but rather a sprawling space in several buildings with entire departments devoted to different crafts of the area. The section of the store farthest from the entrance is a ceramics shop. There's a linens department with exquisite work (some of it deservedly very, very expensive), a portion of the store that sells the local inlaid wood marquetry, and some touristy souvenirs near the entrance.

EFFE
Corso Italia 206

This is clearly the local Furla shop; I don't know why it's not called **Furla**. Furla is a handbag maker that I have always enjoyed, especially in Italy where their prices are half what they are in the U.S.

ELLE
Via Fuoro 2

Not to be confused with Effe, this is one of zillions of ceramics shops on the back alley; it just happens to be one of my favorites.

LIMONORO
Via Fuoro 22

This is my favorite Lemoncello factory; it's pretty—lots of white tile—and has a great selection. There are many different sizes of products, gift packages, and beautiful lemon-laden wrapping paper.

STANDA
Corso Italia

Standa is a chain of stores, with branches in virtually all major Italian cities and formerly owned by one of the big Italian department store families. It is now owned by one of the French department store families (Pinault), and may become a FNAC or anything else at any minute. Stay tuned. I like to shop Standa in just about any town I visit; it is especially refreshing in Sorrento because it's not a tourist venue. It's a dime store.

The store is not large, but it has a selection of Italian beauty products (try the Venus brand of skin care), linens, housewares, pots and pans, kids' toys, and even a grocery section. I can happily spend an hour here.

POSITANO & THE AMALFI COAST

The famed Amalfi Drive begins shortly after you bypass Sorrento and enter the kingdom of the curves, a twisty road that skirts the coast from above and often makes me queasy . . . and very grateful for my regular driver, Franco, who is always booked for me by the Hotel Le Sirenuse.

I never need go further than Positano, but one can go all the way to Salerno, shopping as you go. Me? Bury my heart in Positano, where it simply can't get much better. And everyone speaks English.

Visitors say Positano; locals say Posi. So, while a day in Sorrento is a pleasant enough way to spend some time, if you're a do-everything kind of person on a cruise or a limited schedule, you can get through the pleasures of Sorrento (pleasurably) in 2 hours, and then be on your way to Posi, via the Amalfi Drive.

Cruise passengers can rent a car for the day, or take a taxi. There's even a public bus from Sorrento for the truly determined (one-way fare is less than $2).

Some of the stores in Posi close for lunch at 1pm and will not reopen until 3 or 3:30pm, so you want to make sure to allow time for shopping before lunch.

On the other hand, you can avoid the pressure by simply booking yourself into town and staying for a few days.

The Lay of the Land

Positano is one of the famed hill-clinging towns; it is literally dug into the side of a cliff and terraces itself from the beach to the top of a small mountain. There are some main streets, but most of the shopping is along pedestrian alleys and walkways. What I call "uptown" is the Via Colombo; what I call "downtown" is the Via Mulini. In this city, you are either up or down (or prone). Certainly the land lays between the black sands and Le Sirenuse; the crippled, infirm, short of step or breath, or simply lazy might want to reconsider. The lay of the land is vertical, not horizontal.

Snack & Shop

The best bet on a one-day visit is to work your way up the steps and then, if you can afford the best, have lunch at **Le Sirenuse,** the posh villa-turned-hotel, where you can eat on the terrace overlooking the sea. Lunch here is a tad pricey, but not over the top, especially if you just have a pasta or a simple lunch without going the whole route—$25 a person will make you feel like royalty.

If that's over your budget, **Chez Black** is down the hill, on Via del Brigantino (no number), where food starts at $10 per person, and they serve pizza. *Note:* This restaurant is closer to the beach and catches the in-crowd in summer; a reservation is a must (☎ **089/87-50-36**), and tell them I sent you, which won't help if they're busy. I ate lunch there with my girlfriend Abby; we had scampi on the grill and salads and desserts, and the bill was $70 . . . so don't give up Le Sirenuse and then be shocked at Chez Black.

There are three or four other beach cafes in a row surrounding Chez Black.

Sleeping in Positano

LE SIRENUSE
Via Colombo 30

I would tell you maybe I am partial to this hotel because I have a long history of coming here and of visiting with my late husband, who adored it here. But since the hotel has been named the number-one best hotel in Europe by *Travel & Leisure*, well, I think the secret is out. Built into what was once a private villa, the hotel is drop-dead gorgeous in its perch on a hillside. You can sit by the pool and stare down at town or out to sea. You can also enjoy the new Aveda spa (built by Gae Aulenti, no less) or touch the antiques that are spread on the multilevel space and placed on the hand-painted ceramic green tiles. The hotel is open year-round; there are packages in the off-season. They always book my car and driver for me and do transfers to and from Naples airport, and anywhere on the Amalfi Coast.

Book through Leading Hotels in the U.S. Local phone ☎ 089/87-50-66; fax 089/81-17-98; e-mail: info@sirensue.it.

The Shopping Scene

If you haven't already learned the International Rule of Inaccessibility, this is a good time to learn it. What makes a city into the kind of haven the rich and famous like to visit is its inaccessibility to the masses. All the great resort cities of the world, especially in the Mediterranean, are hard to get to.

This understood, you can understand that Positano is the center for the rich and famous along the Amalfi Coast. It is adorable, and its stores sell fun things. There are very few TTs and no branches of The Gap. On the other hand, the selection gets to look uniform in short order; there are only a handful of stores that sell designer clothes or nonresort items that you might wear in the real world if you don't live in the U.S. sunbelt.

The scene is antithetical to what's happening on Capri. Here it's more laid back, and the look is sort of rich-hippie casual. It's a movie set, and stores display their wares to enchant . . . and sell. Flowers pour out of flowerpots, dishes are piled up on stairwells, cottons fly in the slight breeze, and lemons are dancing everywhere.

Dishes and pottery are a big thing; many stores sell them, and all stores seem to sell so much of the same thing that you soon get dizzy. There aren't as many jewelry shops as in Capri—the emphasis here is less on the body and more on comfort or home-style. There are bathing suit and clothing boutiques, but they sell funky fashions and comfortable things, even comfortably tiny bikinis. Many of the stores specialize in what I call Mamma Mia fashions: clothes made for short, wide women with a large bosom. I buy these clothes because they hide the waist and hips and allow for great comfort and eating space. Pass the pasta please.

Shopping Hours

Stores open at 9am and close for lunch around 1pm. They reopen at 3, 3:30, or 4pm, and stay open until 7 or 8pm. Many stores are closed out of season, from mid-October until after March 15. Stores are open on Sunday and on Monday morning.

Finds

Emporio de Sirenuse
Via Colombo 30 (across the street from Le Sirenuse)

This is where I first discovered my idol, Lisa Corti (see chapter 8, p. 230), and where I first fell in love with my dear friend Carla, who buys for the shop and has the eye of a maven, whom I trust with all things Italian. The tiny shop is a mélange of gorgeous tiles set into the floors, hand-painted cabinets and armoires, and merchandise in gorgeous colors, all chosen to reflect the energy of the resort and the passion of the sea.

While perhaps 30% of the merchandise is from Lisa Corti (thank God), the clothes come from Missoni, Etro, and many smaller designers that Americans might not have heard of. Prices are fair, certainly no higher than elsewhere, despite this being a fancy resort. Although I had bought a mound of Corti things in Milan, I ended up with three more tablecloths—different designs I could not live without.

This is one of the best stores in Italy and is worth the trip to Posi if you love color and flair and the art of the unique. There is also a catalog and online business: **www. emporiosirenuse.com**.

DELIKATESSON
Via dei Mulini 5

Just as the name implies, this is a deli, or minimart. I must admit to being outright shocked that they had sexually explicit–shaped pasta, but I'm sure they will sell out before you get there. This is a tiny little place, but you can buy lemons (a great gift to take back home if you don't live in the U.S.), snacks, water, soft drinks, picnics, etc. Open Monday morning; closes on Sunday at 1pm.

CERAMICA ASSUNTA
Via Colombo 97

Just a few doors downhill and closer to town from Emporio de Sirenuse, this large shop has a wide selection of local ceramics in assorted styles. Most of the ceramic shops sell more or less the same wares, but this store is large enough for you to see everything. They pack and ship and will deliver to your hotel; **www.ceramicassunta.it**.

MENA CINQUE
Via Mulini 30

This is my favorite of the clothing stores because their linens have a lot of style and can be worn in the real world. I bought an electric-blue linen dress, very baggy but chic, for $110. To dress it up, I wrap a tablecloth from Emporio Sirenuse (Lisa Corti) around my shoulders as a shawl.

Chapter Ten

....

MEDITERRANEAN DREAMS: ITALY'S PORT TOWNS FROM TOP TO TOE

MEDITATIONS

I am dreaming of a hillside village, clinging to cliffs above the deep blue sea. Hmmmm . . . maybe it's turquoise. I know, I see it more clearly now—it's deep blue with streaks of turquoise in the places where the water is more shallow.

I know you see my vision in your mind's eye because you, too, are dreaming of the Italian shores of the Mediterranean and Adriatic—whether you're renting a yacht, taking a cruise, driving around in your rental car, or merely perching on the back of Giancarlo's Vespa.

With Italy's location as the boot into the sea, many cities are port cities; many are cruise destinations. The larger cities have their own chapters in this guide; this chapter mentions the smaller ports that few guide books talk about.

COME SAIL WITH ME

In the last few years, the cruise business has gone nuts, adding more and more ships and juggling routes to give more people the chance to cruise the Mediterranean in grand, but afford-able, style. Dubrovnik has just been reopened, putting even more pressure on Italy, with Venice usually as the turn-around point for cruises that visit Slovenia and Croatia. Not to be left out, Rome's port city has spent the last two years tearing up the roads and making dust to pour money into its dreams of sea-faring glory.

There are now several routes that give passengers a lot of Italy in a week or 10-day cruise: There's a northern Italian Riv-iera itinerary from Rome to Monaco, which may or may not include some French ports. A southern routing departs from either Venice or Athens and travels around the boot of Italy to Rome, with plenty of southern Italian destinations, includ-ing a possible sighting of Stromboli and the Dalmatian coast, which includes Slovenia and Croatia.

Genoa is reinventing itself to compete for cruise business on the Italian Riviera; several ships are calling there for the first time. Catania, which has been included as a destination for many years, is really going to town and taking on many designer shops that were near there before. A **CK Store**—yep, a Calvin Klein shop—opened.

Definitions, Please

I was just reading one of my favorite travel magazines, and it had one of those gorgeous four-page color inserts from a cruise company that announced "The Rivieras." It then went on to define the Riviera as beginning in Lisbon and ending just shy of Athens. I find this a bit of a stretch, but I mention it because there is a lot of confusion out there, and there are people sell-ing with the word "Riviera" because it sounds so glamorous.

Technically speaking, the French Riviera is a confederation of Cannes, Nice, and Monaco that banded together as one des-tination in order to get Americans to come over and sunbathe topless. It became such a hit that the Italians, just down the coast a sneeze, decided that they had the Italian Riviera.

Now cruise ships will tell you that any port city on the Mediterranean side of Italy is "the Riviera." Oh well, use sunblock, put on your sunglasses, and smile for the cameras. Lunch will be served at 3pm. This is glamour and this is what you came for; who cares what they name it?

Getting There

Depending on which parts of the Mediterranean coast you plan to explore, you have several transportation options. I am forever reminding people to look at a map and understand that the Nice Airport, which is technically in France, is really the gateway to northern Italy. If you are coming from a European hub city and are using regional aircraft, there are small airports that you can fly into—from Turin to Genoa to Pisa and on into that not-at-all-small airport in Rome. Of course, once you're in Rome, you're halfway down the coast.

If you're on a cruise ship, or joining a cruise ship, you will most likely board at Monaco, Rome, Venice, or Athens.

You can also explore the coast by car, using the big international airports as gateways. But don't underestimate the use of trains, buses, and even ferries.

Several famous resort towns are just a hydrofoil, ferry, or bus ride away from the major cities, so that you may want to leave your rental car at your hotel and take day trips to some of the more exotic spots, like Capri. In the Amalfi region, you may indeed be terrified to take on the infamous Amalfi Drive in your rental car. (Don't look down!) Rest assured that you can enjoy all the splendors of the region without the risks.

Getting Around

If you come on a cruise ship, getting around in port is limited to cruise tours, foot power, or whatever rentals you have arranged ahead of time. The concierge onboard your ship can have a rental car waiting for you, although it will cost less if you arrange for the car in the U.S. at promotional rates.

If you are driving, you want to remember that the reason your rental car had so many extra insurance riders is that car break-ins are a way of life in Italy. Make sure your belongings are secured in the trunk and that nothing at all is inside the car; the car should be locked at all times. To avoid aggravation, use a car park that has an attendant.

My method is a little more expensive, but it's foolproof—I drive to the fanciest hotel in town and let them take the car. They park it, guard it, and take responsibility, and bring it back to me when I'm ready to leave! Money might not buy happiness, but it buys a parking place, even in Naples.

Taxis abound, especially at train stations, although you can expect to be cheated by taxi drivers, especially in Naples. But that also happens in Rome and just about everywhere else in the world.

Do note that while you may think that a local or regional train connects all the parts of Italy you want to visit, in some cases, there is no train service, or the train service is limited (or on strike). Consider a bus!

SITA buses (☎ 055/21-47-21), originating in Genoa, service the full length of the Italian Riviera, in both directions. In fact, it's best to arrive in Genoa by car, plane, or rail, then rely on the bus to take you up and down the coast. SITA buses also service the Amalfi Coast, originating in Sorrento.

Shopping Hours

Store hours in southern Italy are Mediterranean, which means that virtually everyone closes up for lunch and, possibly, for the rest of the afternoon if it's hot enough. However, there is tremendous variety and no lack of creativity in the store hours in each port city, so ask when you arrive.

While northern Italy has more sensitivity toward business and business hours, don't think Milan here. Mediterranean is Mediterranean, from the French border to the toe of the boot.

Note: If you buy a lot and decide to leave your packages at a store so you don't have to schlep them in the heat all day, you need to know exactly when the store will reopen after lunch so you can retrieve them before you leave town. I was once onboard a yacht that couldn't leave port because the big-time shoppers had left their haul behind closed doors that would not unlock until 5pm!

Money Matters & Scams

I don't want to be rude about this, but I found myself more frequently cheated and scammed in southern Italy—especially port towns—than anywhere else in the country. I realize that tourists are fair game all over Italy (and I have had my share of dirty tricks played on me in Milan and northern Italy, too), but in southern Italy I noticed every trick in the book: I was given change from under the bottom tray of a cash register; the money had, of course, been out of circulation for two years and could only be exchanged at a bank. I've also received the wrong change, or was charged surcharges and commissions, and extra taxes. If you care about these things, pay attention in all your transactions.

There are convenient American Express offices in most Italian tourist cities, so if you need to cash a check, get an advance, or change money, you know you'll be safe.

Also remember that you can always walk into a good hotel to change money. You'll get a lesser exchange rate, but you won't pay commission and you won't have to deal with crazy banks or storekeepers. You need not be a hotel guest.

PORTOFINO

....

Portofino is postcard perfect—indeed, any time you see an ad about Italy, or a cruise through this part of Italy, there's always a full-page photo of the harbor at Portofino. Dream on.

The tiny harbor is surrounded by pastel stucco buildings, many of which are stores. There are itty-bitty **Hermès, Trussardi, Gucci, Armani, Stefanel,** and **Paul & Shark** boutiques as well as a few tourist traps (TTs) and street vendors who will happily take your cash.

Portofino is beautiful, but after about an hour or two you may be wondering what to do with yourself. Answer: Take the public bus to **Santa Margherita,** a town about 2 miles away. There's not a lot of shopping, but it's real and funky, and it's fun to walk around for an hour or two.

In Santa Margherita, there is a street market with gorgeous vegetables, there are pasta shops, drug stores, ice cream places, and, of course, shoe stores. But, there's nothing that you really have to buy; no must-do stores. This is more the place for window-shopping, strolling shopping, and for feeling the power of the streets, resorts, and the vibes of rich Italians. You don't have to spend a single lira to enjoy it.

Shopping Hours

Stores in Portofino and Santa Margherita open at 9am and close at 7pm Monday to Friday; some close for lunch.

A Warning About Ventemille

Because I was going to be in Portofino on a Friday and I know that Friday is the day of the market in Ventemille on the France-Italy border (where they sell all the designer fakes), I thought it might be fun to head off on an adventure.

I was on a cruise at the time, with a limited amount of time in town, and I surely didn't want to miss the boat, so I discussed all the details with the concierge on the ship and the port agent. The agent warned me against going, saying that in summer the traffic from Portofino to Ventemille can make the drive 3 hours long (each way)! I heeded his advice. If you are driving, however, and want a small adventure, there is a market in Ventemille on Tuesday and Friday and in San Remo on Saturday. This is the market that is famous for the fake designer goods, where the Louis Vuitton fakes have been known to pass muster with the rich and famous.

LIVORNO

If you're on a cruise and you come to port at Livorno, please note that this is neither a resort nor a tourist town. It's an industrial port not too far from Florence, which will be your destination for the day. No one driving the area would ever make the detour to Livorno. For Florence, see chapter 6. You may also want to contact Maria Teresa (see p. 113), who does a lot of programs for cruise passengers coming into Livorno.

SARDINIA

Ah, Sardinia sounds so romantic, so sophisticated, so private. It's so private that the first time my cruise ship pulled up in Porto Cervo I didn't know how to pronounce it (*Porto Chervo, cara*), and I didn't know the difference between Corsica and Sardinia, other than that Corsica is part of France, and Sardinia is part of Italy. I'm learning, but still can't claim to feel that Sardinia is part of heaven.

Sardinia is a rather arid little island with not too much of anything except glamour—you come here to chill out at the drop-dead gorgeous resorts that overlook the sea. There are only one or two little funky villages, not much to tour, and only a little shopping.

But what shopping it is!

Porto Cervo was built by the Aga Khan, as were many of the resort towns on Sardinia. If you remember my rule of inaccessibility and exclusivity, you get the drift here. Although this is a fake village, manufactured and built to be charming and cute, it's also pretty hard to get to.

The proper arrival and departure point is the pier, as the Aga himself created this town to be reached by those visiting on private yachts.

Few Americans go to Porto Cervo unless they are on a cruise that makes a stopover here. The only other way for mere mortals to reach the resort is to take the FS (Italian State Railways) ferry from the mainland (departures are from Civitavecchia) to Golfo Aranci on Sardinia. From Golfo Aranci, it's a short drive to Porto Cervo. For more information, call ☎ **0766/232-73** on the mainland, or 0798/468-00 in Golfo Aranci.

The Lay of the Land

The good news about Porto Cervo is that it's a mall. The bad news about Porto Cervo is that it's a mall. But if you've come to this isolated-yet-glamorous island looking for something chic to do, you have found it.

The entire town is a tiered development that includes a gorgeous hotel and a lot of stores. At the back end is the parking lot for locals. At the front end is the marina, for those who come by yacht. Frankly, my dear, I wouldn't recommend a trip to Sardinia just to visit this town and shop here, but that said, it does have some of the best designer shopping of all the ports, particularly for Italian big names, and the shops are open late at night. It ain't bad in one of those perfectly fake kind of ways.

Built as a stucco village, with long terraces and piazzas and even views of the sea, the mall leaves plenty of space to stroll. There are stairs here and there that lead to other levels, so you can wander and explore a little without feeling boxed in. If you're thin and tan and love the good life, you may like it here. If you prefer the back streets of Brooklyn, this is not your kind of place.

There's a post office and a place to make phone calls. There's also a newsstand or two selling postcards and two pharmacies. But mostly there are designer shops—**Gucci, Prada, Missoni, Nazareno Gabrielli,** and **Versace. Artigianato Sardegna,** one of the stores in the mall, sells local handcrafts.

My favorite store is actually in the rear of the mall: **Supermercato Sarma.** This is a large (by Italian resort standards) supermarket, which is air-conditioned and stocked with food and some dry goods. I bought plastic jellies for the beach for 5,000L.

Shopping Hours

Stores are open from 9am to 1pm and 5 to 10pm. Everything is closed on Sunday, and in the morning on Monday.

TAORMINA
· ·

Taormina is a Sicilian coastal town, located just south of the Straits of Messina—that's the narrow piece of water between the toe of the boot and the island of Sicily.

Although Taormina has plenty of TTs and can be crowded in season and unbearably hot in summer, there's something glamorous and a little bit funky about it that delights me.

Maybe it's the fact that the world-famous shoe designer Manolo Blahnik summers here each year, and has even named a pair of shoes after the town. Or the fact that Taormina has a somewhat unusual history—a Greek influence that few other cities in Italy have. So I welcome you to a different part of Italy; a refreshing difference if it's the first port city you visit.

Taormina is a town that has charm almost down perfectly; a town that mixes and mingles a variety of cultures—and has shopping souvenirs to go with it. Yes, this is the town where you can buy a Madonna inset into a piece of lava from Mount Etna. But it's also where you can buy antiques (real and fake), faience, Sicilian folk crafts, a variety of foodstuffs (marzipan!), and a few pairs of shoes. That's not bad for an afternoon's work.

Getting There

Most people visit Sicily by taking a ferry or hydrofoil from the mainland to Messina; the ferries, which also transport cars, depart from Villa San Giovanni and Reggio di Calabria, while the hydrofoils depart just from Reggio di Calabria. Call ☎ **0965/89-81-23,** 0965/89-40-03, or 0965/295-68.

To continue on to Taormina for a stay or a day trip, take either the train or the bus. You can, of course, drive as well,

heading south from Messina along *autostrada* A18. If you take
the train, note that the train station is a mile from the heart
of Taormina, but buses waiting at the station will take you up
the hill.

Many visitors arrive by yacht or cruise ship.

Time in Town

I'd call Taormina a good half-day town. That means you can
go on a tour in the morning and prowl on your own in the
afternoon, or spend the morning exploring it on your own and
be ready for a late lunch by 1:30 or 2pm.

If you're on a cruise, be sure to get the shuttle bus timetable,
because it's a good 20- to 30-minute ride from town to your
ship, and you may be tempted to return to your ship for a free
lunch onboard.

Phone Home

There are a few pay phones about half a block from where cruise
ship tenders come to port; some of these phones take an Italian phone card. You can buy a phone card in town at any *tabacchi* (tobacco shop), marked outside with the letter T. News
agents do not sell phone cards in Taormina.

The Lay of the Land

Taormina is a hillside village that overlooks the sea from its
perch in the middle of coastal Sicily. The destination actually
has two parts: upper (the town) and lower, which stretches
around to include several spans of beach.

If you arrive by ship, there are two different ways to get to
town: 1) by shuttle bus (cruise ships provide them); or 2) on
a cable car, which departs from the other part of the beach—
which may not be convenient to where your ship comes in.

If you're driving on your own, you will come over the top
of the hills on the A18, which connects Taormina to both Catania and Messina. You can miss the beach. If you are indeed

driving, you want to park at a hotel in town: My pick is the
San Domenico Palace, Piazza San Domenica 5, right off the
main part of town. You will pay about $20 a day for parking
but can negotiate for an hourly rate if you're visiting for only
a few hours. Say you're lunching at the hotel.

In town, there are two main shopping areas: the main
street, a pedestrian-only thoroughfare called **Corso Umberto,**
and the **Via Teatro.** The latter begins on your left as you enter
town from the pier. It can be hard to find. Ask—it's worth doing.

Getting Around

Taxis make regular runs from the major taxi stand at the
intersection of the Corso Umberto and the Via Teatro. Usually 15,000L will get you just about anywhere you want to go
in town.

If you come by shuttle bus from a cruise ship, you will be
dropped at the bus stop right below the city. From here, you
take the stairs up from the parking lot, walking to your right
until you see the town gates. The stairs are a bit steep.

The Shopping Scene

Like every resort town, Taormina is filled with shops that
cater to tourists. Taormina is a very famous resort city (don't
ask me why) and has some out-of-season convention and
meeting business, so there are shoppers on the prowl constantly.

The best thing about the mix of stores and merchandise here
is that it's totally different from what you'll see elsewhere. They
have found their own niche with crafts and antiques; there are
few designer shops. Forget your Pucci and your Gucci.

The TTs are just about everywhere, but they're especially
dense on the Via Teatro. You'll spot them easily: Just look for
shops crammed with coral necklaces, cameos, pieces of lava
from Mount Etna, "Etruscan" vases, faience tiles and pottery,
and reproduction antiquities—everything but a copy of the Blue
Grotto.

Among the most frequently seen items:

Antiques Who in his or her right mind would buy antiques in a resort town? Yet there are scads of so-called antiques shops on the main drag, Corso Umberto. Watch out for some of these items—many were made last summer in Thailand.

Bread Famous for their intricately braided and decorated breads, Sicilians now sell these loaves to tourists.

Cameos All of southern Italy is Cameo City.

Greek motifs Because of its close proximity to Greece, many of the things to buy in Taormina display a Greek influence in style or design.

Lemons Don't laugh—you're now in the land of the lemon and Lemoncello. I like the local Mount Etna brand.

Marzipan I don't care if you eat this stuff or not, but you are certainly going to want to photograph it! Absolutely gorgeous marzipan is sold from several shops on the Corso Umberto.

SHOPPING HOURS

Stores usually open at 9am and close at 1pm. They reopen at 3 or 3:30pm. A handful of stores will only close for an hour during lunch to take advantage of the cruise ship traffic.

Banks are open from 8:30am to 1:30pm, and do not reopen after lunch.

Note: Because of the summer heat, it's nice to get into town early, shop early, and then get out of there.

PERSONAL NEEDS

The British Pharmacy is located on the Piazza IX Aprile, right off the Corso Umberto. It is closed on Thursday but open on Sunday. They have a computer that can translate your American prescription to the proper Italian medication.

Finds

ARTE ANTICA
Corso Umberto 27–29, Taormina

This is one of the first shops I discovered on the Corso Umberto, and it's continued to charm me on subsequent trips. They sell some antiques, true, but what I love are the wrought-iron sconces of lemons or pansies. Other flowers are also available.

SALUMERIA DA PAOLO & CO.
Corso Umberto 129, Taormina

This store sells prepared foods and foodstuffs. The find of my last trip was located on its shelves—local honey with pistachio nuts. I bought some for Alain Ducasse and for Patricia Wells, my two cooking mavens, and neither had seen anything like it. A great gift for $6.

Size Conversion Chart

....

WOMEN'S CLOTHING

American	8	10	12	14	16	18
Continental	38	40	42	44	46	48
British	10	12	14	16	18	20

WOMEN'S SHOES

American	5	6	7	8	9	10
Continental	36	37	38	39	40	41
British	4	5	6	7	8	9

CHILDREN'S CLOTHING

American	3	4	5	6	6X
Continental	98	104	110	116	122
British	18	20	22	24	26

CHILDREN'S SHOES

American	8	9	10	11	12	13	1	2	3
Continental	24	25	27	28	29	30	32	33	34
British	7	8	9	10	11	12	13	1	2

MEN'S SUITS

American	34	36	38	40	42	44	46	48
Continental	44	46	48	50	52	54	56	58
British	34	36	38	40	42	44	46	48

MEN'S SHIRTS

American	$14\frac{1}{2}$	15	$15\frac{1}{2}$	16	$16\frac{1}{2}$	17	$17\frac{1}{2}$	18
Continental	37	38	39	41	42	43	44	45
British	$14\frac{1}{2}$	15	$15\frac{1}{2}$	16	$16\frac{1}{2}$	17	$17\frac{1}{2}$	18

MEN'S SHOES

American	7	8	9	10	11	12	13
Continental	$39\frac{1}{2}$	41	42	43	$44\frac{1}{2}$	46	47
British	6	7	8	9	10	11	12

INDEX